For Ron Lytle
— obscene
nine-letter word!

[signature]

The best
of Bragg

By Addison Bragg

*A collection of columns from
the pages of The Billings Gazette*

Unicorn Communications

Billings, Montana

ISBN 0-913311-01-4

Cover and inside illustrations by Andy Schoneberg

To Don Anderson, publisher, editor,
reporter — and well remembered friend.

Addison Bragg

Contents

Chapter 1: Nostalgia
Page 1

Chapter 5: Family
Page 123

Chapter 6: Characters & V.I.P.s
Page 143

Chapter 7: Potpourri
Page 161

Chapter 8: Friends Departed
Page 215

Foreword

Since it's customary for books to have forewords, I prefer to do the job myself so — as Mark Twain once said — I can rely on getting in all the facts.

There's another reason, of course.

Dick Wesnick, the guy I have to thank for most of the back-breaking and brain-busting that went into putting this thing together, from copy to galley proofs, from indexing to chapter headings, told me to write it. Since he's my editor, I could hardly say no.

Let's just say that I started out in this business 66 years ago in Ohio where I was born and learned to read and write before I started the first grade.

I wound it up in 1980 when, after 30 years on The Gazette, I retired. Sort of.

In between, there was growing up in Kansas, serving in two wars — WW II and Korea, marrying a girl from Butte whom I met in 1942 at Ft. Leavenworth and helping — as much as a newspaper man back then could help — her raise our four kids.

I suppose my mother — who wrote for a living herself after she got through being an actress — started me on the road to perdition that led to a newspaper career. "You like to read," she told me once, "and you like to stay out until all sorts of ungodly hours — and you can write. You should go to work on a newspaper."

My dad didn't push me one way or another. "Just find something you enjoy doing and can earn a comfortable living at," he said, "and count yourself among the lucky people in the world."

That's what being a newspaper reporter means to me. I've been fortunate enough to work at a job that has never really been a job to me and, though some times were tougher than others, we never wanted for the really important things.

And notice I said newspaper reporter.

I've never called myself a journalist.

And the word columnist — even after nearly 25 years at being one — still doesn't roll all that easily off the tongue.

My life in this business — which began in earnest back in 1947 when I went to work on the Wichita Eagle — has been literally a window on the world. I've met presidents, I hugged a lion, I was adopted by the Sioux — and the only reason I wasn't all that clumsy the night I danced with a French countess was being able to remember that only a couple of years earlier I'd danced with a Thai princess.

There was the night Eleanor Roosevelt and I sat in a hotel lobby and talked until 3 a.m. one morning.

There was the time I told Adlai Stevenson where he could go.

And there was the time I kissed June Allyson.

But that's another story. It has also been a door to new places, new things — and new friends who over the years have become old friends.

I think of Arch O'Bryant, my first (and toughest) city editor. I think of Hal Seipp, who gave me my start with The Gazette. I think of Russ Hart, who nearly 20 years ago asked why I didn't put a collection of my pieces into book form.

And I think of Don Anderson to whom I've dedicated this book.

People have asked me — still do, in fact — about my reasons for writing a column.

That answer doesn't come easy. I have no burning desire to reform. I don't try to preach. I have no mesage. I'm a partisan of nothing and an advocate of everything — including an individual's right to be either anti-or pro-neutral.

Call me, rather, a ham. I love entertaining — and if these pieces do that then they have served their purpose.

Addison Bragg
Billings, Montana
December 1984

Editor's Note:
Addison Bragg, whose retirement from the Army Reserve as a lieutenant-colonel, coincided with his retirement from The Gazette, lives in Billings and his column still appears as a regular feature of The Gazette. A son, John, is a news photographer with the Corvallis (Ore.) Gazette-Times. His daughter, Beth, is a sports writer for the Great Falls (Mont.) Tribune.

Introduction

Addison Bragg is probably the best known person in Eastern Montana and Northern Wyoming — a household name, a familiar figure in the cities, towns and hamlets of this vast area where Bragg's column has been a reading habit for a quarter-century.

Herein is a generous and representative sampling of Bragg's labor of love. It started out as "Bragg about Billings," but soon developed into Bragg about everywhere and everything in the 80,000-square-mile empire The Billings Gazette calls its circulation area.

He writes about people, great and small but always interesting. He writes about places, where he always manages to find something interesting. He writes about interesting things, interesting times, interesting experiences from his childhood to his present state of maturity.

Bragg is a popular speaker as well as a writer. He also is something of a bon vivant, a raconteur and a connoisseur of Irish whisky. (If you're buying, he'll settle for scotch or bourbon, except on St. Patrick's day.)

In this collection, you'll discover Addison Bragg's versatility as a reporter and writer. You'll also learn some things about the writer himself — his love of his family, his country, his profession, and his affection for and mastery of the English language.

George D. Remington
Publisher, The Billings Gazette
January 1985

Nostalgia

CHAPTER 1

Thirty years
in the twinkle of an eye

I T WAS JUST 30 years ago last Thursday I walked into the city room at The Gazette and Hal Seipp took me over, showed me a desk and a typewriter and told me they were mine as long as I felt like staying on.

The typewriter was sold a long time ago when we moved into our new building.

Heaven knows what happened to the desk.

Hal retired about 10 years back. We still get together every now and then.

And I'm still here — but not for long.

There comes a day, I think, when one of the best things you can do is to look around and say to yourself it's time to move on.

In a sense, that's what I'm planning the end of September.

And the 30-year mark seems as good a time as any to make it official.

One of the first things I'll do is sit down and look back over the years with a deep feeling of gratitude — and with what still is to me a great sense of adventure.

Now I'm not going to talk about how the town has changed since I came here that June 19, 1950. I'm not even going to talk about how The Gazette has changed.

I just want to let you know what being a newspaperman in Billings — and Montana — has meant to me.

The guy who came here back then, three years out of the Army, married, with a young daughter, a son on the way — and two more daughters in the future — wasn't exactly a stranger to a newsroom, nor was he filled with more than the usual number of illusions about the business.

I had no deep sense of reform, no desire to crusade or urge to shock. I only wanted to write news stories and, for the frosting on the cake, an occasional feature.

Fortunately in the years that followed I was able to do both — and a little more.

Also fortunately, in the course of it all, I was able to do part of my growing up with the town.

I guess that's why I like being here — and why I'm going to like staying here.

When I walk or drive around town today there are a lot of things I miss.

The old Gazette building with its dingy walls, wood floors, noisy machines and general air of make-do modernization and piece-meal repair that went into carrying a half-century-old structure into the present is only one of them.

I miss the wide sidewalks, the bells that rang at street corners for "Walk" and "Don't Walk," and the neon signs which once made bright every downtown alley.

I miss the smell of coal smoke and the sound of steam and the chuffing and clanking of switch engines that once meant railroading. Their ghosts, I feel sometimes, are still there on dark, rainy nights at the 27th Street crossing.

And I miss the people I used to talk to and see every day who aren't around any more but who were a lot of help to me and whom I'll never forget.

They were oil men, politicians, lawyers, policemen, doctors, schoolteachers, businessmen, working girls, ranchers, cowhands, bartenders, waitresses, priests, ministers, gamblers — and neighbors.

Without them it all wouldn't have been so possible or so memorable.

And I guess somewhere in here I'll have to say what part my family played in all of this — and you can damn well guess it was plenty.

Having a newspaperman as a father — or a husband — wasn't the easiest job in the world.

There were times that were good and those not so good. There were bright days — and dark days. But we managed. And I guess it's partly because of them that today I can do what I'm doing.

Still, all of the things I miss and all of the things I remember and all of the things I cherish are sort of woven into and around a newspaper called The Gazette.

It has been good to me, from the Anaconda Copper Co. past to the Lee Enterprises present, and I've tried to be good to it.

Sometimes I wasn't as good as they thought I was — and sometimes I was better. But we got along over the years.

I'm leaving in September for no other reason than, as I said, I think it's time to go.

And I think this is a good time to tell about it.

I've got a few things I want to do, a few things I'd like to try — and now seems like an appropriate time to start.

You know, about 10 years ago I wrote an anniversary piece and called it a love letter to a town.

Some people said that's what it sounded like.

You can call this a postscript to it if you want — because it's more of the same.

And there are two reasons why I'm writing it now:

The first has to do with that old newspaper tradition where, when a

4

reporter has finished a story, he writes "30" at the bottom of his copy to show that it's ended.

The second I talked about at the beginning of this column.

I've just finished 30 years with The Gazette.

And since I like putting things neatly and simply, it all seems to fit here.

What more can I say?

It's "30"at 30 ... With all my love.

Not another farewell column!

WELL, IT'S ABOUT that time.

At risk of being accused of making as many farewell appearances as the late Sarah Bernhardt — or Old Blue Eyes hisself — I've got to talk for a minute or two about the Gazoo (as some of us, with affection, call The Gazette) on the eve of my last day here as a full-time employee.

(Editor's note: Whaddye mean, full time?)

Let me say at the outset, it's been fun. Absolute, positive, whole-hearted, unmitigated fun.

I've had my problems with editors, sure.

I've even had my problems with publishers.

But once they saw things my way, it was Freedom Train from there on.

Being a newspaperman isn't hard.

The country clubs you can join are limited — along with the week-ends you can spend in Mazatlan.

Good heavens, I can even name (without stopping to think) a dozen or more reporters I've worked with who have never — even to this day — owned their own plane.

But I wouldn't trade the last 30 years for anything.

(Editor's note: How about a case of Chivas Regal?)

And I'm not just talking about a newspaper — even The Gazette.

Billings has been pretty good to me too.

I think of the people who helped me when I came here. And the people I've met since. I think of those who aren't around any more.

And I wonder how in the name of heaven I even thought once — and, to be truthful, I did think once about it — of leaving here.

Native Ohioan and Kansas transplant or not, here, if anyplace, are my roots.

(Editor's note: Call 'em roots if you want. We call 'em barstools.)

I'd miss this place if I left.

As I was telling Red Burnett at the Northern the other day, I even miss this place when I go on vacation.

Red blew a gasket at my remark.

"Vacation," he snorted. "How can anybody tell when you're on vacation?"

(Editor's note: Red Burnett knows you better than we do. And no wonder).

If I weren't so good-natured I think I'd resent some of these comments.

The concensus around here seems to be nonetheless that retirement won't make all that much difference — to me or to The Gazette.

Ellie Posey said as much not long ago.

"We see as much of you around here when you're on vacation as we see when you're working," she informed me.

Oh, well.

And Oscar Chaffee — who I thought was a better friend of mine than that — wrote me a nice note when he heard I was leaving.

Oscar, who was my city editor for years and years before he pulled the plug here, said it was "always a pleasure" to see me come to work.

"Because," he added, "often you came in for some other purpose."

There was some talk at the Golden Belle last week about putting a brass plaque on the end of the bar where, beginning about 15 or 20 years ago, I always sat.

They'll have to get my elbow out of the way first.

(Editor's note: Thanks for coming in to do this last one. We've missed you.)

Inspired by a giant

THERE IS PROBABLY not a working newsman — or a retired one, for that matter — in the country who hasn't heard of William Allen White.

The former editor of the Emporia, Kan., Gazette, dead now for nearly 40 years, was as good an example of a giant in the profession as I can think of — and as great a man as I have ever met.

I was still a decade and more away from even thinking about newspaper work as a career when I first met him — but I'll never forget the time he sat with me in his office and talked about Kansas, about politics, about newspapers and books — and about what a goggle-eyed high school sophomore wanted to do with his life.

Our class had taken a trip to Emporia to visit the teachers college there, and I — thanks to my mother's insistence — had the foresight to bring with me a letter of introduction from my hometown editor, a long-time friend of White's, to a man I was told I should meet even if I decided later on a career other than writing.

The March day I walked into the front door of the Gazette on Commercial Street was warm and sunny.

It matched exactly the dispositon of the man I met when, directed on my way down a corridor smelling of ink, paper and hot metal, I turned left and walked into his office.

His tilt-back chair squeaked as he turned around from his rolltop desk, smiled one of the happiest smiles (on one of the happiest faces) I'd ever seen, brushed a pile of papers from a chair and asked me to sit down.

I suppose I was a bit awestruck — and rightfully so.

Here was the man who had put himself — and his newspaper — on the map with his famous "What's the Matter With Kansas?" editorial, a piece of writing which brought nearly every politician in the country — including members of Congress, even presidents — to his door.

Here was the man who wrote so touchingly on the death of his daughter, Mary, that the piece became almost a standard in every book of American literature in high schools throughout the country and only a year ago was dramatized on network television.

William Allen White. A country editor, as he liked to call himself. An elder statesman of his profession. A legend.

And a kind and gentle man.

I'll never forget the disarray of that desk of his. Papers, magazines, books and correspondence spilled over each side. The top was piled with books, some of which stood properly upright, some of which lay on their sides.

If I ever went to work on a newspaper, I told myself, eyeing the monumental clutter, I'd want a desk just like that.

Not surprisingly, the walls of the small cluttered officer were lined with photographs, not the least among which was a cabinet portrait (autographed) of President Theodore Roosevelt.

There were statesmen and rulers, authors and actors, captains of industry and military leaders.

But the white-haired, friendly man in the squeaking chair dominated them all.

He acted as though he had all the time in the world for me — and he talked as though what I was doing and what I planned to do were the two most important things in the world.

William Allen White even got up from his desk, waved a genial hand at his typewriter and told me I could use it to drop a postcard home. "I'll be back in the pressroom a few minutes," he said. "Make yourself at home."

That was only the first of several meetings with White as a result of my quick acceptance of his invitation to "call me any time you get through Emporia."

I met his wife, Sally, later when I was a guest in their home one Sunday afternoon.

And among my most prized possessions were the books he sent me (White was a panel member of the Book of the Month Club) whenever he ran onto one in which he thought I'd be interested.

The last time I talked to him was when I was stationed at Fort Warren, Wyo., during the war, shortly before he died. I recalled that first meeting of ours — and he recalled it in the short note I got later.

"I enjoyed meeting you," William Allen White wrote, "possibly even more than you could have enjoyed meeting me."

There are a lot of people in this business who have looked at William Allen White as an inspiration.

I count myself lucky to be able to say he, more than anyone else, had a direct influence on my deciding to make newspapering my life's work.

A career which included, I need hardly add, a desk always considered the most cluttered in the newsroom.

Pay was lousy,
the job was fun

T HE YEARS I'VE put in at this business that I remember best are, not surprisingly, the early years.

The pay was lousy .

But the job was fun, sheer fun from the time you sat down before a typewriter (which you shared with two other reporters) to the time you put away your notes, clippings and sundry other impedimenta of the trade in the one desk drawer you called yours and headed home at the end of the day.

I don't think there was a time in my life — excepting the Army where I made $50 a month — when I earned less but enjoyed work more.

And I don't think there was a time in my life where I found myself surrounded by more characters — or more confusion.

Walk in any newspaper office today — including the Gazette — and you'll see what I mean.

Save for the still-cluttered desks, the telephones and the day, week or month-old papers flung about at random, today's city room could well be the loan department of a bank, an insurance adjustment office or a mail order firm shipping department on a busy day.

Isolated pockets of confusion may exist — but it's hard to pinpoint them.

Disappearance of teletype machines into a soundproof area along with the replacement of clattering typewriters by video display terminals in large part account for the strictly-business sound of modern city rooms.

The ultimate, irreversible sign of change came, of course, with the laying of carpet. It made some of us — especially those of us who'd never been there before — feel like we were working in a church.

Today's city room is clean, comfortable, comparably quiet and orderly.

No longer does one stow a telephone away in a desk drawer to allow more room in which to work. Gone is the water cooler that went blup-bub, blub-bup every time you took a drink. Vanished in the past as well are the metal wastebaskets which in times of emergency conferences with the city editor served as seats.

(Wastebasket fires, incidentally, were common occurrences in the newsroom I grew up in — and no one complained overmuch. It would have done little good anyway since our leading arsonist was a pipe smoker named Dick Long who also happened to be our managing editor.)

Reporters no longer cross the room by walking on desks to reach a ringing phone more quickly.

Many of them don't even put their feet up on desks — but I suppose there's a good reason for this.

There are as many skirted reporters today as there are reporters in pants and somehow skirts just aren't built for that sort of relaxation.

Even photographers — once looked upon as a cut above the aborigine or, at best, chronic disturbers of the peace — now act, talk and dress like real people. Sometimes they are mistaken by even the discerning for reporters or editors.

The story, getting it on time, getting it right and writing it right, was the main thing. But once the printers upstairs, whose heavy machines caused a portentious but interesting sag in the ceiling just over the city desk, got hold of it our work was done. We forgot about it and went on, sometimes to a cold beer down the street, sometimes to the bourbon bottle in the darkroom — and sometimes, even, home.

There were no post mortems. There were no elaborate planning sessions for the next edition.

And I can't remember in all those years anyone, editor or reporter, who gave a moment's thought to reforming the world, reshaping the nation, turning the rascals out in state government or cleaning up city hall.

Still — and to be completely honest about it — there was the occasional call from a disgruntled reader who ended his complaint with an order to cancel his subscription.

The story goes that our city editor, Arch O'Bryant, was always ready with his reply:

"Cancel your own damn subscription," he'd roar.

Like I say, we never got rich.

But things never got dull.

Tough editor
kept track of news

W HEN THEY TOLD ME a column on Doc Bowler might be appropriate, I didn't argue the point.

After all, he was my editor. He was — and still is — my friend.

And he's also the most stubborn, irascible and opinionated old so-and-so that I think I've ever encountered in the news business.

When we got word at The Gazette that Doc was headed out our way, the grapevine reports were mixed.

He's terrible, some of my friends in Helena told me.

He's great, you'll like him, others said.

There were as many who thought Doc was the greatest thing that happened to this business since the invention of movable type, as there were those who were of the opinion that Attila the Hun could have taken lessons from him.

But, over the years, Doc and I got along.

He wore a crew cut when I first knew him. He prided himself on the fact that, of the four suits he owned, not one was less than 10 years old (a not uncommon boast among many newspaper men) and that, despite his having arrived at (and passed) that time of life when bifocals are more or less mandatory, he still managed without them.

But that was the Doc Bowler who wore a pair of reading glasses (for checking copy) and carried another pair in his coat pocket for checking up on reporters more than four feet away from his desk.

Eventually, of course, Doc switched to bifocals.

After all, a 10-year-old suit-coat pocket can stand only so much wear and tear from glasses-switching.

In addition to working with the guy in a city room as long as I did, Doc and I managed to roll up a few miles of travel together.

We went to Chicago. We went to Dallas. We spent time in Wyoming. We traveled eastern and northern Montana more times than I like to think of.

You can trace our journeys, I'm sure, by the empty beer cans left in our wake.

That was one thing about traveling with Doc. You had to drink beer as though the future of the American brewing industry depended on it.

I spent a lot of time with Doc — and without him — in Scobey, his home town.

I knew Doc's folks, I knew the people he grew up with and the people he went to school with. I know his children, his in-laws — and I've even met a few of the dogs he's been on speaking terms with.

Over the years we've known each other — and over as many beers as it would take to float a battleship — Doc and I have discussed politics, religion and the military — and we're not any closer together on any of these subjects than we were the first time they came up.

But I'll say this for Doc:

The guy had a sense of what constituted a hard-news story more, I think, than anyone else I've known in this business — and he was both bullish and bearish enough to smoke, prod and break it out.

Sure, I've got mad at the guy myself — and he had it coming. I think.

But I learned from him — and that's what any editor worthy of the name should pass on to people on the other side of the city desk or outside the walls of the glassed-in office.

No one ever said editors have to be all sweetness and light — and Doc Bowler is living proof of it.

But when it comes to passing out Mr. Nice Guy awards, Doc'll be up there with other city-room legends all over the country who put newspapering first and popularity contests second.

There's a story I've told several times about Doc and, at risk of boring those of you who've heard it, here it comes again.

About a year after Doc came here a friend from Helena talked to me about him.

"How do you get along with Doc?" he asked.

Fine, I told him.

"You what?" he said. "You get along with that guy? I don't believe it. Not Doc Bowler."

But, he added, if I did get along with him, I was one of the very few.

"How on earth did you manage it?"

It was simple, I told him.

"You see," I said, "a long, long time ago I removed a thorn from his paw — and he's never forgotten it."

Stop the quills!
It's another scoop!

THERE IS ABSOLUTELY no truth to the report that I started in the newspaper business at a time when editors were still yelling "Stop the quills."

As a matter of fact — and at risk of shattering a few illusions about this game — I never once heard an editor order a press stopped the way Hollywood showed it.

I remember asking my first city editor about it once — and getting in reply a half-patient, half-exasperated look.

"No such a damfool thing ever happened here," said Arch O'Bryant. "When we have to stop a run for whatever reason, we pick up the phone, call the press room and tell 'em to hold it a minute."

Anyone yelling "Stop the presses" in HIS city room, Arch implied, would end up in the same doghouse with reporters who tried to write as though they worked for Time Magazine — and editors who tried to act as though they did.

Legends and myths about newspapers and the people who worked for them persist, however — thanks (I guess) to both movies and television.

I never heard anyone pick up a telephone, call his paper and yell "Gimme a rewrite!"

I never saw a press card stuck in a hatband.

And, after nearly 40 years as an ink-stained wretch (which is what reporters were once called), I've yet to hear an editor bellow "Tear out the front page, we're going all out on this one and to hell with the mayor."

There was, however, still a telegraph key in my first city room and there were still two people there who could use it — but it didn't work anymore.

There were still two telephones sans mouthpieces, one of which was on one of those accordion-like extensions enabling the user to get 10 feet away from the desk before being brought up short by turn-of-the-century technology.

And we still had an editor who'd pick up a metal wastebasket to swear into — just to make certain he was heard throughout the room.

There are times, in this day of video tubes, tapes and computer memory discs, I long for my typewriter.

After all, a typewriter had to go pretty wrong before it took an expert to set it right again. Keys piled up, you pulled them apart, bent them back and went on with the job. A ribbon wore out, you changed it. Type got dirty, you cleaned it.

Walk in a newsroom today with its plethora of electronic marvels and you feel for a moment as though you'd blundered into Mission Control during a moon shot.

Except that it's quiet.

I guess I still miss the clatter of teletypes, the tapping and ringing of typewriter keys and bells, the hollow sound of footsteps on a wood floor — and the occasional anguished wail of a copy editor who has seen "judgment" spelled wrong for the third time that month.

I almost forgot one more important city room sound.

It was the congenial blup-blup-burble of our inverted five-gallon water jar drinking fountain, a departmental fixture which, needless to say, we didn't get from watching Hollywood.

Hollywood got it from watching us.

Even our publisher, down the hall in his mahogany paneled sanctum sanctorum, would leave his silver carafe and crystal glasses to drink water out of paper cups with the rest of us.

It was, he said once, the only place in the building where he could find out what was going on outside.

Undeniably, changes have come over the years — whether you're in the business of reading a newspaper or publishing one.

But it's fun to think, sometimes, of what it was like once.

Like I say, I miss the typewriters.

Hell, I even miss the quills.

Where the *&%★&★ is that ★&*%! copyperson?

I N A WORLD in which change is the only constant, it shouldn't surprise anyone to learn that newspapers aren't exempt from keeping up with the times.

But I'm not talking about teletype machines replacing the telegraph, computer terminals occupying desk space once reserved for typewriters — or even the quiet demise of that photographic workhorse, the 4x5 Speed-Graphic .

Carpets now cover city-room floors where once the spittoon was king. Reporters, once a breed which never took off a hat ANYWHERE, today not only go for the most part bareheaded but have been known to show up at work with permanents.

And it's been eons since I've seen a desk man with a green eyeshade.

Change in the newspaper business is more than physical.

In the news business they don't even talk the way they used to.

Some of this I blame on the public-relations people.

Advanced technology — "state of the art," it's known as now — can account for some of it.

What blame is left can be laid at the door of the guy who used the word "deskperson," "copyperson" or "legperson" for the first time.

I take some comfort, of course, in being able to report that editors still swear at reporters, reporters still swear at editors — and both join forces to swear at the advertising department.

There is, in short, a vestige of times-as-they-once-were in the city room that only profanity and invective, properly used, can provide.

There the resemblance ceases.

A newspaper today, for example, is referred to, not as a newspaper or even a paper, but as a product or a package.

(My paperboy — or should I say package boy? — missed my door the other morning when it was raining, and my morning product was sopping wet.)

With the advent of computerized typesetting (and no type, in the strictest sense of the word, is set, also in the strictest sense of the word, any more) the filler became as much a part of the past as the spittoon.

Fillers, some of you may recall, were those little tidbits of information about the rainfall in Bergen, Norway, or the period of gestation for the lesser kudu, that printers dropped in to fill out a story that didn't run quite long enough.

And in case you're wondering, printers also have all but disappeared.

Once the only thing an editor had to worry about — aside from keeping his reporters sober and covering their beats — was the press conference.

Modern terminology has had its way as well with what once was a simple meeting called by a public official, a politician, a business executive or a celebrity of sorts at which photographers took pictures and reporters asked questions.

And sometimes a pretty decent news story came out of it.

The press conference has now become — in Madison Avenuese — a photo opportunity or a media event.

And it's often about as newsworthy as last month's National Geographic.

City editors no longer call reporters "sweetheart" or "baby" the way back in the rough-and-tumble days of this business, they once did.

And there seems to be an increasing tendency among reporters to refer to themselves as journalists.

A journalist, I learned when I started out in this business, is anyone who keeps a diary. A guy who writes stories for a newspaper is called a reporter.

But I guess one of the greatest changes has been in the darkroom — or rather, the guys who come out of the darkroom.

News photographers today can — and do — pass easily for normal, civilized people.

And, come to think of it, you can say the same for city editors.

Sports editors
are living martyrs

OF ALL THE JOBS on a newspaper I wouldn't take — if I were either in a taking position or a taking mood — that of sports editor probably heads the list.

Publishers have their problems, true.

And editors are well up there in the ranks of martyrs.

Even advertising managers, I have little doubt, arrive at those occasional dark nights of the soul when they wish they had joined either the Foreign Legion or gone into bank robbing as a more lucrative and less nerve-racking a profession.

But sports writers, surely, are those not only in the middle but engulfed — even swallowed whole — by it as well.

I know whereof I speak.

Take a police reporter, for example. Or a business writer. Or even film critic.

One has only to worry about what cops say about his stories. Or the lawbreakers.

The business writer in the course of a normal day's work deals with only two adversaries, competition — and the paper's advertising manager.

The film critic stands aloof even from these.

He may not know movies — but he knows what he likes and doesn't like.

But, alas, the lowly sports editor, whose head is filled with statistics and whose mind is obsessed with only one thought:

How did he get the job in the first place.

More than anyone else on the paper, a sports writer is confronted with experts who, once having gained their expertise by reading other sports writers, use it like a switchblade knife.

The guy who sits on the sports desk can be knowledgeable in any number of sports, beginning with basketball, football, track and baseball.

But somewhere out there in the circulation area there'll always be a lacrosse fan (even though he never spent any time in Wisconsin) or worse, a jai alai devotee who can't find the scores in the paper.

And if there's one thing that sports-desk people learn before they learn to walk — let alone write — it's that each fan thinks his sport all-important.

If you don't believe me, try reasoning with a Little League parent whose son's game was left out of the paper because of the coverage given the Indianapolis "500."

Or consider how you'd deal with a modern-day musketeer — or cardinal's guardsman — who can't find the results of an Ivy League fencing match.

But even if — through some miracle of communications and technology — sports people were able to cover it all, they'd still find themselves beleaguered by transplanted alumni of, say, Baker University in Baldwin, Kansas, who couldn't find a Baker-Slippery Rock (Pa.) score in the Saturday morning Gazette.

Or suffer the excoriation of a retired lieutenant-commander trying to learn the winner of the Atlantic Fleet middleweight boxing finals by poring through his morning paper.

But sports editors, after all, are only human.

They have their favorites, too — though for the most part they manage a creditable degree of objectivity.

One of my favorites is a former Gazetteer who was asked by the man who hired him if he'd ever covered sports before.

His answer was no.

The editor next wanted to know if he knew anything about sports?

The answer was the same.

Finally the editor wondered if he would be interested in covering sports.

A third no.

It was on the basis of these three questions that he was promptly assigned the job of sports editor.

And Roy Anderson, for as long as he was around here, did a pretty fair country job on the desk.

Which, in itself, I guess, says something about sports writing.

Society Editors
have been transformed

I PAUSE FROM TIME to time to mourn the passing of some of the once great institutions of the newspaper world — the paste pot, the green eyeshade and the managing editor's cuspidor to mention only a few.

Paste pots disappeared, of course, about the time we

changed from typewriters and copy paper to video display tubes.

The green eyeshade — with one notable exception right here at the Gazette — became a museum when lighting experts started moving fluorescent tubing into newsrooms.

I'm not sure, however, that in some obscure corner of some littered office occupied by some individualist in this business there isn't that once familiar item of brass still serving its traditional function.

I'm certain, on the other hand, that if such is the case, you'll find not too far away a modernist whose desk is graced with a sign that thanks you for not spitting.

All these, however, are incidentals. We can live as comfortably without them as we did with them. They leave no empty places nor do we experience any deep sense of loss.

We mourn their passing, in short, but do not grieve it.

Our tears are for that one-time giant of the newsroom who was known as the Society Editor.

There are no Society Editors any more.

Changing times have done away with both title and image.

In place of a Society Editor we have today — or most newspapers have today — a women's editor. She goes by other names as well but when she edits lifestyle, homemaking, club, organization or engagement-wedding stories her job is comfortably summed up as women's editor.

Most women's editors look about the same as any other female reporter. They dress about the same. They act about the same.

I guess what I'm trying to say is that the most traumatic change is in the image.

The society editor of days gone by looked like a Society Editor.

And, by Heaven, she acted like one.

None of this hobnobbing about the water cooler with the peasants, be they editor or reporter. None of this cheery chit-chat over a cup of coffee.

Ask anyone who grew up in the Society Editor era and they'll tell you it was like trying to work in the same room with Madame Nhu, Perle Mesta and Queen Marie of Rumania. Society Editors were, in effect, royalty.

They came in the office looking like they had just come from a state dinner or were on their way to one.

They acted as though the newsroom were a necessary stop, like the confessional for a penitent, on their way to cleaner, brighter and certainly more respectable places. They held themselves aloof — and their hauteur was magnified and buttressed by the desk set apart from all others, the fresh flowers which graced it daily — and the dignified arrangement of engagement books, letter holders (for invitations) and souvenir programs which silently proclaimed the esteem in which she was held by the social pillars of her world.

She moved in another plane — and the rest of us were happy to let her.

I guess the nicest thing about Society Editors back then was that they were so busy moving in Society Circles they didn't spend too much time at the office.

Which was great with us. At least, it gave us a chance to do the one thing that forced her from time to time to notice that we were also in the world, though possibly not of it.

Whenever a Society Editor got too uppity we just waited until she left the office.

Then we moved the managing editor's spitton over by her desk.

Silence hangs heavy over the old newsroom

BACK IN THE OLDEN times — which is how those of us in the business refer to newspapering as it was — the one question most often asked by a city room visitor had to do with noise in the office.

And, come to think of it it was noisy.

There were no such animals as silent typewriters. Wire machines (teletypes to you) set up a constant clatter. A police radio squawked. Editors yelled at reporters. Reporters yelled back.

Leather heels clumped over bare wood floors. Telephones jangled constantly. And an hour never passed without someone slamming a desk drawer or kicking a metal wastebasket.

Even the perfume worn by our society editor was loud.

She left it behind her like a wake, wherever she went in the plant — and the story was true that when you wanted to find her all you had to do was to walk out in the hall and sniff your way along until you caught up with her.

"How," visitors invariably asked, "can you concentrate on writing with all this noise and confusion?"

But I'd trade that any day for the noise and confusion going on here at The Gazette as a result of some interior remodeling that's been in progress the past month or so.

Jackhammers explode under your feet or against a nearby wall with nerve-jangling irregularity.

Assorted craftsmen bore holes in ceilings, cut doors in partitions where doors never existed and thump monotonously on carpets with hammers.

Holes appear in floors through which yards of wire are pushed in and out.

"You're going to be moved," an editor said to me some time ago. "We don't know where but you'll move someplace." It's like being back in an army replacement center, waiting for overseas orders — except that here, for all intents and purposes, you're already in a combat zone.

Even this would be bearable, I suppose, were it not for the suspense engendered by the periodic conferences held by the people who are tearing up the pea patch here.

They call their meetings to order just out of earshot. They're in white overalls, blue workshirts, collars and ties. They look up at the ceiling, point to a wall and get down on their hands and knees. They rattle blueprints and alternatively shake or nod their heads.

Once agreement is reached — and of course you NEVER know on what — they break up or go their various ways in silence.

And a jackhammer explodes beneath your feet again.

I suppose, looking at it from a philosophical viewpoint — which at this point in time is about the most consoling place you can look at it from — the current architectural Sturm und Drang is part of the price we pay for progress in this business.

Maybe — just maybe — The Gazette's brave new city room world won't be so bad after all.

But I don't know but what I'd just as soon trade it for the clatter, the jangle, the tiny sound of a wastebasket rolling into a corner — or even Ilma Harlan's perfume.

At least a guy knew where he stood (or sat) back then.

My dark night, however, is not without one ray of hope.

Happily, I've discovered one constant in this welter of variables in which I come to work every day.

And while I'll admit a men's room isn't exactly a pot of gold at the end of a rainbow, it's still comforting to know that when you need it, it's right there where it's been all these years.

Treasure the moments
of a grand Old Year

THIS IS PROBABLY a bit late to be writing a New Year's Day column.

And that, in itself, is sort of funny.

We say "Happy New Year" beginning — more or less — on the last day of December and, depending on how things work out, manage to carry the greeting clear through the first day of January.

Then, as is too often the case, we forget.

Once New Year's Day is past, it becomes a part of the dead past.

For too many of us, the second of January is like the fifth of July — or the 26th of December.

But we still remember, I like to think, some of those famous "resolutions" we all make once the hands of whatever clock (or watch) we happen to be watching begin to close, like inexorable scissors, on the hour of midnight.

I've never been much of a New Year's resolution type.

I suppose it's because I am — and have been — too much of a sentimentalist.

When it gets close to that magic hour on the last day of that year we'll never see again, I think not so much of the year ahead as I do of the one just ending.

New Year's Day — or New Year's Eve — has never been to me so much a time to resolve as it is a time to remember.

And in a way that magic and sentimental moment, when the band is playing "Auld Lang Syne" and people are hugging and kissing people they wouldn't remember if they met them on the street the next day, is a time for remembering.

Looking ahead to a New Year is great.

Looking back on the one just ended is better.

Sure, we all can think of how it could have been better. We all can think of times when we could have been more considerate, more loving — and more honest.

But we can, as well, treasure the bright, the happy and the wonderful hours that that Old Year, characterized as he is by the white-robed old man with the long white beard and the scythe, brought us.

We've all of us lost some friends in the year just past.

But we can all treasure their friendship in the New Year — and in all those years which are to follow.

We've all done and said things for which we are sorry.

But, remember.

We have a year, and more, to make up for our shortcomings, as well as our misgivings.

We have a year behind us from which we've learned.

And we have a year ahead in which we can benefit from our learning.

And, finally, we have just ended a year after which, for all its highs and lows, for all its dark times and all its bright times, we're still here to be thankful for it and the opportunity we're given to greet the one ahead.

And this, I guess, is what nothing more than a simple date on a calendar is all about.

It's a chance to begin, not again, but anew.

And, in looking toward the new, draw upon what is past.

That's what, in a way, I think about when I find myself joining in at (approximately) midnight on an earnest, though somewhat off-key, chorus of "Auld Lang Syne."

I've never objected to ringing out the Old and ringing in the New.

But I've always felt that the exuberant shouts that accompany the clanging of bells and the blowing of whistles as that one hour approaches should be joined as well by a heartfelt thanks that we've been given one more year to do with what we will.

Good evening
Mr. and Mrs. America

ALONG WITH THE other changes which have taken place in our society, I can't get over the way radio stations look today compared to how it was back even in the not-so-early days of broadcasting.

For one thing, they moved to the suburbs long before the shopping centers, long before the branch banks or the service clubs.

It's the rare station today you'll find broadcasting from the top floor of a bank, a hotel or a department store. Yet there was a time when any building owner in his right mind would be proud to count a station among his renters.

There was, as a matter of fact, a six-story building in Wichita, Kan., which went through a name change when the town's first radio station set up business there in the 1920s.

Last I heard it was still the KFH Building.

In its salad days, radio was happy to let a suitably awed public in on the new art.

Announcers at WIBW in Topeka went through their daily and nightly chores behind a large picture window which overlooked the lawn of the state capitol through which any passersby could watch them in action.

And there were plenty who did.

The biggest change, though, came inside the stations themselves.

Imposing, heavily draped and thickly carpeted "studios" large enough to hold a high school marching band gave way to acoustic tiled cubicles referred to casually as "booths".

Even the tomb-like silence which once enveloped the inner sanctum of broadcasting is a thing of the past.

You rarely see a closed door in the business today — unless the front office gang is noisier than usual.

Nor do announcers — and there are still a few around who go by the name — take themselves as seriously as they once did.

I remember one veteran at KFH who never sat down at his news microphone without a jacket and tie — and who spent the five minutes before his broadcast pacing the floor, smoking furiously, thumbing through copy stripped from the teletype machine, sipping from a glass of water and cocking a nervous eyebrow at the monster clock on the wall behind him.

Now whether he would have done this had there not been visitors at the station watching their first "live" radio broadcast I don't know.

But it was part of the business at the time.

Another thing that seems to have disappeared now that radio has come of age is that old bugaboo called mike fright.

Almost everyone who stood before a microphone got it, in one form or another.

It was something you read about. It was something everyone was supposed to get. It was the electronic age equivalent of buck fever.

And I haven't heard of anyone getting THAT for years.

I guess I got mike fright — of a sort — the first time I stepped up to a microphone and started reading a script. (That was back in the days when you let your copy drop silently to the floor as you read it so the rustle of turning pages wouldn't be picked up.)

But mine would more properly be called "reverse mike fright."

I wasn't a bit afraid of all those people out there in what was then called "radioland" who were listening.

What scared me was the thought that maybe no one was.

Time marches on

THE RAILROAD, I suppose, isn't really to blame.

Northern Pacific officials, according to reports, are "amending the rules" which will permit employees to use wrist watches.

So there's another piece of the good old American scene that we can kiss goodbye.

After all, there was something dignified, almost classic, in the time-honored ceremony that ensued when a passenger asked a conductor or a brakeman for the time.

Back went the brass-buttoned blue coat as a hand came up and dipped into the pocket of a vest — also brass buttoned — and withdrew what, for sake of a better word, we're forced to call The Watch.

The railroader's watch was a long way from the paper-thin, microscopic bit of jewelry by which modern man tells time.

It was as substantial as a baked potato, as dependable as taxes and had a dial that a blind man could read on a foggy afternoon.

Next to the courtly bow and the swirling cape, there was nothing that caught the eye as much as the simple act of a railroad man looking at his watch.

Once out of the pocket and flat on the palm of a hand, The Watch was subjected to careful scrutiny by its owner. A finger would touch the heavy crystal and the stem would be given a token turn.

A railroader never told you it was ten-fifteen and let it go at that.

"I have," he'd say, after a long look at the massive hands, the bold figures and red second gradations, "ten-fifteen and — 32 seconds."

Another pause.

" — now."

It was enough to make a wrist watch wearer wish he'd chosen a sundial instead.

Once the time had been given, back into the pocket went The Watch to rest at the end of its gold chain until another traveler, groping through life, measuring only hours and minutes and letting seconds go hang, asked for enlightenment.

And the whole ceremony would be repeated.

I'm going to miss railroad watches.

They aren't as noisy, of course, as were steam locomotives, nor do they have that comfortable smell of coal, paint and oil about them — but railroading is going to be the poorer without them.

I suppose, too, these wrist watches can be automatic — and that makes it all the worse.

From now on when you see an engineer, a fireman, a conductor or brakeman waving as a train passes by, you can't depend on its being the traditional railroad greeting.

He may be only winding his watch.

Ageless books revive imagination of youth

THE MAILS TODAY are full of opportunities, bargains, privileges, not to mention treasures — if, that is, you believe all the sales pitches you get from the book club crowd.

But I've yet to see one with enough sense of tradition to

make the truly timeless — or should I say ageless? — books available to someone who wants to read them.

I was struck by this not long ago when I tried to pick up a copy of "Treasure Island" for a kid I know who'd never gotten around to reading it.

Maybe there's one around (and I'm sure to get mail if there is) but I still haven't found it.

An ageless book by my definition is one that appeals to a fifth grader every bit as much as it appeals to his grandfather.

Like "Twenty Thousand Leagues Under the Sea."

But you don't find kids any more who read Robert Louis Stevenson or Jules Verne.

We can lay part of the blame, I suppose, on teachers who spend more time learning how to teach than they do learning what to teach.

And we can put the rest on parents who look at a blank space against a wall and decide to pick up a bookcase to fill it — and enough books to fill the bookcase.

If there's one thing that chills me in this day and age it's talking to a high schooler and learning he's never read a Sherlock Holmes story, has never heard of "Quentin Durward" — and who thinks the "Midnight Ride of Paul Revere" is a book about living on the road with a rock band.

What happened, for heaven's sake, to reading for entertainment — and reading again for sheer joy?

If, for example, I hadn't got hold of a copy of "Captain Blood" in grade school I'd have never dreamed of a possible career as a pirate.

And if you think this is soul searing, I'll give you a whole day — along with odds — and bet you can't find a kid in junior high school who's ever heard of Tom Sawyer or Huckleberry Finn, let alone "Innocents Abroad" or "Life on the Mississippi"

It's all very well, I suppose, for producers of today to make R-rated musketeer films.

But how many kids are around who've read enough Alexandre Dumas to know that D'Artagnan was not one of literature's most famous trios?

With the possible exception of "Gone With The Wind," seeing the film is not like reading the book.

There are, however, glimmerings to light on the horizon.

We've seen phonetic spelling go down the drain.

And long ago we heard clods dropping on the coffin of the New Math.

I'm even a bit encouraged by the rumors going around that Latin may one day be taught again in high school.

It could turn out to be a whole new ball game.

Who knows?

Once kids start reading again, the possibilities are limitless.

They might even learn to spell.

Treasure hides under garbage can covers

I MIGHT AS WELL confess and get it over with.

I'm a Pavlov dog where garage sales are concerned.

The mere hint of one in the neighborhood is enough to start me on my way.

And I guess it comes from all the time I spent in alleys when I was a kid.

Trash barrels were the version of the garage sale back in Kansas.

A drowsy summer day — and word that a family down the street was moving — was enough to get us started.

And we made the rounds almost every Saturday morning, especially during spring house-cleaning time.

Of course, at the garage sale of today the merchandise is more neatly displayed.

Trash barrels, on the other hand, didn't cost you a cent.

And you could end a morning of alley-grubbing with a collection of household jetsam ranging from old medicine bottles (from which we were sternly warned not to drink) to discarded toasters.

Medicine bottles were good to keep mercury in — which we got from discarded thermometers or dead batteries.

Toasters that didn't toast had a poor market.

But they did have cords and any kid knew that if you strip the insulation off a toaster cord you ended up with three or four feet of bright, shiny copper wire that might come in handy for doing something with.

Burned-out light bulbs always showed up — to be promptly popped against a rock.

And once in a great while you found an alarm clock which, though it didn't keep time, nonetheless clanged satisfactorily when you turned the "Alarm Set" knob in the right direction.

We were often criticized for bringing trash home.

Which just goes to show how insensitive and unaware parents are.

What we brought home was not trash.

It wasn't even junk.

It was, as we pointed out frequently to grownups, real good stuff.

Some of it was good stuff that we needed.

Some was stuff that could be used — maybe — someday. Probably.

And some — very little, surely, but some — literally fell into the category of treasure.

Crystal doorknobs, hair clippers, radio tubes and books made a whole summer of alley-grubbing worth while.

I found a bird cage once and used it to keep bats in.

25

And we didn't confine our activities to residental alleys.

Stores threw things in trash barrels, too. And doctors.

Finding a flashlight that didn't work, a carton of warped tongue depressors or a solid wood cigar box could make a kid's day.

And you could always count on the boxes behind the bakery for broken cream puffs from the night shift.

The sequel to alley-grubbing, of course, was the trading sessions that invariably followed. And I guess this was what finally brought the parental foot down on it all.

Our folks started getting their own junk back.

Of mice
and men

WHAT I'M ABOUT to say should in no way be taken as an attack on Saturday morning television.

I'm talking about the cartoon shows, of course — because if there's anything else on Saturday morning television I haven't as yet been able to find it.

While the elbows-down-on-the-rug position may be appropriate and popular enough for members of the present generation who find time hanging heavily on their hands on Saturdays I still find myself aligned solidly with audiences of another era, another medium — and sponsors other than toy manufacturers.

I'm talking about the Mickey Mouse Club — are you listening, Charmain? — which is not to be confused with another television show called the Mouseketeers.

The Mickey Mouse Club, among the earliest of Walt Disney's forays into the world of commerce outside his Hollywood studio, was born in the early 1930s and, by the end of its first season, threatened to surpass in both numbers and fanaticism any political or social movement then in the news — including devotees of that newest parlor craze, Monopoly.

The Mickey Mouse Club met in the theater on Saturday morning, sang the club song, elected officers, watched a Disney cartoon and a grade B film and got home in time for lunch.

It was a noisy, crowded, milling throng of grade schoolers who for the first time in their theater-going experience didn't have an adult next to, behind or before them telling them to sit still, shut up or both.

Mickey Mouse Club members didn't fool around with such artificialities as mouse-eared hats — and they especially didn't waste time singing about Y they LIKED you.

A Saturday morning session of the club was in effect an exercise in survival because once those theater lights went down it was every man (or Mouse) for himself and devil take the hindmost (or hindmouse).

You paid $1 for the card which not only admitted you to 10 shows during the summer but identified you as well as a full-fledged member in good standing of the Mickey Mouse Clubs of America. It also gave you the privilege of greeting other members as "Mickey" or "Minnie" Mice as well as granting you full voting rights at the monthly election of a Mickey and Minnie who presided — if that's the word I want — over the weekly mayhem.

The accoutrements of office donned by the successful candidates were "Mickey" and "Minnie" jackets which were turned over to the theater manager once the session adjourned.

The manager held the title of Chief Mickey Mouse.

The policeman who stood by — just in case — was called simply "Chief" — because that was who he was.

We learned all the important aspects of theater conduct at MMC meetings like stamping on the floor, whistling and screaming when the cartoon came on (or the film broke), throwing popcorn, putting ice down shirt or dress collars and generally behaving like a pack of hyenas.

I can't recall any of the shows I saw as a full-fledged member in good standing of the Mickey Mouse Clubs of America.

That, however, is understandable. We were all kept too busy learning the club song to concentrate on Bob Steele, Johnny Mack Brown or which horse Gene Autry was singing to.

The penalty for failure to learn the song was — naturally — suspension of membership privileges for a week.

I, accordingly, submit the following as evidence of my dedication as a pioneer Mickey Mouser:

I'm the guy they call little Mickey Mouse.
Got a sweetheart down by the chicken house.
Neither fat nor skinny, she's the horse's whinny.
She's my little Minnie Mouse.
When it's feeding time for the animals,
And they howl and groan like the cannibals,
Both the crow's caw-caw and the mule's hee-haw,
Gosh, what a racket like an old buzz saw!
I have listened to the cuckoo coo his cuckoo,
And I've heard the rooster cock his doodle-doo-doo,
But the cows and chickens, they all sound like the dickens,
When I hear my little Minnie's "Yoo hoo!"

In the case against Saturday morning televison, the plaintiff rests.

The old home town
is never the same

GOING BACK TO the old home town — as I did last week — can be a nostalgia trip in more ways than one.

Not only are the people changed.

Not only is the town itself changed.

You're apt to discover — as I did — that you've changed along with them.

It's nothing to worry about, of course. Nor is it anything to feel defensive over.

We all live where we want to live — whether it's staying home and growing up with a town or moving away and relegating it to a part of our past.

But it's always good for those of us who said goodbye to a place that did much toward forming the attitudes, ambitions and plans that shaped our later years to return every now and then as I do.

In a sense it's sort of like time travel — backwards.

Iola — for those of you who don't know about it — is a town about the size of Laurel, maybe smaller, in southeastern Kansas. Our river is the Neosho. Our creek is Elm. One borders it on the west, the other runs through the south end of town.

It's built, as many Kansas towns are, on a square, the courthouse in the center. The main streets are named after presidents as are the grade schools.

Iola's streets are wide but shaded — in many neighborhoods, completely arched — by elm trees. Sidewalks are about balanced between brick and cement and lawns, flower beds (or gardens) and shrubs are carefuly and proudly tended by owners, however old or young they may be.

My home town has a grapevine that won't quit. You can't buy a new car, check in the hospital, get married, spend a weekend in the Ozarks or, for that matter, die, without the news being all over town by the time it makes the evening paper. My sister's retirement after 41 years of teaching school, the occasion for my recent visit, is a perfect example.

It was announced one night at a faculty end-of-school dinner and dance for the first time. By the next afternoon the whole town knew about it.

Iola changes as all towns do. Though the population is about the same as it was when I was growing up there, Iola has twice as many homes, three times as many businesses as it had then.

But the familiar names are still there. The signs on doctors and lawyers offices, on grocery stores, jewelry shops and many other business firms bear the names of sons — and in some cases, grandsons — of those I knew when I lived in Iola. The Register, for example, is published by the grandson of the man who founded it who, I remember well, talked to me about a career in the newspaper business.

I did the things you usually do when you go back home as I did. I went by the steep driveway where I broke my arm — trying to skate up it. I looked for the old taxi shed where we used to buy bootleg whiskey in high school. (It was gone.) I went by the low-water bridge where we fished. (It was gone, too.)

One pilgrimage took me to an old girl friend's home. She'd been gone as long as I have but the house she lived in was still there at 217 South State St. We've kept in touch over the years and I can tell you this much:

She's in one helluva lot better shape than that house is.

The high school I graduated from still has the same battleship gray floors and walls, students change classes to the same paper-tape operated clock and bells. The flagpole's still there. And I even made a quick trip to the restroom where we used to sneak a quick cigarette between classes and lit up — just for old times sake.

The last time I did that I got caught and kicked out of American history.

This time I was home free.

All in all, it was a great trip and a good week.

And maybe neither Iola or I have changed all that much.

But I was still asked the question while I was there:

Tell us, what is the biggest change in Iola from what it was like when you lived here to what it's like today?

My answer was quick — and simple:

Today I know a lot more people in the cemetery there than I did when I was growing up.

The arms race
slowed down to a walk

O F ALL THE WEAPONS systems developed by what I'm forced to call the youth of my generation, the rubber gun was probably the best answer to the security of any back yard or barn.

It had simplicity of design.

You took a half-inch piece of wood, maybe a foot long, and nailed a block of the same thickness, about three inches long and two wide to one end. Then you prowled through a pile of junk in a garage until you found an old inner tube from which you proceeded to cut bands of rubber, about a half inch wide.

A snap-type clothespin — which you either begged or swiped — was then bound firmly to the rear of the wood-block butt, business end up and you were ready for action.

There was little production time lag in equipping Saturday morning troops with weapons.

There were, of course, refinements indulged in by the individualists in the crowd. There were rubber guns painted black and there were rubber gun stocks carefully carved to represent pistol grips.

No one ever knew exactly what the notches stood for — but there wasn't a gun over 24 hours old without them. (One reckless adventurer vowed the single notch he boasted represented a direct hit on an English teacher who was walking away from him at the time. It was, however, difficult to prove.)

There were two types of ammunition — the single, untreated band, used generally for potshotting at curtains, lampshades, newspapers, (with someone reading them) cats, small children and, possibly, parents — if they were in a good mood at the time. The second type, the anti-personnel band, was the one used in rubber gun wars which were standard recreation every Saturday morning.

This was developed simply by tying a knot in each band, enabling it to carry farther. The deadly effect, of course, lay in the knot itself. If it hit just right it'd sting.

Generally, there was little objection to rubber gun warfare from grownups — even the day we decided to start testing in the atmosphere.

They were quiet. (This, I've discovered since becoming both a grownup AND a parent myself, is a prime consideration in assessing the benefits or evils of any recreation.)

They were harmless — relatively.

I remember, actually, only one casualty resulting from the rubber gun — and this one was, you might say, indirect. It happened to a kid with the only peg tooth in the neighborhood who cut up the wrong inner tube in his father's garage. It looked, he told us later, like an old one to him.

I suppose the tubeless tire was what put the rubber gun on the skids — that and the development of what we all realized at that time was truly The Ultimate Weapon.

You see, you take a Y-shaped branch of a tree and skin all the bark off and then you take an old shoe and cut a piece of the tongue out to make a kind of pocket and then you stake these two rubber strips and ...

Arch enemies
will never die

WERE I TO PICK my favorite villain of all time it wouldn't be the man Sherlock Holmes called "the Napoleon of crime," the infamous Professor Moriarty.

Nor would it be Jack the Ripper.

As a matter of fact, my world champion meanie isn't even Caucasian.

Almost from the time I started to read I became a fan of that arch enemy of the Western world, the evil genius of the Orient whose creator, Arthur Sarsfield Ward — better known as Sax Rohmer — called Dr. Fu-Manchu.

FuManchu, for those members of the congregation who were dozing when he first came on the literary scene back before World War I, was — as Rohmer characterized him — "a sinister Chinaman."

His mission, assigned him by a super-secret cabal known as the Si-Fan, was to keep China for the Chinese — and to dispose of her enemies by a wide variety of unorthodox, terrifying and exotic means.

FuManchu, who commuted from Peking to London and back as the mood (and the activity of the white enemy) inspired him, was never without a scorpion, a mysterious insect whose bite was known as the "zayat kiss," a dacoit, a hamadryad or a evil-tempered baboon when occasion required their services in keeping missionaries, archaeologists, diplomats, scholars at home where they belonged instead of probing the secrets of an awakening China.

FuManchu, as described by Sir Denis Nayland Smith, the head good guy in a war that extended over 40 years in a dozen books from Rohmer's prolific pen, represented "the Yellow Peril incarnate in one man."

And when the Perils had a guy like FuManchu on their side, one man was all they needed.

As casual as he was with life, as great a threat as he posed to Western civilization, the evil doctor had one good point which lasted from his debut in "The Insidious Dr. FuManchu" to his swan song in "President FuManchu."

He was a man of explicit and implicit honor when it came to keeping his word.

Even Smith came to trust him that much, along with Smith's friend, Dr. Petrie, a sort of Watson-type chronicler of adventures which took them from London to Paris, Cairo, Ispahan, Washington, New York — and back to London through all the years.

FuManchu had a slave girl, one Karamanch, who after years of serving her malevolent master, finally left to marry Petrie. Among their wedding presents was (of course) one from FuManchu.

He also had a daughter, Fah Lo Suee, who fell in and out of love with Smith and who eventually was consigned to a fiery furnace by her father after she unsuccessfully conspired with his rivals to take over control of the Si-Fan.

FuManchu wasn't only mean. He was impartial as well.

I don't know, really, what happened to the man who, for all his malevolence and fanaticism, for all his assasinations and bloodshed became a lovable sort of villain.

At least — and even his worst enemies admit this — you knew where FuManchu stood all the time. And once he gave his word on something, good or bad, you could count on it.

Perhaps, as he said in one of his several farewells, FuManchu, Lord of the Fires, has returned to the fires from whence he came.

But still, after a late night reading of the battered and time-worn volumes on my FuManchu shelf, I feel myself listening for a muffled click of a box opening to loose a deadly insect upon my study carpet, peering at my window to make certain a pair of hideous yellow eyes aren't watching my every move, sniffing the air for the tantalizing hint of mimosa, a fragrance favored by the violet-eyed Karamaneh, or hearing the abrupt rapping on my door that tells me Nayland Smith is there, once more on the trail of his, mine and — if you were among those lucky enough to know him — your favorite sinister Chinaman.

A castle guarded by quiet memories

T HE DOOR TO THE bone-dry, dusty stairway was the least-used one in the house — but behind it and above lay a mysterious, dingy place of wonders and memories where a child could leave behind the new, bright, noisy world of everyday.

It was quiet in the attic.

You heard the warped flooring creak under your feet as you walked around and the sounds of people moving down below seemed to come from far away.

You watched dust motes dance in sunlight slivers that streamed through the boarded window at the far end and you sniffed the mustiness that mingled with the smell of mothballs and drying paper.

No one, in the days of attics, ever threw anything away.

Old clothes, as strange to touch and hear as they were to see, filled the quaint old trunks without which no attic was complete.

A jumble of wheels, springs, stands, shades, slats, cushions and chairs were the living rooms, dining rooms and bedrooms of a generation and more ago.

And there were piles of magazines and books — magazines with their strange advertising and books with faded writings in the front that said "Merry Christmas from Aunt Clara — 1882."

An attic in the summer could be an insufferable place — but sometimes you went there anyway to find a book, to rummage in a trunk-tray with its tangled mess of beads, ribbons, pins and quaint old photographs of people who you knew of but never knew. Or sometimes you went there to cry because of the collapse of a part of your child's world that seemed important at the time.

Whatever the reason, when you came down the steep stairs to the coolness of the house, there was sweat on the collar of your shirt and your face was smeared with dust.

But you had what you'd gone up there for, whether it was a book, an old convention badge — or the dusty comfort only an attic can afford.

A child could be king or queen in an attic when the shingled roof rustled with the noise of rain and he sat with a book and an apple and read through a long Saturday afternoon.

This was the kind of day attics were made for — and the kind of day you remember most.

The storm outside, somehow, made the old chromos and paintings in their heavy, gilt frames brighter. There was a freshness in the smell of rain that came through the window that drove the oldness of the place away for a while.

The heaped up furniture and the magazines and books seemed not so dusty, not so old and not so dry — and the clothing in the trunks whispered at your touch, a gentle sound instead of the harshness you once heard.

Fire traps, they call attics now.

But you remember when they caught only memories.

He couldn't get his tutu on straight

I SUPPOSE I HAD JUST learned the meaning of the term "shanghai" when my mother, aided and abetted by other conniving mothers in the neighborhood, shanghaied me — along with a half-dozen or so of my peers — off to dancing class.

We wailed, of course, and loudly.

Dancing was — as any kid with a grain of sense knew back then — sissy stuff.

If you had to put your arm around some old girl the place to do it was out someplace where no one could see you or catch you at it and not fer gosh sakes out on some dumb dance floor where everybody in the world was watching and waiting to laugh.

As for getting dressed up and walking around in time to music with somebody you hardly spoke to in school (let alone thought of putting your arm around), what wouldn't mothers think of next?

But, alas, no. Dancing class was starting, and for every Monday night the next six weeks we were going to be there.

"We're not going to argue about it," my mother told me with an air of finality. "Dancing is a social grace and one which you should be expected to know and you should be thankful for the opportunity.

Back then there were no such things as last-minute reprieves. Which is how we found ourselves at the appointed hour in the appointed place, ready, in effect, to seize this particular social grace by the horns and dispose of it as quickly and as painlessly as possible.

That first night, as I recall, we learned such non-physical aspects of ballroom dancing as the proper way to ask for a dance, the importance of escorting your partner to her seat once the music stopped, thanking her for the dance (and thanking her escort as well), and such sundry caveats as not watching feet, not counting time aloud — and developing the art of small talk during the dance itself.

One thing I remember well:

Since dancing was a social obligation, one danced with any and all if asked — and one asked any and all.

Just because a girl was class president, led the honor roll, was a mathematical genius — and had a face to match — was no reason to pass her over when looking for a partner.

On the other hand, girls were told, pimply faces and big ears do not necessarily imply clumsy feet. If invited to dance by the Ichabod Crane of the sophomore class, one could only accept politely and hope, like Scarlett O'Hara, that tomorrow would, indeed, be another day.

Somehow we managed to make it through the six weeks.

We learned to foxtrot and to waltz.

We were initiated into the arcane mysteries of how to keep from crushing a shoulder corsage, how to avoid sweaty, clammy palms — there were a lot of them during those first few lessons — and how to manage backless formal dresses.

We even learned how to fill out — and interpret — dance cards.

That summer we learned to dance — as we all had to admit later — was one of the smarter projects our mothers were responsible for.

And everything worked out just like they said it would.

We got invited to parties. We made friends. We influenced people — in some cases, to leave the dance floor and head for the parking lot.

34

In time we broadened our terpsichorean horizons to include such diversions as the tango, the rhumba, the Big Apple, the Lambeth Walk, jitterbugging and, later, the Bunny Hop.

And it was, of all things, during a Bunny Hop in my later years that I turned suddenly, hopped in the wrong direction, slammed into a bunny and broke my glasses.

But, looking back, I guess it was all for the best.

I haven't crushed a corsage in the years that saw them go from 75 cents to $7.50.

My palms no longer sweat or get clammy.

And I can't remember when I last looked at my feet on a dance floor — especially in days like these when dance floors are so small and so crowded one has difficulty in seeing one's hips, let alone hers.

I do, however, find myself wondering at times.

Looking at the way some people dance today, I think my mother might have another word for it.

And it wouldn't, I'm sure, be "social grace."

Just a small
town boy at heart

CITIES ARE GREAT places to live — but only if you're already grown up.

For growing up, give me a small town every day.

Small towns like the ones I remember have things that cities can provide only in zoos, museums and parks.

I'm not criticizing cities, mind, or the people who live in them.

Behind all the noise and hurry there are good, decent people.

They just don't have as much time to get out — or get close.

When I look back over the things I have to be thankful for I always think of a small town in Ohio and another, not quite as small but still small enough, in Kansas.

And I'm glad I grew up where I did instead of in Chicago or New York.

I'm glad I can remember things like sailing tiny boats on a mill pond in the summer or skating on it once winter came and it was frozen over.

And every time I see people at a crowded airport who came out just to watch planes land and take off I remember the handful of regulars who showed up each evening at a tiny depot in the shadow of a water tank to see the northbound on its brief stop on the way to the city.

It's too bad, I think, that sometimes the only way city kids know the seasons are changing is when they see the changes in department store windows.

In country towns you feel it in the air, hear it in the night sky as geese head south or see it in the haze of burning leaves at sundown at that time we called Indian summer.

I could be wrong, of course — but I don't think many city kids got a chance to cut through a haunted house on their way home from school.

An empty tenement, perhaps. A deserted warehouse. But no haunted houses.

I had three of them where I grew up, two in Ohio, one in Kansas.

And the best time of all — as any small town kid knows — is making that short cut at the time of evening where there's still enough light outside to see windows but not enough to drive away the shadows in musty hallways or echoing, darkened rooms.

Granted, a city kid is close to where the action is.

They see things like visits by royalty, great sports events and places made famous in films and novels.

We hunted (and found) arrowheads. One of our playgrounds was an impressive monument to the dim past of the Mound Builders.

And across the street from where we lived was a house identified by researchers and historians as a station on the "underground railroad."

It hasn't been too long ago since we bought milk in bottles. Even city kids remember them.

But where in either Manhattan or Chicago was there a town pump? A courthouse park big enough for a kid to run around in but not so large that he could get lost there? A stream shallow enough to wade in, deep enough to fish in and pure enough to drink from?

We never thought of walking back to town from Elm Creek just because we were thirsty. And we never got sick from drinking from it.

Well. Hardly ever.

I don't mean by all this to be putting city kids — or the city they live in — down.

Maybe they had just as much fun as we did. Maybe their lives were just as full as ours.

But I listen, sometimes, to a city when I go there and all I can hear is noise.

In a small town, I also listen.

And often I can hear the beating of a heart.

Ben Franklin,
where are you now?

FOR A NUMBER OF YEARS now, I've been buying stamps.
I've been mailing letters.
And I've been receiving letters.
I feel accordingly that I can speak with some authority on postal matters.

And I suppose the sum total of my observations on the U.S. Postal Service, of which Benjamin Franklin, the kite flyer, is reportedly the founding father, can be capsulized in seven words:

Things ain't what they used to be.

My first realization that there was such a thing as a post office came when I was a pre-schooler in a little town called North Lewisburg, Ohio — where I was born — and my grandfather is irrevocably connected with it.

That was where he went every morning after breakfast.

"Be at the post office, Florence," he'd tell my mother before settling his straw hat firmly on his head and stalking out of the house.

For my grandfather, in a town so small it couldn't even boast an American Legion post (let alone an Avon lady), the post office was, next to the morning paper, the fount of all knowledge.

Everyone in town showed up, sooner or later, at the post office. They talked politics. They exchanged crop information. They sat in judgment on the peccadillos of their fellow townsmen.

And they even remembered sometimes to pick up their mail.

And I remember one of the proudest days of my life was the morning my grandfather turned to me and growled genially:

"Why don't you come along?"

There were six cane-backed chairs along the right-hand wall as you walked in the door — and they were all reserved.

My grandfather's was the farthest back, next to the door of the office of the postmaster, a gray-haired, salty old woman named Della Tritt whose only gesture in the field of public relations was to give each child in town, on the day he or she started in the first grade, a copy of the Bible.

The black flyleaf was signed in white ink.

All this, of course, was back in the days when post offices ranked with the corner drugstore, the pool hall and the fire station as community institutions.

The post office was — and remained for a long time — as the only arm of the federal government with which anyone had daily contact.

Next to the judge, the minister — and possibly the editor of the newspaper — the postmaster was the most respected citizen in town. He represented political power.

He also saw to it that the mail was delivered.

It was even that way after we moved from Ohio to Kansas.

No one walked into the post office, picked up his mail and walked out again.

Morning coffee dates were made there.

Word of births, marriages and deaths was exchanged, long before it appeared in print.

And well I recall that the best of all character references one could list on a job application was the name of the postmaster — if you were among those privileged to know him.

Today, post offices have all the personality of a bushel basket of fog.

I remember a postal clerk named Ira Snell back in Iola, who, while he wasn't busy weighing packages and selling stamps, played chess — at his window — with postal patrons.

I remember a postmaster named Ev Harlan who not only drank coffee with friends but kept a pot in his office for anyone who dropped in.

And those were the days when you dropped in on postmasters — and they were grateful for the visit.

I never knew a postmaster — and this particularly includes one in Billings named Mearl Fagg — who was so busy he couldn't take time to talk to people.

All of which, I guess, just goes to show how times change.

When I think of post offices today I think more of buildings than of people.

I think of "Enter" and "Exit" signs — and signs saying "Closed — Use Other Window."

And I never dreamed that the day would come — excepting, of course, the Christmas rush — when you had to stand in line to buy a stamp.

Mind, I'm not complaining about deliveries.

And I suppose that, having mailed first-class letters for three cents an ounce for nearly two generations, I shouldn't object too strenuously to paying 18 cents today.

But, as most of us do, I suppose, I'd like to see the post office back to what it once was — an institution filled with people, rather than a building preoccupied with numbers.

I prefer, in short, Benjamin Franklin to that slack-jawed, goggle-eyed symbol we came to know years ago as "Mr. Zip."

And come to think of it, our first postmaster general was the guy who harnessed lightning.

Fleeting fame
on the silver screen

THE NAMES ARE familiar, many of them. The faces, even more so.

But chances are, if you met Harry Davenport on the street tomorrow, you wouldn't be able to say exactly who he was or where it was you last saw him.

And you'd walk away — even if you talked with him for a moment — with the uncomfortable feeling that you should know him but can't think to save your neck why.

The same goes for Addison Richards, Samuel S. Hinds, Paul Guilfoyle and Paul Fix.

Think again, now.

Lawyers, maybe? Doctors? Businessmen?

Maybe some of the more unusual names will ring a bell.

Try Etienne Giradot. Forrester Harvey. C. Henry Gordon. Eduardo Cianelli. Una O'Connor.

If you've given up by now — and for the success of this little venture, we'll have to assume you have — the answer to where you knew them and how is simple.

They've all been in pictures, more pictures, probably, than the stars whose popularity greatly outshines theirs.

Every one, of course, remembers Boris Karloff's monster in "Frankenstein" — but who remembers the actor who played the hunch-backed assistant?

His name was Dwight Frye whose record of films today is probably considerably longer than Karloff's.

Like their better-known colleagues whose names and faces are recognized at once, bit players get typed in a certain part, usually playing out their film careers in it.

Davenport, for example, is a kindly judge or a genial grandfather. Guilfoyle and Fix have spent enough time in tuxedos and wing-collars, saying "Okay, boss" to a screen gang leader, they could have given Al Capone lessons on how to run a mob.

The minute Cianelli and Gordon appeared on a screen you could bet your last kernel of popcorn they were going to cause trouble through the rest of the picture. (Even when they got a rare "good guy" role, it ruined the picture for you — just because you'd learned from experience you couldn't trust 'em.)

Hinds and Richards were diplomatic or industrial tycoon types. No barroom scene was complete without the mustached Harvey behind the taps or gothic-eyebrowed Miss O'Connor waiting tables.

Any time a director got a call for a fiery, temperamental Italian, he sent for Luis Alberni. If the script, on the other hand, called for a bumbling, comical Italian, he sent for Henry Armetta.

Few of filmdom's "old reliables" ever made it on television — but two who did, strangely enough, carved their niches in the same profession.

Remember the incredibly old lama in "Lost Horizon"? Or the faithful water-carrier in "Gunga Din"? You know him today as bushy-haired Dr. Zorba, Ben Casey's stern mentor.

Doc Adams had a lengthy apprenticeship in the aviation business before he finally settled down to practice in Dodge City. Milburn Stone, a Burrton, Kan., boy, was "Skeeter" in the "Tailspin Tommy" series for years before he finally graduated to parts like that of Stephen A. Douglas in "Young Mr. Lincoln."

And Stone, incidentally, has a standard answer to strangers who finally approach him with that haven't-I-seen-you-someplace before look.

"If you had a couple hours to kill," he said once, "and you spent them in a theater, that's where you saw me before — if you looked at the screen at just the right time."

Technology separates
the men from the boys

OUTDOOR MAGAZINES and travel writers can say what they will of the joys of fishing mountain streams or the thrill of trying out the latest lure or the newest reel — but such delights still pale alongside the fishing you remember from long ago.

This was before the day of the nylon line, the glass rod and the plastic plug, a time when you got your "lifelike" grasshoppers, worms and crawdads from fields, manure piles and from under flat rocks in the creek you fished instead of from a card on a revolving rack in a store.

The closest thing you had back then to a tackle box was an empty Prince Albert tin (which you stowed away in a hip pocket) and hooks, lead sinkers and 10 yards of line constituted your sole support of sporting goods manufacturers.

Fishing poles, you'll remember, were an unnecessary bother when you thought of carrying them all the way to where the fishing was. That's why you went, unencumbered, and cut a pole after you got there.

There was always the kid who had a new metal rod with a reel that had little ivory handles and he always looked a little sheepish when he showed up with it — but you let him come along anyway because he was one of you and it wasn't his fault his folks bought it for him when they found out he was going fishing and then made him use it.

A candy bar was all you needed if fishing meant being gone all day — and if you got thirsty there was plenty of water, as long as you drank from where it was running fast and not from the quiet places. No kids in those days was dumb enough to ask if he could drink Creek (pronounced "crick") water. He just kept his mouth shut about it so he could say truthfully that no one had ever told him not to. (And no kid in those days, incidentally, ever got sick from it.)

It's funny how you remember, not the fish you caught, but the things you talked about waiting for them to bite.

It's funny how you remember lying on your back and watching white clouds against a blue sky and then feeling patches of sunlight against your eyelids where it filtered down through breeze-stirred tree branches overhead.

And, listening well, you can still hear the sound of those drowsy, comfortable afternoons of long ago, a mixture of water splashing over rocks, the distant barking of a dog, the rasping of cicadas overhead and the hypnotic hum of insects through the leafy rustle of woods around while you talked and dreamed of how things would be for all of you in years to come.

And it's funny how you remember almost with a start the one thing you all forgot to wish for — a chance to relive a summer afternoon along a sleepy creek bank when fishing was a boy's way of living — instead of a man's way of relaxing.

Autumn leaves
sprinkled with imagination

SINCE WE'RE NOT ABLE to burn them anymore — thanks to the pure airists — there would seem to be nothing more to do with fallen leaves than to package them in plastic bags and dump them unceremoniously into the nearest trash can or alley to await eventual transport to the city dump.

Or else let them rot in the yard.

I emphasize "there would seem to be."

That's because, given the imagination of their elders — and a bit of tutoring on the project — dry leaves on a crisp autumn afternoon can open an entire new world of play for kids surfeited with televison game shows or Pac-Man.

Just walking across a lawn where they're piled high, clearing your way through the crackling drifts by kicking leaves as high and as far as you can is in itself nothing short of sheer delight. (If you don't think so, try it. I did, just the other day on a short cut across the courthouse park and it's still as much fun as it ever was.)

Even raking leaves isn't all work — if you rake with an esthetic result in mind.

Anyone who's ever stomped out "fox and geese" circles in the snow can do the same with leaves and a rake.

The only problem, of course, is finishing the game before the wind comes up.

Rakes are also indispensable in constructing leaf houses — and anyone who's never made a leaf house has missed the best part of building a home.

Now, for those of you who don't know — or can't remember — what I'm talking about:

A leaf house is nothing more than a floor plan, complete with doors and windows, of the house of your dreams. It's made by raking leaves into ridges to form the design you want. Your imagination supplies walls and roof and your sense of honor renders the flimsy outline impregnable. In other words, no fair stepping over a wall. You gotta use a door (or a window) to get out or in.

One nice thing about leaf houses:

They're the easiest way to get a lawn raked that I know of.

Leaf fights are also fun, especially when you pass from flinging handfuls at each other and start scooping them up in your arms and dumping them on the unsuspecting. Cramming dry leaves down shirt or jacket backs is also good — but the itching sometimes cuts the play short.

Getting buried in leaves was, for me, the most fun — but it had its hazardous aspects.

It also required a confederate.

The idea, of course, was to get covered up so completely with leaves that no one could tell you were there.

An important point, as well, was to get close to the sidewalk.

That's so people could pass by within (literally) inches of you and never know you were there.

It was hot. It was scratchy. It was also noisy if you moved.

So, hearing footsteps approaching, you played statue in your leafy concealment.

But, like I say, it had its hazardous aspects.

Every once in a while the person coming along turned out to be some kid — who couldn't resist kicking his way through an inviting pile of dry leaves.

What happened to all those lonely men?

YOU DON'T SEE THEM anymore, those men who would knock gently at a back door and ask for food. You called them tramps. You didn't call them hoboes. And you didn't call them bums.

You called them tramps — and you felt sorry for them as you sat beside them on the porch steps and watched them eat and wondered why and how they came, eventually, to sit there beside you.

There was never, at our house, any thought of turning one away.

And one never left without an extra sandwich — "Just in case," he was told, "you get hungry again."

They all seemed hungry, the young men and the old, as they sat there with a plate of bacon and eggs and the saucerless cup of black coffee — and I remember a dog we had once that didn't leave a plate half so clean as did these hungry men who mopped even the last of the egg yolk up with a crust of toast.

They always wondered, quietly, if they could have more coffee.

And they always said, "Please" and "Thank you."

They didn't talk much at first, not while they waited, sometimes uneasily, as the smell of bacon frying and the sputtering of eggs in hot grease came to them through the screen.

They sat and looked with tired, red-rimmed eyes at the sky, the alley that ran behind the house — or sometimes petted one of the kittens that seemed never to be in short supply at our place.

(One cat we had followed a grey-haired man who said he was from Pennsylvania down the alley as he left. He brought her back — and she followed him again. The second time he opened his arms and spilled her out on the porch he warned us with a smile: "She's gonna end up like me if you don't watch her.")

Without exception, these quiet men would ask for work to do in return for a meal.

It seemed we never had any. Besides, someone would say later, when a man's hungry he should be fed, not worked.

Once I remember a man who sat and ate and talked to us about school and books and told us how important they were and then walked over and began straightening and sorting into piles a winter's accumulation of discarded magazines and newspapers in one corner of the porch.

We told him if he wanted, he was welcome to take some "to read along the way."

He said thanks and explained why he couldn't — and I remember watching him until he disappeared around the corner as though he were from another planet.

He was the first person I'd ever known who couldn't read or write.

You used to see them but you don't anymore today — and you wonder, sometimes, where they went or what they're doing, these men who you would have called lonely, had you known then what the word really meant.

You find yourself wondering if they found what they were looking for — or lost what they were running from.

And you hope, too, they aren't hungry, these lonely men.

School books aren't only for studying

THE TIME FOR A renaissance in school book art is at hand — if only the unbelievers in the audience will accept my premise that studying can be fun.

For too long now that doodle has been gone from mathematics, science and history (particulary history) texts.

For more years than I care to think about has the fly-leaf of a geography book carried only the owner's name, room number and home address.

And heaven knows how many have gone through an entire grade school education blissfully ignorant of the fact that a little imagination can turn a dictionary into an hilarious (albeit primitive) cartoon comedy.

Students of today have no idea how a penciled-on beard can change the appearance of John C. Calhoun. George Washington, on the other hand, becomes a very presentable pirate once you put a black patch over one eye and cover his wig with a three-cornered hat.

Put a mustache on Calvin Coolidge, block out two of Clara Barton's teeth, draw a cigar in John Cabot's mouth and you've material for more snickers than the Mars Candy Co.

There were two ways of identifying yourself as the owner of a book.

One was where you wrote your name, then your address, then "Billings, Yellowstone County, Montana, U.S.A., North America, Western Hemisphere, The World, The Solar System, The Universe."

The other way was to write on the title page "If you want to know who this book belongs to, look on Page 102" and you turned to Page 102 to find word to look on Page 57 and from Page 57 you went to 93 and from there to Page 6 and so on for 30 or more pages until you were sent back to the fly-leaf where you found not only the owner's name but the observation that "this is where you should have looked first, stupid."

44

Dictionaries were best for drawing cartoon sequences (because they had more pages) of little stick men who walked, ran or jumped across the top of the page, pursued by other little stick men throwing rocks, turning somersaults or sometimes rising completely off the page to reappear in front of the stickmen they were chasing. (He, of course, fainted dead away in surprise to end the sequence.)

There were other things you could do with school books, too.

One which proved particularly aggravating to teachers was folding over about a quarter of an inch of each three margins of the leaf, then bending the cover slightly to obtain an air space.

Tapping the cover with a finger resulted in a series of highly satisfactory buzzing sounds.

You could fill in o's, too, if you were the type who cared for detail work.

But even if you didn't care for doodling, cartooning, noise-making or o-filling, school books weren't a total waste of money.

As a last resort, you could always study out of them.

I loved you, Miss Meliza

YOU REMEMBER them.

Every year when school starts again you remember how they stood before the blackboard, chalk in one hand and the other making dark, moist places on the slate as they pointed to the list of books you'd have to buy.

You remember what clothes they wore and how they fixed their hair — and you remember, if it was a man, wondering whether or not he smoked. (A teacher who smoked was the seventh-grade equivalent of a pearl of great price. He UNDERSTOOD how things were.)

And you wonder if today, somewhere, they're still around, these teachers you once knew — and who once knew you.

The fourth grade Simon Legree, for example, who once took a Tarzan book away from me because I read it in class — but who taught me more mathematics than I've learned since. The name is gone, but if she walked in the door this moment I think I'd put away whatever I was reading and fold my hands on my desk.

"Cowboy" Nelson, we called our English teacher — outside of class. She played tennis, walked a mile in ten minutes and, had she taught anywhere but Kansas — would have skied as well. There was a dark suspicion — unconfirmed — that SHE smoked.

A science teacher, naturally, had to have a name like Zenith Mullen. She was a two-finger dabbler, in the aquarium, beakers, turtle-tank or whatever "experiment" happened to be in progress at the moment. Whispered confidences had it that Miss Mullen could dabble in a vat of pure sulphuric acid and come out unscathed — and she had a temper to match.

A patient manual training teacher named Paul Iden spent nine months trying to teach me how to drive a nail straight, then, as I recall, took a job as a salesman. I came out of his class after a year with a "D" and a wobbly flower pot stand — without a pot to put on it.

I think A.E. Garrison, the skipper of our taut little ship, the SS Iola Junior High, was one of the few people I knew who wore pince-nez. The only time I saw him without them was the night he was hit in the face by a popcorn ball at a school Halloween party. It took him five minutes to get them back. It took the school five years to get its parties back.

Millicent Voorhees, our penmanship teacher, was the only one who ever caught me shooting paper wads. Actually, she didn't catch me. I'd loosed this one at my best friend, sitting across the room, not because I wanted to hit him, merely because, according to my logic at the time, he WAS my best friend and therefore wouldn't tell on me.

He told.

An estimated nine out of every ten boys who had classes under Jean Coghill, her sister, Esther — both blondes — or Jimmie Lou Calloway, who wore a boyish bob, wanted to marry one, if not all three of them.

I was, of course, one of the nine. The holdouts weren't anti-teacher. It just happened THEY were in love with Miss Voorhees.

There were others. The redheads, like Pauline Rodeal. The lip-pursers like Doris Cota. Grace Reno, who cured me of drawing airplanes in class by making me do long-division after class. And Ethel McCoy who, year after year, won the "Good Joe" award from every kid who knew her.

But, most of all, I remember Miss Meliza. Dorothy was her first name and she taught history.

She was a teacher. She was a friend. She was a guardian. There was very little nonsense about Miss Meliza. No one called her a Good Joe. No one hit her with a popcorn ball.

No one shot paperwads in her class.

But no one ever left her at the end of year without knowing that he had learned — because she had taught.

Miss Meliza quit teaching a long time ago and went to Alaska. She'll probably never see this — but in the event she does, it's time she knew.

Of all the teachers I had, she's the one I remember best — and the one who, now I know, I loved the most.

Thank you again, dear Miss Meliza — for everything.

Technology failed
with the pencil box

NOW THAT THE back-to-school season is upon us I can't help wonder what role the pencil box will play in this day and age. The pencil box — for the uninitiated — was once considered a sine qua non for kids headed schoolward, regardless of grade.

Everybody got pencil boxes.

Basically, they were imitation leather boxes to carry pencils in.

They lasted, with any sort of luck, about a month.

By that time the snap fasteners with which you closed them wore out.

The ends and sides got bashed in from being crammed in a desk.

Or the lid, through innumerable openings and closings, cracked and eventually was detached.

Most of the money invested in a pencil box went for frills.

Like the erasers that wouldn't erase anything.

Or the ruler which was okay as long as you needed to draw a straight line not more than six inches long.

Or the pencil sharpener that never worked.

There were usually three pencils — one with soft lead, one with hard lead and a double-ended one that wrote red or blue.

That was the one which, by the magisterium which forbade writing in any color but black, you threw away.

The others broke or splintered early on.

The pencil sharpener worked pretty good when you wanted a crayon with a sharp point — but it chewed up more pencils than a second grader trying to learn two times two.

Most pencil boxes made their way to the waste basket because too much was expected of them.

Pencil boxes were for pencils, okay?

So you jammed pencils in them until they literally bulged at the seams.

I can remember three-pencil boxes that held as many as a half-dozen or more before they cracked.

So what else was a kid to do?

He junked the pencil box and started carrying pencils where they belonged:

In books.

Making money
hand over handbill

THE WAY A KID used to earn spending money was like this:

He mowed lawns in the summer.

He shoveled snow in the winter.

And between the times when the grass wasn't tall enough to mow or the snow wasn't deep enough to shovel he put out handbills or sold bottles.

I was neither a mower nor a shoveler. (And, my wife tells me with a trace of rancor, I've done little to change my ways.)

But I was very good in the handbill and bottle division.

A kid who put out handbills that went out of town could always count on (a) a long ride, (b) a free meal and (c) passes to the show the handbills were advertising.

A kid who scrounged alleys in his neighborhood for milk or pop bottles could depend on earning a piece of change without getting blistered hands or cold feet.

Mowing and shoveling, we felt, were "working jobs."

Handbills and bottles, on the other hand, were jobs carrying both adventure and excitement.

A kid never knew when he'd get caught stuffing a dozen flyers in a screen door instead of just one.

A kid never knew when he'd get yelled at for grubbing in a trash can — either by the people who owned the trash or the man who collected it.

We could get two cents apiece for pop bottles, a nickel for a milk bottle and — if the day's hunting were really good, a dime for a gallon jug.

In season, burlap sacks were worth a nickel — if you could find one without any holes.

There was, however, a certain status to the mower or the shoveler that we in the ash-can set failed to achieve.

Theirs was a front-door clientele.

Sometimes we couldn't even get up to the back door.

All of us, though, aspired to what then was the elite corps of the job holder — those lucky enough to have paper routes.

These included, in my day, the banker's son, the sons of the town's two car dealers, a lawyer's son and son of the only man in town who owned his own airplane.

The one kid we thought should get a paper route — if anyone should — was the boy whose dad owned the paper. Apparently, though, his heart wasn't in the business.

He was having too much fun passing out handbills and rummaging through trash cans for bottles with the rest of us.

Montana

CHAPTER 2

Interesting Facts and Priceless Information

T HE FOLLOWING Completely Memorable History of Montana is designed for the tourist who, by careful study of the Interesting Facts and Priceless Information contained herein, may learn to talk as glibly about the Treasure State as though he were a native (or cutthroat).

HISTORY

Montana's history began with its discovery by a Spaniard named Oro Y. Plata, a hard drinker who, when younger, was frequently seen out on bats. Today, however, he spends all his time on a Great Seal.

PERSONALITIES

Montana is noted for its colorful personalities such as Vigilantes, Russellers, Copper Kings, etc. The Vigilantes were people with beards who hung around Virginia City or any place else in the neighborhood where they could find a convenient tree. (Virginia City later became famous for tourists who came to visit the Vigilantes' old hangouts or string-ups.)

Russellers, who live both in and out of Montana, are noted for their zeal in collecting oil paintings by an artist-cowboy who came out here from St. Louis and became a cowboy-artist.

(The true Russeller is not to be confused with the rustler who, having no appreciation of fine art, collects only cows.)

Copper Kings — of which there were three — lived around Butte where they fought wars and became memorable for finding copper by mistake while they were looking for gold and silver. They sold the copper back East, however, for gold and silver so everyone in Butte was happy — except the Copper Kings.

POLITICS

Montana politics can be summed up in the following sentences:
"The Democrats have ruined the State." (Signed: The Republicans.)
"The Republicans have ruined the State." (Signed the Democrats.)
"Both the Democrats and the Republicans have ruined the State." (Signed: The Taxpayer.)

MEMORABLE CITIES

There are several Absolutely Memorable Cities in Montana, including Butte, Anaconda, Miles City and Billings. (There is no truth to the rumor that a city called "Great Falls" is located in Montana. Those responsible for this are thinking, of course, of Little Falls, which is in Minnesota.)

Butte is populated by mine shafts, Democrats, Irishmen and one Republican who comes out only on election day and votes as often as he can before getting caught. (There is a place in Butte where Irishmen go when they want to drink which is called, appropriately enough, Dublin Gulp.)

Anaconda, located near Butte, is best known as the first Montana city to hire a full-time policeman. He later became famous as the First Anaconda Copper.

Billings is Thoroughly Memorable because of its founding by a man with a beard who was not a Vigilante. It is also memorable because of Grand Avenue which, like the Red Sea, is opened up from time to time to let people pass.

Miles City is memorable for many things (among others) but mostly for the people who visit there who call it Funtown, U.S.A.

New traditions
with new generations

FOR THE FEW STILL here to celebrate it, the Year of the Tiger came in quietly.

It wasn't always this way, any one of the dwindling Chinese population of Billings will tell you.

Back in the 1920s — or earlier — when nearly 150 Chinese worked and lived in Billings the arrival of the New Year was something big.

There were no parading dragons that other Chinatowns in the nation still cling to for benefit of tourists — and few firecrackers.

There was, however, all the celebrating Oriental required in the way of drink, food and music.

The Chinese Masonic Lodge, one of China Alley's more prominent buildings, was a center of merry-making. The two-story brick structure, torn down only a year ago to make way for a parking lot, was the scene of the midnight banquet which climaxed the celebration.

Every Chinese in town took the day off. The truck gardeners who earned their living growing vegetables on tiny plots near the Great

Western Sugar Co. factory, the restaurant workers — even the herb doctors whose tiny shops were located along Montana Avenue.

They always managed to find a band to play appropriate music for their New Year's dance.

They always managed to have fun.

The town was wide open then.

One of the less-than-three-dozen Chinese left here talked about how it used to be, squinted down the sun-drenched street and shook his head.

"Lots different now," he said. "Lots different. This time, this New Year's, all Chinese restaurants had a special meal for their employees. Nothing else happens. Real quiet."

He lit a cigarette with nervous hands, blinked at the bright sky and said softly:

"New generations come — old traditions go."

West of the city in the weed-grown southeast section of Mountview Cemetery, the traditions lie buried with the generations who kept them.

Barely legible today are the painted Chinese inscriptions on the weathered board markers and the smell of burning joss-sticks which once rimmed each new grave is lost now to even memory.

The new generations of Chinese who call the city home are also fading — fading like black-brushed writing, in the sun and rain, fading like the scent of sandalwood in the wind, fading even as the echo of a New Year's greeting.

Cowboys will never become extinct

WELL, I SEE THEY'RE doing the old cowboy obituary thing again on the talk show circuit.

At least, that's the impression I got from trying to listen to television in the other room yesterday morning while I was scrambling eggs in the kitchen.

It seems there's another book out designed to answer the question once and for all as to what the cowboy was and what his prospects are for the future.

The author — assisted by his television host — got across his contention that the cowboy of a century ago was "nothing much more than a common laborer" and that his descendant of today has come upon parlous times what with the decline in beef prices and the gradual disappearance of the open range.

During the talk about the two species — the cowboy primitive and the cowboy endangered — there was discussion of the cowboy of "myth and legend," accompanied by slides of a fringe-jacketed Buffalo Bill and a sequin-shirted Roy Rogers.

Well.

Of course, anyone who's spent any time at all living and working around Montana and Wyoming, anyone who's ever spent any time on a ranch, at a rodeo, at a livestock yard — or at a bar in Jordan — knows better than to try to measure cowboys in sociological terms. But most easterners (and most sociologists) try it anyway.

I think most of us out here know the difference between the cowboys of western films and those who got their start in the business on the Antlers Ranch out of Sheridan just as anyone knows real-life police-women don't look a bit like Charlie's Angels — even on one of their bad days.

So I'm not worried — as were the talk-show people — that one day I'm going to have to go to a museum to see a cowboy in wax standing there alongside such other distinguished extinctions as the dodo bird or the passenger pigeon.

Cowboys are going to be around as long as there are cows because of their very nature.

For heaven's sake, who ever heard of an extinct cow?

Or, for that matter, a retired cowboy?

Montana can't be wrapped in a package

A TRAIN CAN TAKE a lot of Montana back to New York.
It can carry people — and hospitality.
It can carry guns and arrowheads and paintings — and the hint of adventure and history that surrounds them.
And it can carry silver dollars and horses and music and fun.

But there are some things a train can't carry back to New York, not if you made it a mile long and filled every car to the ceiling.

Try building a display case, for example, that will hold the beauty of sunlight on snowcapped mountains or the sweeping loneliness of a sunset on rolling plains.

Take the biggest frame you can find that will fit in a car on your train — and try to fill it with just the smallest piece of a blue summer sky or the velvet black of a winter night when stars hang so close a man can reach out, almost, to touch them.

Try to find a place on your train where you can bottle the smell of a valley in the springtime when the grass starts feeling soft beneath your feet — but leave room, if you can, for the sound of wind that scatters dry leaves down the empty street of a deserted mining camp.

Montana is many things you can't get on a train.

It's a feeling of warmth and closeness and of fullness and emptiness — all at the same time.

It's people knowing people — and liking them whether they know them or not.

It's Butte Hill and its lights on Christmas Eve — and it's Miles City on a hot July afternoon.

It's the sweep of the Missouri at Great Falls, the crooked, impossible streets of Helena and the gentle ghosts that still roam the weathered buildings of a score of long dead towns.

It's a man with oil on his shirt and a dressed-out deer on top of his car — and it's a woman whose face is as beautiful as her hands are worn.

Montana is a song you sing and a place you come home to — whether you ever lived here before or not.

And it's many things a train can't carry back to New York — not if you made it a mile long and filled every car to the ceiling.

We could use more Uncle Georges

THERE ARE THOSE today who may wonder what a chunky little German immigrant has to do with the Fourth of July.

That was years ago, they'll say, when you tell them about it.

Who cares about a fireworks display now — even though the guy did pay for it himself?

There are much more important things to do on the Fourth. Like mow the lawn. Like have some friends over for beer and barbecue in the evening. Like go fishing.

Besides, they'll add, so few remember now why the firecrackers pop. Who wants to bother with it?

George Bennighoff, for one, wanted to bother with it — and those who remember what the Fourth of July was like when he was around are glad he did.

They called him "Uncle George."

They called him other things, too, the sheep men and the cattle men who made his hotel their headquarters at the turn of the century.

But no one laughed at Uncle George when he tried to say what he felt about his adopted country — even though his English, after nearly 50 years here, was comically broken.

The fireworks, in the street outside the hotel at First Avenue North and 27th Street, were but one expression of his love for the United States.

No one remembers now what first gave Uncle George the idea that resulted in his first order for "lots of fireworks" from a firm back East.

They do remember the whole town was invited — and the whole town came. They blocked off streets in preparation and men, women and children crowded the long steps that led up to the hotel porch and overflowed into office windows that overlooked the intersection.

A concrete block in the middle of the street provided a convenient pedestal for the firing of some of the more spectacular displays. And through it all the genial figure of Uncle George moved, blue eyes dancing behind his glasses and drooping mustache quivering in a constant grin.

It was this way for almost 30 Independence Days — until 1917 when wartime restrictions banned the use of powder for fireworks.

There was one more in 1920 — and Uncle George's fireworks became a part of our town's history.

No one knows, for certain, why they stopped — but those who remember wish, sometimes, they hadn't.

The country, they say, could use more Uncle Georges.

No one had to ask a second time for his help in any community cause. No one had to explain to him, during the first World War, what a Liberty Bond was or what it could do.

George Bennighoff, born a subject of a foreign prince, lived most of his life and died as a free man.

He knew liberty as few men did — and he wasn't ashamed to let people know what it meant to him.

Maybe that's how the fireworks idea began.

It's been a long time since the last sputtered its flaming trail across the night sky above the city — and those who watched it can't be blamed, perhaps, for feeling the old Grand Hotel corner is, for all its lights and people, a darker, quieter place on the Fourth of July than it was once.

The veil of dishonor
is removed from Major Reno

CROW AGENCY — The tawny bluffs that rise above the valley of the Little Big Horn River echoed to the sound of rifle volleys and the clear notes of a bugle Saturday as they buried an officer of the 7th U.S. Cavalry — 91 years after the battle he fought here.

The mouldering remnants of clothing, the buttons and the bones that are all that is mortal of Maj. Marcus A. Reno were laid with military ceremony in the grave assigned to him, close by the cemetery's flagpole where the flag he fought under whispers its unceasing requiem over the brave men who lie in its shadow.

Reno died in Washington, D.C., in 1889, an officer not considered worthy of honor of his comrades in arms.

It was all forgotten on this day as hundreds stood around a tiny green plot to watch old wounds healed — and old wars forgotten.

They listened, red man and white, to the 11-gun salute accorded Reno, restored to his Civil War rank of a brigadier general of volunteers. They stood quietly as the three rifle volleys sent birds up from the pine branches in the cemetery to wheel against a gray sky and disappear over a distant ridge.

And even the children, who sat wide-eyed and silent on the grass, lowered their heads at the first clear note of "Taps."

Before it all came the funeral service at the First Christian Church in Billings and the military procession through Hardin as Major Reno, cleared last May of charges which resulted in his dismissal from the service, began the last leg of his long journey that began, nearly a century ago, on a sun bleached hill not far from where he now lies.

The dirgelike strains of "Holy, Holy, Holy," played by the 46th Army Band, marked the bronze casket's removal from the church, and as the procession moved off, muffled drums set the slow beat to Chopin's "Funeral March."

It was the same in Hardin where people lined the town's main street to watch what Edwin Peterson of Logan, Utah, national vice commander of the American Legion, called "the righting of an injustice."

Many have felt, since the controversial battle, that Reno's conduct which resulted in two courts-martial, stemmed from bitter criticism of his actions during the fight.

Until the Pentagon hearing which cleared his name, leading to his removal from an unmarked grave to the place of honor where he now lies, few have known that the very court which convicted him recommended leniency, along with the convening authority and the judge advocate general of the Army.

It was President Rutherford B. Hayes, who disregarding the recommendations, ordered Reno's dismissal.

Saturday all that was past.

It was past in the black riderless horse, boots reversed in an empty saddle, which followed Major Reno's casket.

It was past in the red flag with the general officer's single white star, signifying Reno's restoration to rank, which was carried in the cortege.

And it was past in the lilting music of "Garry Owen," the Seventh's regimental song which Marcus Reno, in happier days rode to.

"There's no occasion for sadness," the Rev. Gene Robinson said during Major Reno's eulogy. "It is a time of remembering — and a time of honor."

As the Rev. C.A. Bentley of Crow Agnecy began the prayer consigning Major Reno's body to its second grave, his words punctuated by the flapping of the cemetery flag in the wind which rose up from the valley, Indians and white men listened — and watched.

From where they stood they could see the meandering stream where it all began, that June day in 1876. They could see in the distant haze the hill where the man they were burying fought — and the ridge where his commander died.

But their eyes came back always to the flag-draped casket at their feet — and to a soldier at long last home from a war that followed him, even in death.

Then came Saturday — and to the troubled spirit of Marcus Reno, peace.

Jumping on the centennial bandwagon

H EAVEN KNOWS, I'VE NEVER considered myself in any sense a historian — but now that Billings is getting up steam for its 100th birthday celebration I find myself increasingly involved in climbing aboard the bandwagon.

And bandwagons, especially the centennial kind — though you may have noticed already — are easier to get on to than off of.

For example, I've committed myself to a couple of articles and at the moment am putting the polish (such as it is) on three talks, all of which involve getting up before historical groups, school assemblies and service clubs to talk on what I know of the town I've called home for the last 30-odd years.

And here, I'm afraid, is where my fleeting resemblance to the figure called "historian" ends.

As a friend of mine, himself a historian of sorts, once said;

History belongs to the man who tells it first.

To which I would add — with a touch of irreverence — most history, whether it involves the American Revolution, the Norman conquest or how Billings got where it is today, is stuffy.

My kind of history, I hope, is the kind that'll keep you awake. You may not learn much — but you won't get much sleep either.

Let's start with G. Hermann Smith who not only ran the oldest undertaking business in town but who was also a pretty fair football referee.

Afternoon football games, however, interfered sometimes with afternoon funerals — but G. Hermann, with the spirit that helped win the West, was equal to the occasion.

In those early days when funeral directors turned out in top hats and frock coats G. Hermann wore his black and white striped shirt under his coat, changed clothes in the hearse on his way back to town and had the driver drop him off at the football field in time for the kickoff.

His son, Howard, who later took over the business, didn't referee games. He played them.

And one of Howard's memorable games involved a black cat — and a funeral car outside his father's chapel while the service was in progress.

What better place, thought young Howard, for a black cat than in a funeral car?

Everything went according to plan, including the emergence of a yowling, spitting cat when the car door was opened for the pallbearers, the confusion among the startled mourners — and even the subsequent disciplining of young Howard in the proprieties of the profession.

History? Maybe not as important as the arrival of the railroad or the installation of the first telephone — but history nonetheless.

Then there was the time in the mid-1950s when Deaconess Hospital went through one of its early expansion programs. Unearthed in the excavation was a bronze marker for a flagpole which, it seemed, had been given the hospital 30 years earlier.

"What shall I do with this?" the contractor asked.

The hospital administrator suggested a) that he throw it in the Yellowstone River and b) that he keep his mouth shut about having ever seen it.

The bronze marker — and its accompanying flagpole — were given to the hospital by the then active Billings klavern of the Ku Klux Klan.

One of my favorite bits of history not told often enough is about the arrival here of Samuel Cardinal Stritch of Chicago during a jubilee celebration of the Catholic church in eastern Montana.

The Cardinal's plane landed in one of the worst electrical storms in the city in years — and one in which, for the first time since its construction, the Shrine Auditorium was struck by lightning.

I didn't find out about it, naturally, until years later — and for good reason.

"We knew what you'd do with a thing like that, Bragg, if you ever got wind of it," one of my Shriner friends told me. And they were right.

Because I did — even though it was years late.

Sacrifice Cliff sounds good — and it's as historical sounding a name as you can think of. Good enough, in fact, for an early day televison performer in Billings to call himself.

But it wasn't, according to Earl Snook (who should know), what the Indians named the rimrock promitory across the river east of town. To them it was always Three Dance Cliff. But then — who ever heard of a country-western singer called Three Dance Cliff Larsen?

And while we're on the subject of names, let's look at Billings — Frederick K., to be specific. Our town was named after him only in a sense.

Billings, then president of the Northern Pacific Railway, directed his engineering crew to plat a townsite on the Yellowstone River at this point.

Included in his order was one additional item.

The new town was to be called Billings.

We did a lot of things right getting to where we are as a city and community today.

Stars &
Stripes

CHAPTER 3

Forgotten enemy
remembered friend

EVERY YEAR SINCE 1941, reporters on newspapers all over the country have sat before typewriters with an assignment staring them in the face: Do an anniversary piece on Pearl Harbor.

It was easy at first. You wrote about what people remembered of the day. You wrote about where you were when it happened, about people who recalled hearing that first broadcast. Then, as years went by and the world slid from the days of an uneasy peace to the tension of an undeclared war, you tried finding someone who was there when it happened.

The story, by those who lived through it, was always better than an I-remember-when account — and it got you through another year, another anniversary.

But now I'm tired of writing Pearl Harbor stories that, when it's all said and done, are just rehashes of a hundred memories, a hundred sorrows, a hundred minutes of the day which would — we were told — live in infamy.

That's why, with Pearl Harbor now 19 years in the past, I like to remember a boy called Hiroshi Sasamoto.

Hiroshi was 14 when we first met — through a foreign "pen pal" correspondence column that appeared in the Christian Science Monitor. I was the same age.

And the letters started. We wrote first about our hobbies, Hiroshi and I, then about our families and, finally, our hopes and ambitions. The letters went back and forth, from 401 S. Elm St. in a little Kansas town to 450 Mabashi, Suginami-cho, in Tokyo, through the years. I remember when his sister was married, I remember his entering medical school and the picture he sent me — a young, dark face, the half-smile and eyes bright behind dollar-round horn-rimmed glasses.

Hiroshi — who never forgot a Christmas greeting or a birthday card — wrote me once in his cramped, studious hand on the tissue-thin paper on which his letters always came of the walks he and his family took on summer evening "with the country-side dancing with lights of fire-fly-lanterns and the air full of gentle Japanesy emotion."

I remember how we laughed at the expression, "gentle Japanesy emotion."

The years went by and letters, always warm, always gentle, came

We're forgetting
our great heritage

DON'T ASK ANY kids why they do fireworks on the Fourth of July.

Chances are no one will come up with the right answer.

Which, of course, involves the signing of the Declaration of Independence.

On the other hand, don't blame them too much for not knowing.

Five'll get you ten that Independence Day, along with Armistice Day, is one of those forgotten holidays as far as source, tradition, legend and meaning is concerned.

Times, it seems, have changed.

I know where of I speak.

Back in those years when I looked forward to the Fourth as a time when we could make all the noise we wanted without being scolded for it, the only thing we worried about was how much money we could spend on fireworks — and how early could our celebration start.

It usually started a day or two before the Fourth when my father took us down to the fireworks stand — there was only one in the small town we lived in — gave us the money and stood by while we spent it.

That was the day of the "spitting devil," a red disc which, when rubbed on the sidewalk, popped, flamed, smoked and behaved most satisfactorily — considering the fact that it cost only a penny.

It was a time when you could buy a "torpedo," a ball-shaped bit of explosive which produced — really — more noise than you bargained for. And all it took was a toss in the air, a throw to the pavement or — if you were that daring — placement under a car tire. (The tire was never damaged).

And who, I wonder, remembers "lady fingers"?

They were the tiny firecrackers, around 200 in a single package, which you either fired all at once by lighting the single fuse that connected them all — or held one at a time, pinching the base tightly as they went off with a tiny pop.

We have to be careful, though, when it came to such items as "flash crackers" and "salutes."

An ordinary firecracker could blow a tin can five feet in the air.

A "salute" could rip the same can to shreds.

And I'm not just talking about firepower.

A package of ten flash crackers could cost as much as 25 cents.

A blue cardboard box containing three "globe flash salutes" could cost even more.

Back then they were considered pretty heavy stuff.

I guess they'd get the same sort of respect today.

But, aside from what the day — and the fireworks accompanying it — represents in most younger minds now as compared to what it represented originally, there's another way to measure it.

There are a lot of us still around who can remember coming home from a fireworks stand with a sack bulging with firecrackers, rockets, Roman candles, torpedoes, lady fingers, spitting devils, snakes, fountains, flash crackers, pinwheels and salutes, enough to last through the day and into the night.

And you still had enough change left from a five dollar bill to buy punk with.

Except for one thing:

Back in those days you got punk free when you bought fireworks.

And if you have to ask what punk is — well ...

That's another way in which the holiday has changed.

Proudly
she waves

I'M GLAD THERE are still people around who don't think flying a flag is old fashioned.

They do it on July 4.

They remember on Memorial Day.

And Monday, I think, will be another time that some neighborhoods throughout our town will be a little brighter because of such people.

Unfortunately, holidays like Flag Day tend to be overlooked by lots of us.

We're busy. Stores aren't closed. Mail is delivered and banks stay open.

It's a holiday, yes.

But not one, apparently, to get too excited about.

A personal observation is due at this point:

I still get a little excited — though that's hardly the word — when I think about Flag Day and why we observe it.

I am, in short, one of those people who can't see our flag without getting sentimental about it.

The feeling goes back a long way — I think to as far back as the first time I read a story by Edward Everett Hale called "Man Without A Country."

You all know it — or at least you should know it.

Philip Nolan, a young lieutenant, was tried and convicted for treason and, on being sentenced, told members of the military court "Damn the United States! I wish I may never see or hear of the United States again!"

His wish was granted. Until the day Nolan died he lived on ships at sea where all news, spoken or written, of his homeland was kept from him.

I read, long ago, the fictional Nolan's tribute to his country's flag after long years away from home and as he was nearing death.

There hasn't been a Flag Day since that I haven't thought of it.

Seeing those red and white stripes and those white stars on a blue field for the first time when you're away from home — and particularly for the first time the country is at war — is an experience not easily forgotten.

The meaning came home to me the time I saw our flag flying over a tiny piece of rock in Manila Bay called Corregidor.

I felt it one cold, dark night in Washington, D.C., when I walked by the White House, looked up and saw it, rippling in a chilly April wind.

The feeling was there at Arlington National Cemetery one day at the funeral of a friend.

And it was there at my first retreat ceremony in the service when the sunset gun echoed through the hills around an Army post and a regimental band played our national anthem.

It's still there at every parade I watch.

I remember flags on Memorial Day and on Independence Day.

I remember flags flown in victory — and I remember flags folded in mourning.

And for me they all mean home and country.

I guess that's why "The Star Spangled Banner" is something special, no matter how poorly it's played or sung sometimes.

And I guess that's why, all these years, I remember those words — pure fiction, of course — of Lieut. Philip Nolan:

"And for your country and for that flag, never dream a dream but of serving her as she bids you, though the service carry you through a thousand hells. No matter what happens to you, no matter who flatters you or abuses you, never look at another flag, never let a night pass but you pray God to bless that flag."

Sentimental? Sure.

But I find it hard to let a Flag Day go by without reading those words once more.

And it helps bring new meaning to the day — as well as to the flag it honors.

Veterans Day
dims memory and honor

FOR MANY, THURSDAY will be just another day on the calendar.

Others will think of it as Veterans Day.

And not a few, I'm sure, will wonder what, exactly, which term is right.

Veterans Day?

Or Armistice Day?

I was among those who grumbled a decade or so ago when they changed the name of the day from "Armistice" to "Veterans" and moved the observance to the nearest weekend to the November 11th date.

I wrote no letters, I merely grumbled.

That, of course, was because I was a traditionalist — and still am.

Armistice Day, from the time it was first celebrated, marked the ending of a war in Europe in 1918 in which American soldiers, sailors and Marines fought.

We won't bother with either the slogans or the political results (good or ill) which followed the conflict.

Armistice Day meant that peace had come to Europe, that men were coming home — and that it was a time for gratitude and remembrance.

That was what the 11th day of the 11th month of the year 1918 was all about.

Turning it into a "Veterans Day" dims memory and dilutes honor.

I'm not saying, mind, that those who fought in other wars should be without their day.

They too earned and deserve remembrance and recognition.

But if it comes to creating one inclusive catch-all celebration (or observance) then let them do away with V-E Day, V-J Day and, for that matter, Pearl Harbor Day as well. And, as long as they're at it, forget such names as Yorktown and Appomattox Courthouse.

They could even get rid of Independence Day setting it on a weekend in tribute to everyone in the colonies at the time who disagreed with George III.

But I wouldn't like it and I don't think anyone else would.

Maybe that first Armistice Day didn't silence the guns as long as we hoped.

Maybe it didn't make the world safe for democracy.

And, surely, it wasn't the war that ended all wars.

But it's still a day when a flag flying in the morning breeze and the sound of a bugle by a Soldier's Monument takes on special significance as it moves a nation back to one day, one month and one year in its history and to the memory of the men who made it all possible.

We are, as a people, grateful to all veterans of all wars.

But we should honor, as a nation, those to whom that first Armistice meant so much — and those for whom the guns fell silent long before 11 o'clock on the morning of November 11, 1918.

They earned the day.

Let it be theirs.

Mother's cooking was never like this

I'D BEEN IN THE ARMY, I daresay, all of one week before I learned about rectangular pies — and subsequent developments proved to me that pies like mother used to make weren't the only items on civilian menus I'd come to remember with a pang of nostalgia.

There was a practical reason for the square pie, of course, since no mess sergeant in the country had the time or the inclination to prepare five-slice circular pans for hundreds of ravenous troops.

But I still wonder why the mess hall version always had to be either cherry or unsweetened lemon meringue.

Thanksgiving and Christmas, when every commissary in the land decided to put a dent in canned pumpkin stockpiles, provided the only respite in the parade of red and yellow desserts.

Passing the drink was another mess hall innovation I had to get used to.

One never asked a person to pass the lemonade, the orangeade, the cherry, grape or lime concoction that accompanied everything except breakfast.

This was because it was served in aluminum or stainless steel pitchers and you never knew what you were getting until you poured it. Sometimes you weren't sure even then.

Aside from getting a seat at the end of the table (where you had only one fatigue-clad elbow to deal with), the most coveted thing when it came to eating in the army was an early chow pass.

Its advantages were enormous.

You didn't have to stand in line.

You didn't have to pull a tray from the rack, still beaded with water and so hot from its scalding you could hardly hold it.

And KPs, still relatively new on the job, hadn't as yet developed the technique of lobbing a spoonful of gravy onto your sectioned tray with such dexterity and unerring aim that it covered equally your mashed potatoes, your cole slaw and your left thumb.

But of all my mess hall experiences, I remember breakfast best.

It was where I tasted my first powdered eggs — and one day inadvertently overheard a mess sergeant bemoan his inability to prepare them "so they cook up a little more yellow and a little less green."

Army mess hall breakfasts were where I'm confident the military got rid of food it had been hoarding since World War I.

The man who wished could load his tray with corn flakes, oatmeal, fruit and juice — just for a starter. He then passed on to the grill offerings which included eggs, bacon and pancakes.

But most of all I remember mess hall breakfasts as the time I learned to call a piece of dry toast a shingle.

And creamed hamburger something else.

Look who's coming home from Canada

THE PRISONERS OF WAR are coming home from Vietnam.

And we may as well ready ourselves for another group of homecomers — this time from Canada.

No doubt, now that the war's over, increasing pressure for amnesty for draft-dodgers (and let's be honest and call them that) will make itself felt in Washington.

And there'll surely be those to whom a "forgive and forget" attitude will come quickly and easily.

I hope they are in the minority.

While not denying that there may be mitigating circumstances which argue in favor of a degree of amnesty for some, I feel the majority of those who, having left the country to avoid military service, should accept the consequences if they decide to return.

They had the choice, had they stayed, to register and serve as conscientious objectors. For a long time the law has provided for this.

But those who left took the law, in effect, into their own hands.

And many spoke at the time of the "courage" on which their decision was based.

Let's give them a chance to show us once again the "courage."

Let them come home and accept whatever consequences there may be.

And let's hear no talk of amnesty from these modern day sunshine patriots who feel, now that the war is over, that this country is worth living in — but not worth defending.

Ghosts of war
stalk the Burma jungle

THE NIGHT THEY CALL All Hallows Eve never comes without memory taking me back to a time and a place that was once an important part of my life and the lives of all of us who spent a part of the war in a part of the world called Burma.

I think of the Naga hills on Halloween and I think of the ghosts that surely haunt them even today.

And I thank the impulse that led me to clip what someone long ago wrote — in an obscure newspaper published in a now-forgotten Indian city — about those ghosts and why they are there.

The clipping is yellowed with the nearly 40 years I've kept it.

But I always read it once again when Halloween comes around because some of those ghosts I knew — and it's important, somehow, that they're remembered.

Let me share it with you:

BURMA — There were ghosts in the land last night.

On Main Street, U.S.A., the goblins had their day and the witches made their annual ride on their broomsticks across the face of the moon — for it was that final fated day of October, day of the ringing doorbells and the missing shutters and the snagged-toothed pumpkins — Halloween, 1945.

But on Main Street, Burma — the Highway 66 of this jungle, the Post Road of the Irrawaddy Shore, known to a few as the Ledo Road — a new host of ghosts was abroad.

No witches, these, nor goblins, but the water buffalo crept deeper into the thickets and little Naga children trembled in their mothers' arms and even Shan, the tiger, lay with his belly on the ground and fear in his heart. The land was still and only the ghosts walked.

High in the Patkai Mountains there was a meeting and the hills sounded with the beating of the conversation — for it was the talk of battle, of rifle ball and pistol slug and the deeper, hurried thud of mortars.

The sky was dark, for the moon was on the other side of the world where the witches played, but the sky wasn't empty.

There were ghosts up there in the dark and the sound of their passing was the roar of 1,200 horses and their calling cards dug deeply into the jungle with a boom and a flash.

72

At Myitkyina there was quite a convention. Ghosts with white faces met ghosts whose skins were darker and some whose skins were yellow with centuries of life in the Orient. They prowled along the grass-grown edges of the strip up there and they talked in their own way about Joe Stilwell and Frank Merrill and General Sun.

On down the river at Bhamo they gathered in the dark, these Burma ghosts, and looked silently at the temples and the foxholes beside those temples. There were music lovers among them and these sat in the deserted bomb crater near the mission and remembered a gracious lady from Paris who stood on a hot day in the broiling sun and sang until she could sing no more.

There were ghosts at Mong-yu, where the Ledo trace runs into the Burma Road. These ghosts wore suits of armor — 1945 version — and behind them came four-legged ghosts with big, flapping ears, a bray straight from hell and an inquisitive look straight from Missouri. They wore the scars of sores on their backs and their legs ached with the miles of the mountains.

Yes, ghosts walked in Burma last night. It was Halloween.

And tomorrow night and it won't be Halloween either.

They'll walk there until the road that bore them is nothing but a memory, until the reason they were born and left to be ghosts of this land fills only two pages of a televised or microfilmed history book.

We wish them well, these ghosts, because, but for the grace of God and the breaks that come to a man, we might have been with them and we are glad we aren't.

We hope we'll remember them and perhaps we will — but the memory of a man is a treacherous thing and the chances are we'll forget. Only on dark and stormy nights in a driving rain will we remember and because we hate to remember things we didn't like, we'll turn from the wind and the rain to the lights of home.

But the ghosts are in Burma and because they are there the world is a different place and though we may forget, the ghosts of the Ledo Road will remember, and they'll know — and they'll be satisfied."

It's Russian roulette in the mess hall

I N THIS DAY OF computerized warfare — and the microchips and synthetic materials that go along with it — I often wonder what might have happened 40 or more years ago had our enemies discovered what may well have been their ultimate weapon in achieving victory.

Had they discovered it there would have been no need for an attack on Poland — or a bombing of Pearl Harbor.

Were they only to look in the right place, all the intrigues of Japanese and German intelligence would have been time and money wasted.

For with the leverage this Achilles heel would have provided — accompanied, of course, by competent exploitation — history might have taken an entirely different turn.

I refer — for those of you who might not have guessed by now — to the Army mess hall.

Faced by the powerful mystique of the Army mess, Caesar, Bismarck and von Clausewitz would have been babes in arms.

Recalling, after all these years, the breakfast, lunch and dinner menus of only one week in the service, I marvel that VE and VJ days ever came about.

Consider, for example, powdered eggs, an early-morning staple for the civilian-turned-soldier a couple of generations ago.

They were dry. They were green. And they had a brown crust rivaled only by a piece of French toast that had been left on the griddle too long.

On the other hand, they WERE eggs.

But about the only thing to be said in their favor was that you didn't have to worry about finding pieces of shell in them.

Another source of strength overlooked by our enemies was that delectable entree made up of creamed hamburger on dry (and I mean REALLY dry) toast which was known as something-or-other-on-a-shingle.

I submit — and let the record show — that properly placed enemy agents could have powdered-egged and SOSed us into sitting down at a peace treaty table in less time than it would have taken to say "short-stop."

That was another thing about the Army mess.

Observing its protocol may well have detracted considerably from the war effort.

Aside from going to sleep on guard duty, the next most disgraceful thing for a soldier was to short-stop the powdered eggs — or the SOS — or whatever.

Short-stopping, in short — and no pun intended — meant that when you were asked to pass something down the table you helped yourself to it on the way down.

No one, however, was ever court-martialed for a short-stop.

Cinching was another matter.

That was when you took something from a serving plate and left only enough for one more helping — and the man to take the last helping had to go back in line and refill the plate.

Short-stopping was a clear-cut offense. There were witnesses who caught you at it.

Cinching, on the other hand, involved a matter of judgment.

When, in short — and again no pun intended — was a cinch not a cinch?

I spent half my meal time in the Army listening to arguments on this fine point. And to this day I have little doubt more time was spent in determining who cinched the potatoes (or the powdered eggs, the creamed peas or the drink) than was spent in planning the invasion of Europe.

One always tried to make the mess hall early — only because that assured one of being able to pick a metal tray off the rack without having to wear asbestos gloves.

A rule of thumb in the Army mess hall was that the hotter the tray the better were your chances for getting Jello salad — or ice cream for dessert.

By the time you got to your table you could drink them both.

Mess-hall etiquette being what it was, though, you didn't.

You ate them in the conventional manner, with a spoon — blowing on it only to cool both dessert and salad.

Armies, some great military man once said, travel on their stomachs.

But mess halls — at least the ones I experienced — belie the saying that getting there is half the fun.

A soldier's death is never useless

DEAR FRIEND:

I know, now that peace has come in Vietnam after 10 long years, that your thoughts aren't near so much on those who are coming home as they are on the one who isn't.

He could be a brother, a father, a husband or a son.

He could be lying now beneath the green of a cemetery lot — or in an unmarked grave in God knows what Asian jungle.

And you might well feel beneath the scars of an old pain — or the freshness of grief — a sense of bitterness in loss.

It's over, you keep saying to yourself. It's over and he's not coming back.

And you think of the things that could have been — and the things that were. And the things that are.

And it's understandable, in a way, how you feel.

But don't let them tell you his death was useless. Don't let them tell you he died for nothing. Don't let them, no matter what, tell you the death of any man in any war was a mockery.

The men who died at Lexington, Antietam, Belleau Wood, Bastogne and Iwo Jima didn't ask to go there.

But they went.

And those whose eyes looked for the last time at a blue sky over Korea or who breathed their life away in a tiny village in Vietnam with an unpronounceable name didn't ask to go there either.

But they went.

And the very whisper that their death was for nothing is an affront to why they lived — and why they died.

Useless death?

You can see it on the front page of your newspaper every day if you look. What about the family killed on a highway in a head-on with a drunk driver? What about the innocent bystander caught in a gunman's cross-fire with police? What about the victims of a crazed killer?

These, I feel, are deserving of the term.

But those men, whose flag-draped coffins have been much in our thoughts and memories these past 10 years, deserve much more than the shallowness of the cynic or the vitriol of the demagogue.

For it is to them, as to all those who died before, we owe our strength.

And to deny this is to betray them. To deny this is to mock every grave on every battlefield of every war this country ever fought.

And to deny it would be to forget, in a sense, they ever lived.

For the day we can understand that the only useless death is one that follows a useless life we shall be truly wise.

The Army tells
its side of the story

EDITOR'S NOTE: Addison Bragg, Gazette columnist, is a retired lieutenant-colonel in the U.S. Army Reserve with more than 20 years experience as a general staff intelligence officer at Department of Army level. The following article by him was based on a U.S. Army Command Information Unit publication in his possession, published in Washington D.C.

To keep the record straight — and to be fair — it might be well to set forth the U.S. Army's side of things following last week's visit here by a retired officer who spoke about "dishonesty" and "deviousness" in the service.

Lt. Col. Anthony Herbert, former commanding officer of the 2nd Battalion, 503rd Infantry was relieved of his command April 4, 1969, for unsatisfactory performance of duty.

Five days later he formally asked for a "redress of wrongs" as provided under the Uniform Code of Military Justice. A three-star general called 38 witnesses, listened to them for five days and ruled Herbert's superior officer was justified in his action.

There is no record that at that time, orally or in writing, Herbert raised the issue of war crimes.

On his return to the states, Herbert made his first appeal from the low efficiency report submitted at the time of his relief from command.

This was in September 1969. The appeal was turned down by Headquarters, Department of Army, which determined there was no cause, on the basis of evidence submitted by Herbert, to change the report.

There is no record that at the time Herbert raised the issue of war crimes — or the alleged failure of the 173rd Airborne brigade commander to investigate them.

A second appeal was made by Herbert Sept. 4, 1970, and on May 25, 1971, he was notified that this, too, had been turned down.

There is no record that at the time Herbert raised the issue of war crimes.

Robert Froehike, Secretary of Army, ordered a third review of Herbert's unsatisfactory efficiency report (made in April 1969) in Oct. 1971. The review included consideration of the report itself, the report of the board hearing the original request for "redress" and the two appeals.

As a result of Froehike's review, the adverse report was removed from his 201 file and the file was forwarded to a promotion board.

The earliest official record of Herbert's allegations of war crimes is dated Sept. 28, 1970. This was 18 months following his relief from command. At the time the Department of Army, on Nov. 13, 1970, began investigation of 21 incidents said to have occurred between mid-1968 to mid-1969.

The Army assigned 16 people to the investigation, later expanded it to include 32 criminal investigators and administrative people.

The investigation lasted seven months, ending June 23, 1971. More than 300 people, some of whom had already returned to civilian life, were interviewed by investigators in 30 of the 48 continental states as well as in Hawaii, the Philippines, Vietnam, Okinawa, Australia, New Zealand, Mexico and Germany.

As a result of the inquiry, seven of the 21 incidents were considered of sufficient substance to merit action — or further investigation.

Two of the seven had already been acted on by the 173rd Brigade commander at the time they happened. One resulted in punishment, the other in a general court-martial. Two more involved offenses by Vietnamese against Vietnamese over which the Army had no jurisdiction. The remaining three allegations involved maltreatment of suspected

Viet Cong or Viet Cong supporters. They were, in November 1971, awaiting action by officers with general court-martial jurisdiction.

Late in 1970 and early in 1971, Lt. Col. Herbert was told that investigation of his charges was continuing.

But in March 1971, Herbert preferred charges against both Gen. John W. Barnes and Col. J. Ross Franklin for "failure to report and investigate alleged violation of the law of land warfare and for dereliction of duty."

Charges against Col. Franklin were dismissed July 15, 1971 after an official inquiry lasting two months. It was determined at that time that there was insufficient evidence to show that Col. Franklin had ever been made aware of the charges to warrant a court-martial.

The Military District of Washington looked into Herbert's charges against Gen. Barnes. The investigation lasted six months, included 3,000 pages taken from 52 witnesses and a record that included more than 100 documentary exhibits. The MDW commander announced on Oct. 15, 1971, that evidence was not sufficient to warrant further proceedings. The charges were dismissed.

All of which hardly smacks of either dishonesty or deviousness on the part of the Army. On the face of things, it looks more like an organization bending over backward to make sure an officer relieved of his command deserved to be relieved of his command.

"Whenever someone decides to speak out and make public some outrageous act," Lt. Col. Herbert said here the other night, "people become suspicious of him."

So, whenever someone waits 18 months before "speaking out," be it for an official Army record on the commission of war crimes — or to the larger court of public opinion insured by the hundreds of war correspondents roaming the streets of Saigon during the three months Lt. Col. Herbert was stationed there following his relief, and later in the U.S., we get a little suspicious too.

Friendship flows
down on the Bayou

Y OU'LL NEVER FIND THE Chief of Staff, after a hard day at the Pentagon, hoisting a tall cool one in the Bayou Room — but it won't be because he isn't welcome.

He's probably never heard of the officers club located barely 10 minutes walk away in the ramshackle wing of a transient officers billet on Ft. Myer's South Post.

Which makes the Chief of Staff in the minority.

Bayou Room alumni, the thousands who date themselves from 1950 when the club was opened, are flung as wide as the services they represent — and the more sentimental among them never return to the Washington area without making at least one trip back "to see who's still around."

None can deny that sentiment is the club's strongest drawing card, with informality and the prospect of running into an old comrade-in-arms running close seconds.

It's certainly not the amenities which, compared to rich, refurbished, sedate and aloff Patton Hall across the highway to the north, are Spartan indeed.

When Patton Hall, for example, got its new ballroom, expanded dining area, plush carpets and svelte cocktail lounge a few years ago, the Bayou Room blossomed out with plastic window drapes, six new light bulbs and a new coat of paint in the combination phone booth-cloakroom. (The old walls had gotten pretty well covered with scribbled phone numbers in the 15 years since Korea.)

But there's no jealousy among the Bayou Room's habitues. Live, they say, and let live.

And, despite the creaking of the worn dance floor, the chrome-and-plastic chairs and tables, the drab green walls and the rattling of its window air conditioner, those who frequent the place have been known to do a lot of living there.

Informality isn't only the keynote of the place — you could almost call it a mandate. Not, of course, that anyone would ever be criticized for showing up in a tie — but legend has it that a member who strolled in early one Sunday wearing pajamas elicited no more comment than "Hm, I never knew Major So-and-So wore pajamas before."

Best about the place, perhaps, are the people who come there, be they Army, Navy, Marine or Air Force, reserve or regular, active or retired.

They remember while a Bayou man is gone — and, more important, remember when he walks back in.

And every year around Christmas time the cards start coming in from all over the world to be pinned up around the bar as evidence that, as the club remembers, it is remembered.

It's said the place will be torn down soon to make room for mushrooming Arlington National Cemetery — but members will believe that when bulldozers come to shove them off their stools.

"They've probably forgotten us down here," one said. "The CARE packages we used to get from Patton Hall have even stopped coming."

And so the days go by at the Bayou Room, by all appearances the only officers club in the country that could qualify for the poverty program — but by all experience the one best remembered for its warmth and friendship.

The military stands
tall on the firing line

I CAN'T HELP THINKING of Kipling's poem about Tommy Atkins when I read and hear some of the things that are being written and said about the military today.

It is, apparently, open season on uniforms — especially those with stars on the shoulder straps — the like of which we haven't seen since the late 1920s or early 1930s.

That was when America was too troubled with other things, things like prosperity and things like depression, to be bothered with the Eisenhowers, the Pattons, the Bradleys and all the others — officers and enlisted men — who spent long, thankless years in the service before being accepted finally by a society which once considered them a jot below the sub-human in the scheme of things.

And now we have the same thing happening — and have had it happening for some time. Military men are criticized for speaking their mind — and then criticized for not speaking up.

They are censured for "getting us involved" where we shouldn't be involved by the same people who are equally adamant that civilian authority "should never let the brass hats get the upper hand."

Military men are accused of "brainwashing" the Congress and the public when they appear before committees to plead their case for defense budgets.

And they're accused of being "uncooperative" if they stay away from Capitol Hill.

Charges that the Army, the Navy or the Air Force wasted billions of the taxpayers' dollars on the F-111 fighter and the C-5A transport are common today.

But who, if we may be so bold as to ask, awarded and signed the contracts?

Not, certainly, any member of the Joint Chiefs of Staff.

And what of the increasing hue and cry over so-called war "criminals" in American uniforms — and the silence on the other hand that greets every courtroom decision exonerating them (16 defendants so far in the My Lai "massacre" alone)?

I think it's high time we started looking at some of our generals and some of our admirals and most of the soldiers, sailors, airmen and Marines who serve under them as something more than whipping boys for decisions, both political and diplomatic, which have turned out to be less than wise or practical.

And I think it's time we remembered that there are words in the dictionary just as beautiful (and practical) as "privilege, prosperity and peace."

And I'm talking about words that men in uniform live by — words like "duty, honor and country."

This is why in this day when it's fashionable, even smart, to ridicule the services for their mistakes I'm reminded of a poet's tribute to the British soldier and agree in principle with him that it's better to have an Army that we don't need — than to need one we don't have.

And with Kipling, I hope:

"O, there'll surely come a day

"When they'll give you all your pay,

"And treat you as a Christian ought to do;

"So, until that day comes around,

"Heaven keep you safe and sound,

"And, Thomas, here's my

best respects to you!"

A day devoted to the living and dead

YOU CAN'T REALLY appreciate Armistice Day unless you've lived in a small town back in a time between wars when the word "armistice" was still strange to the tongue.

People then talked of guns barely ten years silent — and never dreamed of a day when men would march once more in Europe and throughout the world.

But it was a pleasant time, this celebration of war's end, in the town you lived in.

It was a day devoted to both the living and the dead.

There were parades and there were flags and there were bands — and even one year a balloon ascension in the court house park.

A state senator or, on rare occasions, a visiting member of Congress could always be prevailed upon for a speech at the informal program in the morning.

That was always just before a member of the Legion post's drum and bugle corps climbed the rickety steps to the clock tower in the court house.

He blew "Taps" at exactly 11 o'clock — that same time on the eleventh day of the eleventh month of the 18th year of this century when the World War they now call the first ended.

And just as on Memorial Day, people made their trips to the little cemetery on the hill north of town and stood for a moment by the uniform rows of white stones broken only by flashes of color where small flags fluttered.

This, perhaps, was what was significant about the way a small town observed Armistice Day.

People celebrated the ending of a war — but they also recognized the contribution of those who fought for the peace they celebrated.

Their parades began with the flag.

Their speeches ended with a prayer.

And no one spoke of the obscenity of war or the uselessness of death or the immorality of America.

This, perhaps, is what you remember most about Armistice Day in a small town back in a time between wars.

And this, perhaps is why the greatness of America today still lies in its small towns where people honor their war dead instead of pity them — and are neither ashamed or afraid to put words like duty, honor and country above words like privilege, prosperity and peace.

A soldier's heart beats ever so proudly

I N ALMOST EVERY town there was a Soldiers Monument.

If it didn't dominate the city square or the courthouse park, it stood high on a hill overlooking the green and white tapestry of the cemetery which surrounded it.

It was either accepted or ignored the rest of the year by the people who grew up with it and around it.

But when, that one day came, the Soldiers Monument with its inscriptions, sometimes simple, often quaint, took on a special significance.

Decoration Day, they once called it. And they still do in many places, especially in the East or South. But even where the celebration long ago became Memorial Day it was special — to the young as well as to the old.

But though it lasted only a few short hours it was much more than just another three-day weekend.

I guess to really understand the day for what it was you'd have had to grow up in a little town.

You would have had to know what an organization called the Grand Army of the Republic was.

You would have had to remember a song called "Tenting Tonight on the Old Campground."

And you would have had to listen in youthful wonder to the still-strong voice of an old man as he spoke to you of battlefields that bore American names.

The Civil War wasn't all that far away back then.

Almost every town had someone who fought in it.

I knew a half dozen or more in the town where I was born in Ohio.

There was one still living right across the alley from us in Kansas where I grew up.

Old men they were for all the other days of the year.

Old men sitting in yards, on porches or on benches in the park.

They talked, they whittled on bits of wood or puffed on pipes.

They generally blended in with the scenery.

But on Decoration Day they stopped being old men and, for those moments of parading, of speaking and singing — and finally, to the sound of a distant bugle blowing "Taps" — they were old men no longer.

They became soldiers.

The brims of their faded campaign hats were limp. The brass buttons on the blue coats they wore were tarnished.

But their step was firm as they marched — almost in time — to the music.

I remember the man who first went with me one bright May morning to the cemetery west of town and told me of what the day meant, how it began and why we should remember.

Remember, he said. That's why they're beginning to call it Memorial Day.

And I remember.

I close my eyes and I can see the blue sky and smell the freshness of the new-mown grass.

I listen and I can hear as though it were yesterday the flutter of tiny flags in the breeze that came up from the river before the hush that fell over the crowd was broken by the crack of rifles firing volleys.

I hear as well the distant sound of a bugle.

It will always be to me what Memorial Day was, is and shall be.

And since that first May morning long ago the day has never come and gone but that I remember who first talked to me of what words like duty, honor and country should mean to those of us who follow those who went before.

And in memory once again I feel a large, warm and browned hand holding mine and I look up — and see my grandfather standing at my side.

You can't change history

I F ANYONE IN the crowd's taking names, he can include mine on the list of those who'll celebrate Armistice Day come Nov. 11.

And I don't care what the date-changers in Washington have to say about it.

They're the same ones, remember, who gave us a second and a third Unknown Soldier at Arlington Cemetery.

And I didn't like that, either.

I think we need only one Unknown Soldier to remind us of all of those who rest in honored glory, known but to God.

I think we need only one Armistice Day to show our high resolve that these dead shall not have died in vain.

Maybe (and in all honesty, it's a pretty valid "maybe") I'm a rank sentimentalist.

But to me, Armistice Day will always be a clear, crisp morning in November in a little Kansas town.

It was a day when flags flew from porches and the radiator caps of cars and the wheels of every kid's bike in town were circled with red, white and blue crepe paper.

It was a time when people came from miles around for the annual celebration which marked the end of a war barely 15 years in the past.

And it was when veterans of the Civil War and the Spanish-American War still could — and did — wave to crowds that lined the square as they led a parade which was the important part of the day.

From the bugle in the courthouse tower which sounded "Taps" as the clock struck 11 — the hour on which guns along the Western Front fell silent that November day in 1918 — to the games, the shows, the dancing and the fun far into the night, Armistice Day was a time of celebration — and remembering.

There were, I know, a thousand "little Kansas towns" all over the country where this happened when the 11th day of November came around.

Maybe they're still here.

And maybe Armistice Day and the things it stands for will be remembered after all.

Like I say, I'm a sentimentalist.

On my calendar Armistice Day will fall on Nov. 11.

And Oct. 25, at best, will be what it's always been — Thanksgiving Day in the Virgin Islands, the day on which all the islanders celebrate the end of the hurricane season.

Old Navy men
always stick together

THE GUY WHO SAYS "sink the Navy" should have his head examined.

It can't be done — as an hour-long interlude in the Petroleum Club proved Wednesday afternoon.

As with so many of the grander projects devised by mind and forgotten just as quickly — this all started with the usual service reminiscences over a convivial cup.

One cup, of course, led to another as talk whirled and eddied and finally settled down, narrowing into discussion of an incident that took place — or was believed to have taken place — a full 17 years ago.

There was, one wearer of the Navy blue declared, only one way to settle the matter.

He picked up the telephone, "Get me," he told the operator, "my old friend, Capt. Fitzhugh Lee."

Capt. Lee, he recalled, was stationed in Pensacola, Fla. — 10 years ago.

Long distance operators from Billings to Miami went to work at running down what proved to be an elusive Fitzhugh Lee.

He was no longer in Pensacola, word finally came back. He was now in Washington, D.C.

"Liberty," said the Petroleum Club caller, jotting down the Pentagon phone number, "5-6700. Get me the Bureau of Naval Personnel."

Now, his friend agreed, we're getting someplace.

The man on the phone listened and smiled.

"My old friend Lee," he said, "is an admiral now."

At the rate it's taking to find him, a listener observed darkly, he'll be retired before the call gets there.

Whoever answered the Navy bureau phone said Admiral Lee had left Washington.

He was now, apparently, in the office of the commander-in-chief, Atlantic Fleet, Norfolk, Va.

"Okay, operator," Admiral Lee's friend said, "let's go to Norfolk."

There was silence for a moment as they tried to reach the admiral in his quarters.

"Whyncha call back the Pentagon and ask to talk to some WAVE there?" someone offered. "They know all the answers."

The man on the phone shushed him.

"Whatzat, operator?" he said. "No answer, huh?"

Forget it, his friend, the man who'd first started the discussion, said. Forget it.

"If ya gotta call someone," he said to the man on the phone, "call Salinger. Maybe he'll know."

The caller said he didn't like Salinger.

"But I know a guy we can the answer from," he said. "Since we can't get old Admiral Lee, he's our last chance."

He asked the Norfolk operator to put him back to Washington. There was a moment before the Washington operator came on the line.

"Hello," said the man. "Operator, where are you?" The operator told him where she was.

"Get me," said the man on the Petrolem Club phone, "John F. Kennedy."

This seemed as good a time as any to draw the curtain on the scene besides, who wants to eavesdrop on conversations between two old Navy men?

Old

Favorites

CHAPTER 4

You can't out-flip
a flip-chart flipper

THE FLIP-CHART, a sales-minded friend said to me one day, apropos of absolutely nothing, is the greatest contribution to civilization since the wheel.

"In fact," he said, warming to the subject, "if they'd have had flip-charts back in those days they could have gotten the idea of the wheel across to the general public a hundred thousand years earlier."

I couldn't argue with him.

From the day of my first experience with a flip-chart — one which showed a disemboweled M-1 rifle in vivid color — I've learned better than to try to argue with a flip-charter. Or is it a chart-flipper?

They drown out your feeble protests with the rustling of paper, flipped up, over and smoothed down with a pointer. (A flip-chart man is never without a pointer.)

I remember one flip-chart man — he tried to sell me a set of encyclopedias — who stirred up such a breeze in the room I went around with the sniffles for days.

If the going gets too rough, remember, the chart-flipper (or flip-charter) can always hide behind his easel, thus offering a poor target.

History, I'm afraid, would have been written differently if the flip-charters had been in charge.

Imagine, for example, Moses at the edge of the Red Sea, setting up the first papyrus chart and using a rod — which he borrowed from Aaron — as a pointer.

It would, considering the presentation involved, have to be a BIG chart.

Going back still further, think how much sooner people might have learned to write if early man had abandoned his solitary efforts with hammer, chisel and stone and spent a few profitable minutes with a junior account executive representing The Writing Man.

"These," the Stone Age flipper would say, pointing — in this instance, with a club — "are letters."

The first page would show a jumbled alphabet.

Flip.

"Letters make words," the second page would read. Flip.

"This is a word." (Under a crude sketch of a sabre-toothed tiger would be spelled out "C-A-T.")

Flip. Point.

"Words make sentences." (At this point there would probably ensue considerable nodding, mumbling and pointing from the hunkering audience, now beginning to catch on.)

Thanks, of course, to the flip-chart.

Flip again.

"THIS IS A SENTENCE." (Repeated tapping with the club at this point to put idea across.)

Primitive man might have learned to write sooner, there's no denying. There's always the danger, however, that he might have gotten off the track and spent the next few ages of civilization making flip-charts.

I pointed this out to my friend who seemed unimpressed.

He wouldn't have been able to, he argued.

"You can't make a flip-chart," he said, "just by watching one being used. You have to —" He broke off at this point, a strange look in his eye.

"It's never been done before," he said, whipping a pocket notebook out and beginning to sketch and letter rapidly. "It's never been done before — so mine will be the first."

Puzzled, I peered over his shoulder.

He was making a flip-chart on how to make a flip-chart.

This Horrorscope
tells it like it is

T HIS IS ONE OF THOSE things that came "from a friend who got it from a friend whose cousin showed her a copy that had been borrowed from a guy who got it in the mail."

So we don't know who to credit for it.

Be that as it may, it's still too good not to pass on — especially to astrology buffs.

AQUARIUS — Jan. 20 to Feb. 18 — You have an inventive mind and are inclined to be progressive. You lie a great deal. On the other hand you are inclined to be careless and impractical, causing you to make the same mistakes over and over again. People think you are stupid.

PISCES — Feb. 19 to March 20 — You have a vivid imagination and often think you are being followed by the CIA or FBI. You have minor influence over your associates and people hate you for your flaunting of your power. You lack confidence and are generally a coward. Pisces people do terrible things to small animals.

ARIES — March 21 to April 19 — You are the pioneer type and hold most people in contempt. You are quick tempered, impatient and scornful of advice. You are not very nice.

TAURUS — April 20 to May 20 — You are practical and persistent. You have a dogged determination and work like hell. Most people think you are stubborn and bullheaded. You are a Communist.

GEMINI — May 21 to June 20 — You are a quick and intelligent thinker. People like you because you are bisexual. However, you are inclined to expect too much for too little. This means you are cheap. Geminis are known for committing incest.

CANCER — June 21 to July 22 — You are sympathetic and understanding to other people's problems. They think you are a sucker. You're always putting things off. That's why you'll never make anything of yourself. Most welfare recipients are Cancer people.

LEO — July 23 to Aug. 22 — You consider yourself a born leader. Others think you are pushy. Most Leo people are bullies. You are vain and dislike honest criticism. Your arrogance is disgusting. Leo people are known thieves.

VIRGO — Aug. 23 to Sept. 22 — You are the logical type and hate disorder. This nitpicking is sickening to your friends. You are cold and unemotional and sometimes fall asleep while making love. Virgos make good bus drivers.

LIBRA — Sept. 23 to Oct. 22 — You are the artistic type and have a difficult time with reality. If you are a man you more than likely are queer. Chances for employment and monetary gain are excellent. Most Libra women are good prostitutes. All Libras die of veneral disease.

SCORPIO — Oct. 23 to Nov. 21 — You're shrewd in business and cannot be trusted. You shall achieve the pinnacle of success because of your total lack of ethics. Most Scorpio people are murdered.

SAGITTARIUS — Nov. 22 to Dec. 21 — You are optimistic and enthusiastic. You have a reckless tendency to rely on luck since you lack talent. The majority of Sagittarians are drunks or dope fiends. People laugh at you a great deal.

CAPRICORN — Dec. 22 to Jan. 19 — You are conservative and afraid of taking risks. You don't do much of anything and are lazy. There has never been a Capricorn of any importance. Capricorns should avoid standing still too long as they tend to take root and become trees.

The rippling
rhythm of radio

WHEN OLDER PEOPLE sit around and start talking about radio — and I'm sure some of you who grew up on TV know about that — they usually go for the serials or the comedy shows.

How often, for example, have your parents — or even grandparents — brought up such names from the past as Amos and Andy, Vic and Sade or Lum and Abner?

And you've had to sit there trying to look interested.

Or how many times have you agonized at not being able to recall — despite those clear memories of your elders — programs like Chandu, the Magician, I Love a Mystery or Lights Out?

In a way, I not only understand your detachment from what was once the big radio scene. I can sympathize as well with your who-really-cares-all-that-much attitude.

That's why I'd like to talk for a minute about what — and how much — radio meant to those teen-agers your grandparents once were.

After, that is, the soap operas, the drama shows and the comedy hours were over for the night.

Radio, back in the 1930s, was dancing — once 10 o'clock came and went.

And there's probably not a disc jockey in the business today — no matter what he's playing or where he plays it from — who can compare with the no-talk, all-music radio of those days.

There were no sponsors.

There was just dance music from practically every radio station or network in the country, from New York to Los Angeles. An announcer came on (right after the 10 o'clock news) and told you who you were listening to and where the music was coming from.

And you took it from there.

The bands you listened to every night — clear up, in fact, until 2 in the morning — are heard now only on record albums.

And some of those albums, believe it or not, were made from "air takes" of those same broadcasts.

The names read like a "Who's Who" of what is now called the Big Band Era.

Benny Goodman, Guy Lombardo, Glenn Miller, Tommy and Jimmy Dorsey, Jimmy Lunceford (anyone rememer him?), Fletcher Henderson, Xavier Cugat, Wayne King, Jan Garber, Jan Savitt, Joe Sanders, Sammy Kaye, Eddy Duchin, Kay Kyser, Artie Shaw, Count Basie, Art Kassel, Blue Barron, Carlos Molina, George Olsen, Red Norvo — and who knows how many others?

92

The music, which came from the Aragon and Trianon ballrooms in Chicago, the Empire Room of the Palmer House, the Coconut Grove and Trocadero in Los Angeles, the Wedgewood Room of the Waldorf-Astoria, the Blue Grotto (near Sedalia, Mo.) and somebody's (I forget who) Starlight Roof, went on for hours.

And you did more than just listen.

There were plenty of house parties which began with the simple process of rolling back a living room rug, turning up the radio — and letting nature (with an able assist from Terpsichore) take its course.

After all, a good radio — particularly one of those "cabinet" models which resembled in size and design the nickelodeon — was better than any phonograph in the business.

(And, as anyone who spent any time at the trade knows, there was nothing better than a car radio when accompanied by a moonlight night.)

But — and you may find this hard to believe — we even managed with a phonograph. And there were always enough wallflowers in the crowd to change records and to wind the thing when it needed winding.

I guess, when you get right down to it, that's one of the things I miss about late night radio — as opposed to late night television.

Late night radio — and those great night bands — were good to listen to and great to dance to.

And TV, advanced though it was and is, couldn't hold a candle to it.

Who, I ask, ever put an arm around a girl while watching "Nightmare Theater"?

And who ever proposed to anyone at 2 a.m. — right in the third quarter of a re-run hockey game?

Every Christmas
is worth remembering

EVERYONE, I SAY, should keep a Christmas scrapbook — even though it's lacking in old cards, the glue to paste them in with and a shred here and there of browning tinsel, faded ribbon and tattered wrappings.

The sort of book I'm talking about is one that won't fit on a shelf — let alone a coffee table — and one whose pages are turned only in memory.

My particular scrapbook is filled with memories of sounds, tastes, scents and scenes.

It starts on one side of the world, moves to the other side and then comes back to that one important place which always figures in every Christmas past, present and — in the words of Charles Dickens — yet to come.

I'm talking about home, the place we all think of at this special time of year.

How often have we listened with envy to those who spoke of "going home for Christmas"?

We can remember our parents who spoke with warmth and love of what Christmas and home meant to them.

We can even remember trying to explain to our children — too young, of course, to appreciate such things at the time — about what Christmas at home was like.

Again, I'm thinking of the sights, the sounds, the scents and the tastes of Christmas in the many places I've called home over the years.

Sleighbells on a cold, moonlit night a long time ago when we were met at a tiny railroad station in Ohio on Christmas Eve by a horse-drawn sleigh to spend the holiday with relatives in the country.

My first look at Santa Claus — whom I recognized right away by his formidable horn-rimmed glasses as a great-uncle — and my reply to him when he picked me up and asked what I wanted for Christmas. I told him to put me down.

My father, a traditionalist if ever there was one, who ruled Christmas with an iron hand when it came to such essentials as trees and gifts. For as long as I can remember there was never a tree decorated or a gift in evidence in our house until early on the morning of Christmas Day. We went to bed, my sister and I, with the house looking much as it did every other day of the year. We woke up (early, of course) to find the Christmas elves or fairies (or whatever) had indeed been at work. The living room was transformed — and the magic of the moment has never left.

(Our tree, incidentally, stayed up until the sixth day of January.)

Long before I even got there I'd read Rudyard Kipling's "Christmas in India."

I spent two Christmases there — and it was the way he told it.

Recalling the time, I think of gongs, tiny candles outlining windows, the smell of incense, an occasional sight of red and green, the shouting people and the crowded streets — and, finally, a Calcutta cathedral choir singing "Adeste Fidelis."

Christmas at home for me really began in Kansas after the war when, though we had no trouble finding a tree for our first Christmas (small though it was) there were no metal tree stands to be had. Our Christmas tree that year stood in a quart milk bottle on my wife's cedar chest, braced with books on either side. I suppose I should have saved the bottle but I didn't.

There have been other Christmases, busy, confused, lonely, joyful, hectic, loud and nostalgic. I remember them all for being a part of them all.

94

And I can recall not a single Christmas that I was not the richer or the happier or the more content for.

And I need no scrapbook to bring them back.

Still, I say again, Christmas scrapbooks are important — even though they are made up of the chapters of memory — and the pages of love.

Press was not fair with Nixon

IT ISN'T THE EASIEST thing to be a voice crying in the wilderness.

But that, among most of my colleagues in the business, is what I've been for the last year or so.

I have, I suppose, some old-fashioned ideas about the presidency — and the President of the United States.

Both the office and, to a degree, the man who holds it, are deserving of respect.

If you're a Democrat and the man living at 1600 Pennsylvania Ave., is a Republican, you have, of course, certain liberties. It works the other way around as well.

But I'm not concerned at this moment with good, traditional American political invective.

I'm talking about the good, traditional American legal concept that a man — whatever his station or office — is innocent until proven guilty.

This, I feel, is something that Richard Nixon, as an American citizen, has been denied for months by most columnists and most radio and television commentators in the country.

With the possible exception of Dwight Eisenhower, there hasn't been a president of this country since — and including — Franklin Roosevelt who hasn't at one time or other committed some act for which he could conceivably have been impeached.

They, however, were fortunate in that they had the media generally on their side. The hue and cry, in short, was not initiated. The public was not subjected to a steady diet of suspicion and innuendo lasting for months and even years involving the unconstitutionality of court-packing, closing steel mills, personal improprieties or amassing personal wealth while in public Richard Nixon long ago inherited — justifiably or not — a bad press.

Thursday his longtime critics had their revenge.

Mind, I'm not sitting in judgment of guilt or innocence. I'm merely

95

saying that, from the beginning, the President was not given the same consideration by the majority of the news media that would be accorded a common burglar awaiting trial.

This is not being written as a defense of the man.

But I think someone — even though only a relative unknown on a paper of only regional circulation — should speak up for a man whose political friends in recent days have behaved more like they're leaving a sinking ship than they have like people concerned with justice and fair play.

I wonder, even, what some of the more widely (and you can bet it was widely) quoted comments from certain congressional leaders would be were these men not running for office this year, two, or six years from now.

As I said, it's not easy to be a voice crying in the wilderness.

But somewhere, someone in this business should stand up and be counted — even though it's only to say that Richard Nixon's "high crimes and misdemeanors," if indeed they exist — and this, a highly vocal opposition to the contrary, is yet to be proved — are outweighed by his accomplishments in other areas.

And they said this about Roosevelt.

And about Truman.

And about Kennedy.

And about Johnson.

But again — they had most of us in this business on their side.

Hopping down the platypus trail

I'VE NEVER BEEN ONE of those to go about smashing icons — but there comes a time in every man's life when he has to make a stand.

Like Custer, for instance.

That time arrived for me about 7:21 p.m., Tuesday, Feb. 1, when a friend expressed a degree of anxiety about the next day's weather.

"I mean I just wonder," he said, "whether the groundhog will see his shadow or not."

It was time, I felt, to speak out. For too long we have been held captive, weatherwise, by whether or not Candlemas — and that's what the day was called before the groundhogs took it over — dawns bright and clear.

And I say the time has come to puncture the bubble.

Groundhogging as a profession may work all right back in Punxatawney, Pa., where the Chamber of Commerce has gotten as much mileage out of its local 'hog as Cody, Wyo., has out of Buffalo Bill.

But let him confine his annual comings and goings (or innings and outings) to Pennsylvania where time and tradition have made his place in folklore secure and leave the rest of us alone.

After all, the groundhog is a frisky, buck-toothed little rascal who, when it comes to predicting six months more of winter or spring is no more (or less) dependable than other frisky, buck-toothed little rascals who do it the year around for televison, radio, newspapers — or the federal government.

Having disposed of the groundhog, allow me, pray, to pass along to the Tooth Fairy.

I've wondered at times — though "idly mused" might describe it better — about whether we have dentists because of Tooth Fairies or whether we have Tooth Fairies because of dentists.

As a parent of four I've been a Tooth Fairy helper in slipping my share of dimes under pillows and about the only good thing I can say about it is that it's a lot easier than being one of Santa's helpers. You don't have to wear white whiskers.

But when I was a kid all I got when I lost a tooth was a hole in my jaw.

I suppose this was because my father didn't believe in the Tooth Fairy.

My father didn't believe in Franklin D. Roosevelt, either — but that didn't keep him from giving me my weekly allowance (equivalent to three Tooth Fairy visits) whether or not I emptied ashes from the stove and water from the drip pan under the icebox.

Now, if you were thinking our old friend, Mr. Longears, whose day will be coming up in another few weeks, was going to get away with a whole skin, think again.

Of them all, I love smashing Easter Bunny icons best — because they really don't have to be smashed.

You eat them, starting with the ears and polishing the rest off as your appetite for chocolate and marshmallow dictates.

But, aside from that rather pleasant (and efficient) way of putting another legend out of the way, I've always been a bit foggy on just exactly what is the Easter Bunny's function in connection with Easter eggs anyway.

Is his job strictly one of hiding eggs?

Or does he lay them first and then hide them?

I can understand, however, that his presence (for good or ill) on the Easter scene is to meet demands of practicality.

We all know the only egg-laying mammal in the world is the duck-billed platypus.

But who ever heard of designing Easter cards with cute, cunning

97

and adorable little duck-billed platypuses (or is it platypi?) scampering about distributing varicolored eggs?

Whose palate would not rebel at the thought of munching upon a chocolate-covered, marshmallow-filled duck-billed platypus?

And what respecting composer wouldn't cringe at the thought of a children's song that began "Here comes Duck Bill Platypus, hopping down the bunny trail?"

So much, then, for the Easter Bunny and his eggs which, if he really brings them for kids, how come he hides them.

Does the Tooth Fairy hide his presents?

And what about Santa Claus? There they are on Christmas morning, right under the tree for everyone to see.

Which brings me to my final icon — but don't get excited.

After the great job the New York editor did in his famous "Letter to Virgina" in proving there was a Santa Claus, there's no way I could contest it without getting the groundhog, the Tooth Fairy AND the Easter Bunny on my back.

I simply — and only for the sake of argument — pose the question:

Is there a Virginia?

Turkey, children and a blessing

IT WAS, I REMEMBER, the first and last time I ever rode in a sleigh — but if you knew Aunt Mary Johnson, you'd never think of getting to her house for Thanksgiving dinner any other way.

She wasn't really my Aunt Mary — nor was she related in any way to the hundreds of people in that part of Ohio who called her that.

She was old, of course, and local legend had it that she was rich as contrasted to "well-to-do" or even "wealthy." The three-story white house with its long porch was the largest for counties around and some said Aunt Mary was the only person in that part of the state who could look out from her big house on the hill and see nothing but land that belonged to her.

When she was a girl, they said, Aunt Mary was beautiful — and though it's sometimes difficult for a child to see beauty in white hair, a wrinkled face or hands that begin to show stiffness, you could tell this when this gracious old woman smiled or spoke to you.

Aunt Mary spent Christmases alone — but a Thanksgiving Day never came or passed that the house wasn't filled with "nieces" and "nephews" ranging in age from six to sixty.

There was snow on the ground this one year — and that's how the people came to be picked up in the sleigh and taken up the long, winding lane to the driveway where Aunt Mary waited at the door.

Children were, of course, shooed at once to the big warm kitchen where cups of hot chocolate waited them after the cold trip and afterwards, somehow, Aunt Mary always managed to find two or three sleds in a barn, left over from a time when her sons and daughters laughed and played on the long, gentle slope of the mile-long "front yard."

The kitchen smells and sounds stay with you longest from such Thanksgiving Days. Turkeys crackling as they roasted in the oven of the big black stove. The tinny whirr of an egg-beater, whipping cream. The rattle of a roller-towel and the sound of silverware against china.

The smells of home-made bread, fresh churned butter, sage and fresh-baked pumpkin pie mingled in the busy air of the kitchen as Aunt Mary moved from table to stove to cupboard, prodding, tasting, sniffing — to see that this Thanksgiving dinner was worthy of both the name and the house.

It was all ready by the middle of the afternoon and they called the children in by ringing the dinner bell on its tall post by the back porch.

And of all the things you remember after a Thanksgiving Day with Aunt Mary, you remember the prayer which came after the last child had been settled in his place, the last chair pushed in and the last candle on the long table lighted.

In a time when the quality of a meal was judged by the length of the blessing asked over it, Aunt Mary's grace was almost revolutionary.

"Praise God," she would say, "from whom all blessings flow. Amen."

But no one at the table thought it strange that, as she spoke the words, Aunt Mary looked — not at her plate or at the food on the table — but at the faces and into the eyes of her nieces and nephews who sat around her.

Leading an art
critic to the Trough

MR. PRESIDENT
Norwest Bank
Billings, Montana
Dear Mr. President:

I suppose this is a letter I should have written you a long time ago but I'm one of those guys who lets letters of congratulation and that sort of thing pile up until something pulls the chain and the dam, as it were, breaks.

I'm talking, of course, about all the pros and cons we've been hearing about "Trough" since you guys dedicated it the other day and I thought I might as well get myself on record, too.

But first things first.

You know, I never got around to congratulating you on getting to be a bank president so — herewith, felicitations.

And going back a bit further — though I did do a column item on it once (or maybe twice) — I let your hole-in-one become a part of Billings golf history without so much as a postcard. (Come to think of it, don't you have more than one to your credit?)

So that takes care of that. Now to the business at hand.

I figger anyone who's a bank president and who can drop an occasional ball in the cup right off the tee knows a little about what he's doing and so I fail to see what all the ruckus is about over your taste in sculpture.

I like it. I don't know art — but I know what I like.

And between you and me, I just as soon have "Trough" sitting there where it is than another hot dog stand or a bicycle rack.

Now, lest somebody out there question my credentials, may I point out that I got back not long ago from 10 days in Rome where they got art (including sculpture) coming out their ears and I spent a lot of time looking at it.

I feel, accordingly, that I can speak with as much authority as anyone.

Admittedly, I got a crick in my neck from the Sistine Chapel and I saw some paintings in museums that I wouldn't have hung on Montana's Centennial Train but, like the man said, "Chacun a son gout." (You can look it up, and I never did dig those Old Masters they way some people think they ought to be dug.)

I heard someone compare "Trough" to Michelangelo's "Pieta" which to me is like comparing apples and oranges. Let's face it, The Billings Sheraton is no Taj Mahal either if that's the way we go about criticizing art.

And I'm not losing a bit of sleep — or peace of mind, for that matter — worrying about what "Trough" is supposed to mean or be.

I've got a bronze longhorn steer on my coffee table which is lying down and I haven't wondered since I got it whether the steer is lying down because he's tired or sick or maybe just lazy and I could care less whether he's looking at the sunset or worrying about what happened to the rest of the herd or, for that matter, whether he's out on some Texas prairie or in a pen at the stockyards.

Also, people pick wallpaper because they like the design or color — but try putting a frame around a piece of wallpaper and someone's bound to look at it and ask what it's supposed to be or what does it mean.

I think this is dumb.

So you hang in there with "Trough" and I think a lot of us will be with you. I don't even require the artist's explanation — which I thought was sort of obscure anyway — about what it does or represents in terms of dynamics or conflict or balance. To me it's just a nice looking arrangment of metal and stone in a space that's big enough to hold it without looking crowded and if anyone's bothered by it they can detour a block or, for that matter, not look when they walk by.

Which, come to think of it, is what they say people who disapprove of porno shops or movies can do.

As long as you can assure me that the thing isn't going to fall on me when I walk through it, I'll settle for "Trough" any day.

Just thought you'd like to know.

Sincerely,

Addison

At last
they knew him

THE NIGHT HAD BEEN cold and the man, chilled by the wind which moaned through the garden, drew his coat closer about him.

It's not much longer, he thought, peering across the path at the dim form of his companion.

He called softly.

"It's nearly morning," he said. "Are you awake?"

The figure stirred and a man yawned.

"I suppose I am — but I wish I weren't," came the reply.

There was a rattle of pebbles on the pathway, loud over the wind in the trees as the tall man got up and walked over and stood by his companion.

He watched the eastern sky, silent a long time as the ghostly fingers of dawn clutched feebly at the dark.

"I'm sorry if I slept," he said. "It was a long night."

It was no matter, the other told him. "Threre was no one here," he said. "I could have slept too if I hadn't been so cold."

The two were silent. As the wind, smelling of rain and greeness of new growth, dropped, their breathing became barely audible.

"I'm glad we were here, after all," the taller man said. "It's a lonely thing for a man to die and be forgotten."

The other cleared his throat noisily as he remembered the hours they spent on a hill not far away and how, once they had finished there, they had been called once more, this time to watch a garden.

"I was thinking the same, sir," the first said quietly. "But even us — well, you couldn't call us friends, exactly. Not after what happened."

Stars hanging low in the east began to grow dim and there came the thin cry of a night bird from high overhead.

The tall man finally spoke.

"We did what we were told to do back there on the hill," he said, nodding toward where the shadows were darkest, "the same, you might say, as he did."

His companion nodded and was about to speak when the wind, like a dying breath of night, came up again.

Sighing, it moved through the trees and blew before it the shadows which throughout the night had gathered, dark and deep in the garden.

Now lifting, it brought from the faintly blushing hills in the east the fragile hint of morning, scattering light on branch and path and touching the two men who stood there with dawn's gentle finger.

And two men watched in silence the birth of day, turning only when the hesitant sound of footsteps on the garden path told them they were no longer alone.

The woman stopped as she saw the tall man who had spoken to her on the hill and her heart beat loudly as she heard his voice again.

It was still firm, as it had been that remembered afternoon but now there was a ring of triumph in words which echoed from the empty rock cave behind him.

"If you seek Jesus of Nazareth," he said, "He is not here. He is risen as He said."

And the woman remembered again the afternoon and the voice which had told her then:

"Truly this man was the son of God."

And for a while there was silence in the valley, broken only by the sound of birds and the singing of the wind in the trees — and the muffled clank of a Roman centurion's armor and he and the soldier walked out of the garden and back into the waking city.

Isn't this much nicer than a card?

HELLO:
Well, here another year has rolled by and we haven't gotten a chance to get a letter off to you so we thought we would just not send Christmas cards this year and would follow the example of a lot of our friends who are doing the same thing.

102

You'll have to excuse us if this doesn't sound like a professional "round robin" because after all it is the first one we have ever written and we might make some awful mistakes like maybe mentioning names of someone you all know or forgetting to sign the dog's name or something like that. But we promise to do better next year when all you nice people will get a holiday letter just chock full of informative goodies with perhaps a line or to at the bottom to make it REALLY personal, you know. (If, of course, there's room at the bottom after Daddy's gotten through running all the copies off on the office mimeograph machine.)

Since we've already mentioned Daddy, we'll start by telling you that he's one year older (Ha ha) than he was this time last year and is keeping busy on the job which, especially since the reorganization which took his department and another phase of the operation and combined the two, has put him in line for ANOTHER promotion. He still finds time though, to play golf and is said to be one of the favorite contenders in the interdepartmental tourney which, as you know, is coming up next April. He has subscribed to the air mail edition of the Manchester Guardian and picks up an occasional copy of "Famous Monsters" from our local newsstand so you can see he has had quite an active year.

Mommy is fine and, what with taking care of the new house (we built after the fire, you know) and keeping track of four active children in addition to her committee work, she wonders whether there's truth in the saying about no rest for the wicked. (Ha!)

She and Jill, the president of her club, are co-chairmen of a pilot committee on invitations, place cards and door prizes and just LOVE working with Hermoine S. (John's wife — he's Daddy's boss.) That's enough of Mommy's year except to add that there's every chance in the world that she will win the election.

(More about this NEXT year.)

Porthos, Athos, Aramis and D'Artagnan have grown so much you'd never know them in all the world. Porthos, our sophomore, made the B squad and is beginning to be interested in girls. Athos is now the proud holder of three merit badges and a junior fire marshal certificate. Aramis spends his time with his bicycle and is beginning to hate girls and D'Artagnan — our youngest — is due back from China just any day now. (If you didn't read about it in the papers let us know and we'll tell you all about it NEXT year.)

Well, that just about takes care of all of us except, of course, Scheherazade, our bird and she'd be heartbroken if she knew she had been left out. We went thought two moults since last December and you've never seen anyone do away with cuttlebone as quickly. Already she's beginning to talk and it just seems like yesterday that we brought her home. Time certainly does fly, doesn't it?

Well this should bring you up to date on the Gleebs and remember the latchstring is always out for any of our good friends who happen to find themselves nearby so please drop in and don't worry about room.

We have loads.
All our love,
Daddy, Mommy, Porthos, Athos, Aramis and Scheherazade Glee.
P.S. Merry Christmas

Summer slips away
more rapidly each year

THERE'S A LOT to be said for the end of summer, that time of year when sunburns begin to pale, early-morning shadows are longer than they once were — and school looms ominously on a youngster's horizon.

For some, it's the most special time of all the year.

It's a time for wondering how many more weekends the lawn furniture will stay out, how you'll get the garden hose back in the corner of the garage where it spent last winter, and where you'll go this year to spend the Labor Day holiday.

But mostly it's a time for asking:

Where did it go so quickly?

Has it really been three months since you watched a high school senior walk across a stage and found youself saying a quiet goodbye to an important part of life?

And that week on the lake — and the other in the mountains — were they all that long ago?

There's a funny thing about summers.

Each one, no matter what your point of view or time of life, passes more quickly than the one before.

Children measure summer by lazy mornings and quiet afternoons.

And before they know it — and before you know it, really — they're a head taller.

The more summers you put behind, the more differently you look at them.

Grownups count the days of summer by the time it takes grass to grow or flowers to bloom and die — and they measure its passage by the nearing of the back-to-school chaos.

But for everyone, however they count its days, summer has always been and will always be a time of memories.

And they begin to pile up when a calendar page is turned and you realize that it isn't that long a time from May to September after all.

Memorial Day was long ago — and only yesterday.

And for some it's possible to look up at a night sky and see the still-glowing trail of sparks from a long-dead fireworks display that marked a Fourth of July now gone forever.

Barely visible touches of brown begin to appear in green lawns.

Flashes of yellow appear in the green of trees.

And there's a chill in the morning air that wasn't there before.

The morning sun has already started its crawl northward on the horizon.

Days grow short.

And memory grows long.

Summer is dying.

Those who mourn the death of a season equal in number those who rejoice in its passing.

But whether you measure the length of a summer in months, weeks, or days, and whether you look upon it as memorable or forgettable, one thing is true of that time of year that begins with vacant windows in a school building and ends with the coiling of a garden hose in a garage.

Summer is always the year at its peak — and the echo of laughter that rings through the months to follow until it comes again.

Forgotten people work on Christmas

J UST AS THERE ARE night people — those whose day starts when the day of the waking world ends — so are there Christmas people.

They're the people whose calendar, year in and year out, makes December 25 a work day.

This is for them.

This is for the men and the women who work the most joyous holiday of the year — that others may enjoy it.

They are many — and they are everywhere.

And too often they're forgotten.

This is for them.

It's for the policeman and the fireman who spend Christmas eve wondering why, when some people are lucky enough to be able to spend the night with their families, they don't do it.

It's for the bartender and the cocktail waitress, the hasher and the cook — and the kid whose best Christmas present is being able to keep the dishwasher job he got a year ago this Christmas eve.

And it's for the janitors, the charwomen and the night watchmen — and everyone whose Christmas in an empty, silent building is particularly quiet, particularly lonely.

It's for ambulance drivers and doctors and nurses and orderlies in hospitals who'll spend Christmas watching life begin — and watching it end.

And it's for the people they care for — and who seemingly no one else does.

It's for the truck driver making his second coffee stop along a mountain highway in the night.

It's for a telephone operator and a night club musician.

It's for everyone in uniform, whatever the service, who drew Christmas as a duty day. And it's for a refinery worker, a sheepherder (whose calling, incidentally, takes on strange significance at this time) and the man at the corner service station.

It's for those people who travel and whose jobs — whatever they may be — find them spending Christmas, all or part of it, in waiting rooms or air terminals. It's for a train crew and a bus driver.

And it's for a man in a glassed-in-tower who talks to an airliner passing in the night, high in the cold sky over a sleeping city — and for the crew whose only Christmas decorations are the red and green lights of the instrument panel in the cockpit.

This shows a little, we hope, that you're remembered.

You and thousands like you.

And so we wish you, in God's mercy, a happy Christmas!

Dandelions are getting a bum rap

IT'S HIGH TIME, to my way of thinking, that a good word was said for the dandelion.

And I, stepping boldly up on my soap box (and out on my limb) propose to say it.

For too long the dandelion has been treated like a double hernia at a weight lifters convention.

It has been sworn at, tramped on and uprooted.

Its name has become a hissing and a byword throughout suburban America.

Volumes have been written on how to get rid of it — and how to keep it from coming back once it's been gotten rid of.

All of which is why I think it's time a voice was heard on behalf of the underdog (or dunderlion).

Let's forget about dandelion greens — which, if you've ever eaten a properly prepared mess of them, in itself is pretty hard to do.

Let's forget about the root which, when dried, roasted and ground up, is a pretty fair coffee substitute.

And let's forget that elixir vitae, dandelion wine.

Let's just talk about the things you can do with dandelions that you can't do with any other flower — and shame on you if your childhood years are so far away you've forgotten.

Dandelions are great, for example, in telling whether you like girls (if you're a boy) or boys (if you're a girl).

You take the bloom, rub it on a cheek and if yellow comes off — there's your answer.

And it does no good to deny it. You can't fool the dandelion.

Dandelion stems could be the subject of a whole chapter, almost.

You can chew on them. You can split them with your tongue into two, four, six or as many sections as you want — and keep pushing them back and watching them curl. (The more spit you use, the more they curl).

And if you blow on a dandelion stem just right you can get sounds ranging from a bass clarinet to a soprano sax.

They also make great chains.

A daisy chain, I grant, is colorful and dainty — but it can't hold a candle to a no-nonsense collection of dandelion links which, by gosh, even LOOKS like a chain.

I remember feeling sad when the dandelions in our front yard first went to seed.

I thought it meant summer was over.

But even dandelions that trade the closest thing the flower-world has to a Smiley button for the fluffy ball that vanishes in the first wind can be of use.

We used them mainly for telling whether or not we were wanted at home.

Blow. Blow hard. If you clean off all the seeds in one breath, your mother doesn't want you. You can stay out.

It didn't, however, always work.

Many a kid of my generation was peremptorily summoned to the house despite the dandelion's assurance that he wasn't needed.

And when he got there, there was always the unperceptive grownup — and the warning.

"For heavens sake, if we weren't having ENOUGH trouble with dandelions already — you have to sit out there in the yard and scatter more seeds around."

Scars were hidden
by his love for man

THE OLD MAN SAT every day in the sunlight and in the shade of the big maple that grew in the yard of his home.

For everyone who passed the little white cabin — for it was nothing more than that — he had a smile and a wave of a thin bony hand. Sometimes, for the school children who walked a few steps up the neat board sidewalk that led to his door and past his comfortable place in the sun there was a spoken greeting.

You had to listen well to hear it, for Albert Green was very old and his voice had grown as thin, almost, as the long white beard that covered his face.

There was no one in the little Ohio town who didn't know Albert Green, who came, they said, not long after the Civil War ended.

He was a preacher. The few times in his life his name got in a weekly newspaper they called him "Reverend" — but to everyone in North Lewisburg he was "Mister Green."

And the Rev. Mr. Green would stand up before his tiny congregation every Sunday in the days before his voice became like the sound of wind blowing over dry leaves and he would talk about the brotherhood of man.

People would listen and would nod and leave, wondering how Albert Green — of all people — could talk like that.

Later, when Albert Green's hands became too frail to hold the battered leather-bound Bible, he spent Sundays with it on his lap, leafing through the pages and reading, from time to time, through the gold-rimmed glasses he always wore.

There were those who swore Albert Green was past 100 and he thought they might be right. He didn't know.

He couldn't say when or where he was born. He didn't know who his parents were. He talked, sometimes, of the war, but never of the days before it.

When death came to Albert Green it came gently and peacefully and the few who passed that warm May morning saw him in his familiar chair with the sunlight and shadows splashing across the grass and thought he was asleep.

It was one of the town's biggest funerals — but only afterwards did people learn the whispers they'd heard all along about Albert Green were true.

The marks left by the whippings were there and that was why, even when standing before his people, his back was bent and his shoulders stooped.

This was the Albert Green whose beard looked all the whiter

against the blackness of the skin on which it grew.

This was the man who spent half his life as a slave and the other half talking of the brotherhood of man.

It used to be
called a meeting

UNLESS OTHERWISE DIRECTED by my city editor, I try assiduously to stay away from any gathering of more than two people.

Not, mind you, that I oppose in any way the constitutional guarantee of the right of the people to peaceably assemble.

It's just that in this day and age one never knows exactly what kind of a meeting he's attending.

Time was you could go to a convention, say, to sit and listen (or sleep) to a parade of speakers. It was as simple as that.

I suppose it was back when the educators started taking over that we lost our simple audience-speaker relationship.

Now we have a choice, ranging from the formal-sounding "conference" (attended by, of course, "conferees") to the formidable "symposium" (attended, in some instances, by Shriners).

Taking part in a conference doesn't worry me. As a matter of fact, I feel rather distinguished at being referred to as a "conferee."

The word "symposium," however, bothers me a little. It sounds more like a public bath than like a meeting. But I still know plenty of people who'd break their necks to get to the more dignified symposium who wouldn't be caught dead at a mere conference.

The "forum" (also called "open forum" or "forum-type discussion") is also high on my non-attendance list.

As far as I've been able to find out it's a Latinized version of the conference or the symposium — with the added disadvantage of having a rather shoddy historical background. Julius Caesar, I believe it was, was on his way to one of those meetings to make the Roman people an offer they couldn't refuse when he met with foul play at the hands of certain local gentry.

I worry, too, about getting involved in the "seminar." From what I've heard, it's not much different from the forum, the symposium or the conference — except that it's smaller, the participants sit around a table and generally have ashtrays and pitchers of water at their disposal.

I realize my concept of the seminar holds shadings of the "discussion group" or the "panel discussion" — therefore I should point out one major factor influencing my attitude.

At this stage of the game, I lack both the interest AND the theology required of a seminarian.

Of all these, however, my pet aversion is the "buzz session."

This — which I consider the nadir of peaceable assemblages — is a modern day outgrowth of the teachers' meeting, the social workers' conference and an array of organizations striving to flee the pomposity of the symposium, the seminar and the forum.

But whenever I hear the word it only conjures up an image of a bunch of honeybees sitting around talking about a cure for hives.

I have been recently advised (by those who claim to be in the know), that yesterday's "buzz" has become today's "rap" session.

But I see little cause for rejoicing.

What, I can't help wondering, ever happened to the old-fashioned "question-and-answer period?"

And the tomb was found empty

TODAY MARKS ONCE MORE a time when Christians throughout the world stand before an empty garden tomb to think again on those events which led them there.

And in the quiet of the morning, if we listen well, we can hear the faint and far off sounds of that first Easter — wind that sighs through tree branches, the rustle of leaves overhead, sandals scraping on a graveled path and the distant murmur of a waking city.

And if we look long enough, if we stand truly before that vacant sepulcher in the rosy dawn that begins to inch its way over the hills and across the sky, we can see, eyes straining in the darkness of the garden shadows, dim shapes and forms of those who were for good or ill players in this greatest of all dramas.

The dead man is Judas, among the first to follow him. Like the others he was trusted. Unlike the others he traded at worst danger, at least unpopularity, for security.

The sleeping men were with him at Gethsemane. All he wanted was that they watch with him for one brief hour. They were willing, but they were also tired.

The men you see running are looking for a place to hide. They stayed with him up to a point but it's all too dangerous now. They don't want to get involved.

The red-rimmed eyes belong to Peter. He cries because he's sorry not to have had the courage to admit their friendship. But what would we have had him do? Say he knew the man and perhaps suffer because of it? It was easier the other way.

The tall, imperious figure with the turban and breastplate is Caiphas, rich, powerful and first among the priests of the temple. Supposing the man were who he said he was? What then would wealth, power and status amount to? The solution, of course, was simple. One deals with a threat — especially a threat on one's power — by crushing it. Verdict — guilty as charged.

His hands are dry — but the man in the purple-trimmed toga keeps rubbing them together as though he were washing them. His name is Pilate and as procurator of Judea his job — as he sees it — is to content the people. Peace at any price, he might have put it — even though the price was that of a cross on a hill called Golgotha. Accordingly, he washed his hands of the whole affair.

Simon, the Cyrenian, rubs his shoulder. It was a heavy piece of wood, he remembers, but he carried it, as history will record. That same history also records that Simon wasn't a volunteer. He was ordered to by the soldiers.

The men in uniform are soldiers, as indifferent to what has happened in the garden this morning as they were two days ago when they knelt at the feet of the man they'd been ordered to kill and cast lots for his clothing. They followed orders, they'll tell you. The rest of it was none of their business.

Joseph of Arimathea is there, too (after all, it was his garden) and the look on his face is one of doubt. Was it right to bury him here? What will people say? Then again, what if it was a new beginning — and he was too late in recognizing it? Joseph's head continues to shake slowly, back and forth.

Of them all, only one figure stands out from the shadows.

As he kneels before the tomb in the growing light, the first rays of the sun gleam on his armour and the garden rings with the words the Roman centurion spoke for the first time that afternoon that seems now an eternity ago:

"Truly this man was the Son of God."

Today if we stand in that garden long enough, listen well enough and see clearly enough we can for a fleeting moment see ourselves — in some or all those figures — from Judas to the centurion.

It's the empty tomb that makes the difference.

Singing the praises
of graveyard stew

I WOULD SING, if you will, the praises of graveyard stew.

Of course, like a lot of things that were once great and could be great again if people only knew about them, graveyard stew isn't around any more.

At least, you can't find it on any restaurant menu I know of.

But it was there once and I don't know how often I've wished it was there again.

That's right, graveyard stew.

Now for those of you who weren't in the congregation when the service began, graveyard stew is nothing more than milk toast. But you won't find that on a menu either.

It was the simplest of dishes to prepare. Two slices of buttered toast, dark, covered with hot milk in which an additional pat of butter floated, a dash of salt and, voila!

It was on the counter within minutes after one ordered it.

And in most places an order of graveyard stew brought you change back from a quarter.

An editor of mine, Dave O'Connor, and I once formed — in the old Turf Cafe where probably the best graveyard stew in town was made — the Association for the Preservation and Advancement of Graveyard Stew in America (APAGSA) when we discovered a mutual admiration for what we considered the ultimate, though generally unrecognized, flowering of culinary genius.

Dave considered it a specific for most ills known to man.

Especially hangovers.

I was a graveyard-stew-on-a-bitter-cold-night advocate.

But there was something about graveyard stew that made it different from anything else.

One could duplicate a restaurant hamburger, egg sandwich, chicken-fried steak or even a bowl of chili at home.

It was and still is impossible — because I've tried it and I know — to bring back the look, the smell, the taste and the solid warmth and comfort of a steaming bowl of graveyard stew served at a crowded lunch counter late on a cold, snowy night.

All the ingredients are there — but there's a difference.

No matter how it's fixed at home there's always someone around who'll call it milk toast.

And there are no real men who eat milk toast any more than there are real men who eat quiche.

The gleam has faded
from the old pool hall

THEY CAN SAY what they want to about the way things have changed but when I start to compare how things are as to how they were, if it's all the same to you, I'll head for the nearest pool hall or bowling alley.

Excuse me. They don't call them that anymore.

Now you bowl at a place they call a lanes — and you play pool in a lounge.

I have trouble sometimes telling them apart. They both have soft lights, carpet on the floor, upholstered seats — and such conveniences as paging systems and snack bars.

You seldom hear the click of balls on felt (which isn't green anymore) and the muted thump of a ball on hardwood is almost as quiet as the muffled clatter of pins falling.

Time was, by heaven, when you knew you were in a pool hall or a bowling alley.

They both smelled of stale smoke, floor sweep and beer.

And they both spurned such amenities as food (unless you count peanuts or candy bars) or cushioned seats.

The philosophy back then was that you came to a pool hall to play pool and to a bowling alley to bowl and if you wanted frills then you went back to the soda fountain where you belonged.

And for a comfortable place to sit there was always a hotel lobby.

Back in Iola — that's in Kansas — we had two pool halls.

Both were dens of iniquity for teen-agers as far as most parents were concerned. Because of this, of course, we teen-agers visited them every chance we got.

The bowling alley didn't come to Iola until the mid-1930s and because bowling was a game played by men who smoked cigars and used strong language — just like pool — it took its place as well on the proscribed list.

I remember John — I think his last name was Reuther but I can't be sure — who put in the first three lanes in town. He smoked cigars and used strong language.

He also bowled like a million dollars.

Even today senior statesmen among Iola keglers remember John's unconventional windup and his underhand delivery that reminded one of a shot-putter standing on his head.

People in Iola had gotten used to having a couple of pool hall owners in the community.

It took them a while to get used to John.

The man who owned the Palace Theater right next to John's place never did get used to him.

During westerns, musicals or war films it wasn't bad.

But there were times — and I remember them well — when it was all you could do to concentrate on Greta Garbo or Robert Taylor with the rumble of balls and clatter of falling pins right next door.

Today the hush in a bowling alley or pool hall compares favorably with some churches I've been in.

Nor, for that matter, does the clientele suffer in the comparison.

As with everyplace else in the country, Iola today accepts not only bowling but women bowlers.

And, speaking for myself, I've never had problems with any of my three daughters complaining that their pool game of the night before was a little off.

But I wish — for the sake of nostalgia if for no other reason — our lounges of today, whether bowling or billiard, would bend a bit and install a reminder of a time when playing pool or bowling was considerably a more vicarious activity than it is now.

Besides, who knows?

A well-placed spittoon just conceivably might be used by a customer who remembers how it once was.

Making a list
and checking it twice

ASK ANYONE WHO knows me.

I'd be the last guy in the world to try to beat the post office out of anything.

Not counting, I should add, re-using stamps the cancellation mark missed.

But the time has come, I think, for all of us — and particularly the big guys — to take a second look at our Christmas-card lists.

For a long time now, it seems to me, the Christmas season has become a handy vehicle to let loose another salvo in the barrage of advertising that keeps us ducking throughout the year.

I'll never forget the first time I went to the mailbox and found a card there from — of ALL people — Continental Oil Company.

It was impressive. At the time I couldn't have afforded a dozen cards of comparable quality.

And it was, to be quite frank, flattering.

I had the feeling that there were all of these executive types down in

Houston who took time out from operating Big Oil all over the world to wish me a Merry Christmas.

In the years which followed I learned that not only Continental thought of me at Christmas time.

So did Northwest Airlines, the Northern Pacific Railway, the Associated Press — and the Defense Intelligence Agency.

Once I was lucky enough to be remembered by the president of the Republic of Andorra, two television producers, a film distributor — and a motel in Arlington, Va.

Needless to say, none of them are or were ever on my Christmas card list.

But there's something about corporated Christmas greetings.

The custom has a tendency to trickle down.

I soon found myself getting cards from real estate salesmen, service stations, an upholstery shop (and I never have anything upholstered), hospitals, service clubs, political parties and the Billings Builders Exchange.

Still remembered is the year and day we went through the mail at home and found a dozen or more cards — and not a personal one in the lot.

A daughter bewailed the fact.

"None of these are from people, Dad," she said. "They're all from things."

And often the enterprising business men and firms didn't stop with cards.

My Christmas loot has over the years included plastic paper clips, golf tees, desk calendars, letter openers, miniature cars, fruit cake, pocket date books, instant coffee (or tea), note pads and car deodorant things shaped like Christmas trees.

There was a time when I got a Christmas card every year from a dry cleaner.

And I hardly ever got anything cleaned.

Today my cleaning bill reads like the national debt.

But not only does he never send a card, he doesn't even call up to wish me Merry Christmas.

I get even, though.

I pick up one of his ball-point pens every time I pick up my cleaning.

But while the Yuletide bric-a-brac still shows up on my desk or in my mailbox there seems to be some light at the end of the tunnel.

Continental's board of directors hasn't thought about me in years.

And the Christmas cards I've gotten so far are evidence that I'm being thought of more by people than by things.

Maybe, to quote an old Gazette editor and friend, we did loose something for a while.

But we seem to be getting it back again.

We supply the booze;
you bring the insults

NEXT TIME YOU find yourself on a things-ain't-what-they-used-to-be kick, you might as well include Christmas.

At least that part of the holiday that was celebrated with "open house" in downtown Billings.

Not, I hasten to add, to confuse open houses with office parties.

Two completely different things.

The office party, though falling in popularity polls over the last decade or so, is still pretty much with us.

The open house was a drop-in type of thing that lasted anywhere from two hours to two days.

It was a boon to reporters who found lunch money in short supply as Christmas drew near. Office parties (generally) featured booze and no bread.

Open houses provided the bread — and plenty of cold cuts to go with it — as well as a nutritious eggnog or warming Tom and Jerry if your thirst ran in that direction.

The qualifications for hosting an open house were about the same as for the office party. Once you had an office, whether it was a 10-room suite in the Midland Bank building or a desk with a phone on the mezzanine floor of the old Grand Hotel, you had fulfilled the requirements.

Office parties were, by definition, restricted to those who worked there.

Open houses welcomed anyone who was hungry or thirsty.

One of my favorite open houses as the season heated up was at Smith's Funeral Home. The ham was great, the turkey plentiful — and I never saw anyone who came there looking for a drink leave looking disappointed.

The Northern Pacific Railway used to do an open house in the grand tradition. There were sandwiches, appetizers, candy, coffee, fruit, a punch bowl for the dilettantes — and a bar for those interested in getting on with the business of the day.

And the thing we all remember about NP's open house was that it was the only one that had real tablecloths and real napkins.

Lawyers, oil men, accountants, insurance agents and real-estate firms held open houses of a sort. It was usually a bottle or two, an assortment of mix, and ice.

If food was your bag, you brought along your own.

Donna Birken's open house at her answering service (when it was on North 27th Street) was another to be remembered. The closeness of the space in which she operated made the lavish decorations all the more impressive.

And with six switchboards going all at once, the event never lacked for conversation.

There was a day when you could hit three open houses in a row and pretty well take care of lunch and dinner. And sometimes all three could be found in the courthouse. Or City Hall. Or the Federal (then the Post Office) Building.

A favorite open house of mine was back in the days when the Air Force had its dispersal base at the east end of the airport. They were always meticulous about including wives and children — AND a visit from Santa Claus, who arrived one year in a jet fighter-interceptor.

Open houses, like office parties, are still around. But they lack character when you compare them with some of the Lucullan affairs of the boom years of the 1950s.

But there's one thing that can be said of them.

At an office party you only have a chance to tell off your own boss.

At an open house you have a choice of several — and not one of them can fire you.

Memories of Christmas past

S O FAR AS I can remember, my father kept himself apace with the rapidly changing world around him. He accepted commercial aviation, talking pictures and even went so far as to vote for Franklin Delano Roosevelt — whom he called "Mister Roosefelt" — the first time he ran.

But when it came to Christmas my father was a traditionalist of the first order — and sometimes he went beyond that.

On his calendar Christmas started the night of December 24 — but only after the children had gone to bed — and not one minute before.

Though he never came right out and said so, I always had the impression that my father — had he his way about things — would have kept even the Christmas cards that came to our house to be opened only on Christmas morning.

My mother, however, overruled him before he got that tradition started.

"There might be," she said, "checks — or money."

My sister and I had a raft of great aunts and uncles who lived out of the state — including one in Pittsburg, Pa., who never remembered either of our names. She mailed us each a check at Christmas every year until she died — and every year my mother took them to the bank with an explanation of how Aunt Clara was about names and how the checks would go through with no trouble and the banker always believed her.

There was, accordingly, an atmosphere — subdued, of course — of Christmas about our house if one looked for the table with the pile of cards on it.

There were no packages under the tree those days before Christmas for inquisitive children to shake or prod in anticipation.

All packages which came to our house were hidden by my father with all the care and stealth of a bank robber disposing of the loot until such a time as it would be safe to return to it. They were high on closet shelves, stowed behind (or in) empty trunks in the basement or taken to the garage.

In some cases, I recall, neighbors were enlisted in the Great Christmas Hiding Caper.

As a matter of fact, we never had a tree in our living room until Christmas eve — AFTER the children had gone to bed.

Christmas, my father used to say, starts on December 25, not before.

And sometimes, even today when I see trees in windows and lights on houses the day or so after Thanksgiving, I can't help but agree — at least in part — with my father.

That's why I can't remember a long ago holiday season at home that wasn't like any other time of the year — until the early dawn of Christmas Day.

Somehow, it did seem as though the elves or fairies or Christmas spirits or whatever you wanted to call them had been at work during the night.

The room which we had left looking quite ordinary and unfestive only a few hours before had literally exploded with light, tinsel, ornaments, greenery, packages and holiday glitter. It was Christmas all at once — and it looked and felt wonderful.

It was, in fact, worth all the waiting — and worth all the explaining we usually had to do with friends who came by in the days before and wondered where our tree was and what happened to the presents. (We had neighbors, actually, who not only put up trees early but who opened presents as they arrived at the house, a custom which, reared as my sister and I were, amounted to almost sacrilege.)

My father's sense of order — and discipline — took no holiday on Christmas morning. Breakfast first in the dining room — and in full sight of the tantalizing tree and all that lay under it — and only afterward, opening of gifts.

We were, I remember, permitted to choose one small present from the tree to open before breakfast — and that was in addition to the crisp, new one dollar bill we always found on our plates as we sat down at the table.

I guess you could call those early Christmases at our house examples of order at its best — even disciplined.

And they didn't stop with breakfast or the tree.

My father, from as far back as I can remember, moved his seat of power from the front of the house to the kitchen once the presents were out of the way and began his ritual cooking of the Christmas goose.

Let others have turkey, he declared, if they must.

Turkeys are for Thanksgiving. Geese are for Christmas.

A great many years have passed since that last Christmas morning we were all together, my father, my mother, my sister and I.

But I can still feel the suspense of waiting through the night and the brightness and warmth of those long ago Christmas mornings.

I can still close my eyes and smell a goose (with oyster dressing) baking in an oven.

And I still, on each Christmas day, think of how lucky we were to live in a home where, of all the good days of the year, Christmas was a day — in my father's words — to be kept and cherished for all time to come.

'Tis the season
for procrastination

THE ROAD TO HELL, someone once said, is paved with good intentions.

Thus has it been with me and getting ready for Christmas — for as long as I can remember.

I don't know how many years have gone by since first I said:

This year I'm going to get the shopping done early;

This year I'm going to get Christmas cards — and mail them out on time;

And this holiday season I'm going to get organized to the point that there'll be no loose ends, no scraping for time and no last minute gift-buying, party-going — or not so much as one moment of regret that I'd left something undone.

I said I didn't know how many years.

Would you believe ten? Or twenty?

I take comfort, however, in the fact that I'm not all that different from most males, most husbands and most fathers.

Women — and let's face it, gang — spoil us, especially at Christmas.

They remember the mailing deadlines for packages as well as cards.

They remember who should be on the list.

They remember to get out and do the shopping.

And, most important, they know how to wrap Christmas packages.

Having spent a large part of my life watching my womenfolks get ready for Christmas I'm convinced that the description "all thumbs" is particularly apt in my case when it comes to further beautifying a gift that will end up under the tree of a niece, a nephew, a grandchild or sundry other family and relatives.

They measure, they cut, they fold, they beribbon and, as though all this were not enough, they label extravagantly.

In years past the thought has crossed my mind that the gift itself is superfluous. The packaging alone is enough, expecially when one stops to think that in the frenzy and excitement of Christmas morning it's going to be ripped to shreds anyway.

My idea — and I'm presumptious enough to think this applies to all us males — of Christmas wrapping is to leave it in the sack (or box) it came in from the store, stick a "Do Not Open Until Christmas" label on and let it go at that.

All this, of course, may explain why I patronize only those stores which feature gift wrapping counters.

Wrapping presents isn't my only Yuletide hangup.

But don't get me wrong.

I think sending Christmas cards is a delightful custom — whether the U.S. Postal Service needs the money or not.

And I love shopping for Christmas cards.

My problem, however, lies in getting them out on time.

I hate the idea of anyone — me included — getting Christmas cards in November.

And I've already gotten two.

So I wait.

And wait.

And — wouldn't you know? — Christmas is right around the corner, so to speak, and all those carefully selected cards are still there in the box.

And it's too late to get them to anyone in time.

This, I'm sure, accounts for the fact that around my apartment this very day are Christmas cards from as far back as ten years ago that I've bought and never mailed.

Maybe, I keep telling myself, next year I'll get with the program.

I've been telling myself that for so long I have a feeling the last program pulled out of the station years ago.

But there's one thing I'm good at.

And on time for.

I'm one of those old fashioned souls who still believes that the feast of Christmas lasts 12 days.

That's why, I suppose, I have no compunction when it comes to saying "Merry Christmas" up until the sixth of January.

To begin with, it keeps my friends from thinking I've completely forgotten the holiday amenities.

And finally — it's a reminder once again that Christmas isn't cards, gifts — or even one day on the calendar.

It's a spirit that should stay with us all through the year.

Belle caters
to kindred spirits

HOLIDAYS SPELL REUNIONS — and vice versa.
Which is why, I suppose, schools and colleges in the country a long time ago figured the Christmas-New Year space on the calendar was as good a place as any to shut down operations for a while and let the kids go home.

And home-for-Christmas reunions are about the best kind there are.

For one thing, they're spontaneous.

No one, really, plans them. They just happen.

You're at the airport in Chicago, headed for Billings and a week with the folks.

And you meet this kid in the bar you went to high school with, forgot about him the day you graduated and there you are, the both you, headed home — and there's not enough time on the flight to catch up on all that's happened in the last 20 years.

Or you wait for a traffic light on North 27th Street — and there's the guy you last saw when you were in the Army. You got out. He stayed in.

And now he's back home, retired, and all there was time for was the wave, the yell and the wide grin before the light changed.

It was still a reunion that wouldn't have happened had it not been for the holiday.

You don't need a hall or a dining room — or even one corner of a bar — for a reunion.

But sometimes it helps — especially the last.

And I guess the Reunion Capital of Eastern Montana has got to be the Northern Hotel's Golden Belle saloon.

What was once said about Times Square — that if you stand there long enough everyone you know will, sooner or later, walk by — can be said about the Northern.

There are those exiles from our town who make it back every year.

Others take longer — but they're never disappointed.

Spend an hour or so there during the holidays and you'll see people you haven't seen in years.

And I'm sure I'm not alone in getting sentimental about Christmas or New Years, just as I'm sure I'm not the only person who figures letting this time of the year go by without an afternoon in the Belle is something one just does not allow to happen.,

There are too many friends, too many memories.

The Belle isn't only a meeting place for celebrants.

It's a rest stop for shoppers, a conference room for the where-do-we-go-from-here revelers and check point for the bewildered.

And reunions, those who know will tell you, can leave some participants pretty bewildered.

I guess one of the most enduring holiday memories of the Golden Belle stems from those halcyon days of the oil boom when the We Wish You A Merry Christmas Gang took time off from the business of finding oil in the early 1950s to serenade the luncheon trade.

Sometimes there were only four.

At other times they rivaled the Mormon Tabernacle Choir in numbers.

Charlie Austin, years ago named director emeritus of the group, was in charge of the program.

It was the easiest job in town.

The WWYAMC gang had only one song — and you can guess its title.

But what they lacked in variety they more than made up for in volume.

Austin's caroleers sang requests, of course — as long as the request was for "We Wish You A Merry Christmas."

And not once was it recorded that any member forgot the words.

There were times when someone was unable to sing the words.

But they never forgot them.

Another holiday regular was the salesman who would spend the entire afternoon at the bar, then would disappear until the following year.

He finally explained one day.

"This is my office party," he told a friend.

The Belle has seen many Christmases come and go. It will see many more.

"The holidays," said a grandmother who was a college freshman when she had her first reunion at the Belle, "just wouldn't be the same without coming to this place."

We have to agree.

It's full of memory, laughter, contentment and warmth — and they're all wrapped around the holiday season.

For, of all the dear ghosts we summon from time to time, the best are those whom we call upon when friends meet friends after many years.

That's why the Golden Belle is haunted — and I hope it stays that way for all of us.

Family

CHAPTER 5

Happy Mother's Day
dear mother-in-law

CERTAIN SOMEBODY WHO lives in Butte is going to be surprised as all get-out when she finds out she was the subject of a Mother's Day story.

But before you start arguing and protesting, Martha, hear me out.

Maybe you're right. Maybe you haven't any place in a Mother's Day story written by your son-in-law.

On the other hand, I'm pretty convinced mothers-in-law are sort of forgotten people on the second Sunday in May.

And I don't think they should be.

After all, mothers-in-law are mothers too.

It figures.

So — no more argument. If you wanted to stop me, it's too late. The paper's already out.

Just you sit back and finish your coffee, Martha — while I tell the people on this bright Mother's Day about my mother-in-law.

To begin, she's the kind of person who takes things in stride and keeps calm in emergencies.

Proof of this, I think, is evident once you learn she never met me until two days before her daughter's wedding — after I got out of the service — and she still welcomed me to the family with open arms.

And if that isn't keeping calm in an emergency I don't know what is.

Another thing about my mother-in-law: For the first four years we were married, she never came to visit us once. I'll concede the fact we lived a thousand miles apart had something to do with it — but even so, this is undeniably a point in her favor.

Martha and I disagree on some things.

Politics, mainly.

This, however, is a thing that always happens to anyone who isn't from Butte who knows anyone who is from Butte.

You're bound to disagree on politics.

Our arguments are always friendly, though.

Well — pretty friendly. Like I said, she's from Butte.

Lots of things we agree on.

Like the Yankees.

We both hate the Yankees, me and Martha.

(This is on account of at home we're both surrounded by Yankee fans.)

125

I submit there can't be too much wrong with a mother-in-law who hates the Yankees. Unless, of course, you're a Yankee fan — in which case you don't deserve a mother-in-law like Martha.

Looking back over the years I've known her, I think one thing that'll always stand out was the time Martha made a cucumber sandwich.

I'd never heard of a cucumber sandwich, let alone eaten one. It's quite an experience.

Martha's slowed down on cucumber sandwiches lately. But not altogether. Every once in a while, she told me, when no one's watching, she'll sneak a slice or two between a piece of bread. That's my mother-in-law.

She's also a warmed-over coffee drinker.

Ever since I first met Martha, I've watched her guard the dinner-time pot to keep anyone from throwing it out. It stays on the stove all night — or at least until very early the next morning — when Martha heats it up for that first cup of the day.

Just wouldn't feel right, she said once, to drink fresh coffee right after waking up.

As a mother-in-law, Martha's as sparing of advice as a lawyer on his day off.

She's just as economical when it comes to visiting.

I have to coax her to come over — and once she's here, I have to beg her to stay.

Now whether all this has convinced anyone that mothers-in-law deserve a piece of Mother's Day, I don't know.

I hope I've convinced you, Martha.

But, if not, I'll tell you what.

You come on over.

I'll lay in a supply of cucumbers.

We'll boo the Yankees.

And I'll try once more to straighten you out politically.

Happy Mother's Day.

Behave, or it's off to the orphans home

I DON'T KNOW WHETHER they have such things as orphans homes anymore and if they do I suppose they're called something other than that.

And I doubt seriously if, by whatever name they are known today, they strike terror into a youngster the way they did when I was a kid.

126

Today, we're told, kids worry about The Bomb.

We worried about getting sent away to an orphans home.

That was the expression they always used. No one ever just went to an orphans home. No one ever lived there. A kid was sent away period.

And no one ever heard of him again.

The orphans home in Ohio — I forget where it was — was a big brick building, surrounded by (and wouldn't you know?) a fence. There were swings and sandboxes and merry-go-rounds and slides and every time we drove by the place on our way to visit relatives in another town and passed by it, all the orphans seemed to be having a great time.

They weren't fooling us.

That's why my sister and I, living in fear of the prospect that an agent of the home would reach out as we passed and snatch us into some sort of institutionalized oblivion despite the frantic protests of our still very much alive parents in the front seat, ducked down below the windows until the forbidding building was far behind.

I don't doubt the orphans home was the most dependable tool in the world back then for keeping kids in line.

"Don't complain about the food," I remember my mother saying more than once. "Just think of what you'd be eating at the orphans home."

Or, on a Sunday when social calls took our parents (and us along with them) to a house in the country for an afternoon of crashing boredom, our pleadings to stay home fell on deaf ears.

"Think of the children at the orphans home," we were told. "They don't get to go anywhere."

Back in those days I think most kids looked forward to growing up for only one reason:

Once you reached a certain age you were too old to be sent to the orphans home. To a reformatory, possibly. Or a prison. Or even a lunatic asylum.

But you were out of bounds — permanently — as far as orphans homes were concerned, a prospect more pleasing than any other.

Achieving orphan status, we gathered, could be accomplished in several ways. Your parents could die. They could disappear. Or they could abandon you.

And, unless there were relatives willing to take you in, it was the orphans home and no way out.

Faced with this grim fact, I remember, my sister and I relished the idea — and sometimes figured our chances of being stolen by gypsies.

I remember we were much less concerned over that or over losing our parents than we were of qualifying for orphan status.

For, both parents being only children, we had no relatives. We grew up with only one grandparent, no uncles, no aunts and no cousins.

Our answer was, of couse, to acquire as many of the foregoing as we could in as short a time as we could. Looking back, I think we chose well.

Cousin Maude was the wife of our family doctor. Cousin Babe owned an apartment building and a beauty shop.

Uncle Jack and Uncle Frank were relatively successful actors traveling with a stock company.

Aunt Mary's husband was one of the most prosperous farmers in the country.

Cousin Bob was a prominent antique dealer.

And Aunt Jeannette, an old school friend of our mothers's, spent her time between Texas and California where her husband drilled for oil.

Looking back, I suppose my sister and I were probably the first pre-schoolers in the country to establish a strategic stockpile of relatives.

We never needed them, of course.

But, when it comes to being sent away to an orphans home, it's better to have 'em and not need 'em than to need 'em and not have 'em.

Family reunion
rocks California

NOW I'M NOT ABOUT to compare the McGrath Family Reunion in Nevada City, Calif., a week ago with the 1905 earthquake and fire in terms of noise, confusion and crowds — but, considering it was only 18 months in the planning, it came pretty close.

I received my invitation — though "summons" might describe it more accurately — in, I think, the spring of 1981 from a McGrath enclave located in San Jose.

It was, you might say, a preliminary nose count.

In the McGrath family, present day members of which range from three months to 63 years, counting noses is but one of several things you do with them. It starts with wiping them and ends with getting them wet.

A grand niece of mine, one Jessica Landon who came on the scene last April, won honors in the wiping division. My brother-in-law, Jack McGrath, who hosted the affair at his home in Nevada City, easily outdistanced the rest of us nose-wettingwise by starting the day before the rest of us got there.

Actually, Jack started years ago — but it doesn't show as much because he's Butte Irish.

Occupying the middle ground were assorted brothers, sisters, in-laws, nieces, nephews, cousins and grandchildren to bring the total to an impressive 65. (Ali Baba, you may recall, could only muster 40 at any of his reunions.)

It was a typical Butte-type family reunion, replete with Irish sons, an Irish flag, shamrocks everywhere one looked, miraculous beer kegs which never seemed to be empty — and green-and-white golf caps as souvenirs of the occasion.

Typical of Butte as well was the confusion which began Friday noon and ended Saturday night in a Nevada City bar called — appropriately enough — the Mine Shaft where at closing time everyone still there assumed that everyone not there had gotten home all right — but weren't all that sure.

The Mine Shaft was packed with backgammon buffs, softball teams, horseshoe pitchers, croquet players and a PacManiac who even brought his portable electronic game with him.

And every one in the place was a McGrath or a derivative thereof.

There were, of course, almost as many cameras at the reunion as there were kids. One McGrath — Pat, from Butte — brought not only a camera but a dog named Sam II. Sam got along with other McGrath dogs already there — and with the several others in the neighborhood who dropped by to see what all the excitement was about.

Jack, the patriarch of the clan — who never, incidentally, tired of reminding everyone there of his title — started things off with a turn around the back yard with his favorite toy, an ancient tractor with tank-like metal treads which he used for hauling logs.

He stopped in disgust when it was brought to his attention that he'd just run over his can of beer.

It was Jack, too, who was in the "Johnny on the Spot," a portable comfort station which he'd had the foresight to rent in view of the crowd, when two sons-in-law, one nephew and a brother decided to do the appropriate thing with it.

And with Halloween three months away.

It all started with Addis and Martha McGrath back in Butte about 60 years ago — and with their four sons and two daughters.

And — with the single exception of my wife, Dolores, who died in 1974 — everyone made it to the reunion. Everyone.

It was a grand time — as long, that is, as I refrained from bringing such names as Queen Elizabeth II or Ronald Regan into the conversation.

You see, I knew when I married into the family they were Irish. And Catholic. But no one told me they were Democrats.

But we get along. Even me and the Patriarch, who told me that as a Cousin Jack — a Butte name for anyone who can't trace his ancestry back to the ould sod — was not welcome but as long as I'd driven all the way from Montana I might as well stay around and have a beer and maybe some of the right politics would rub off on me.

I didn't play ball, pitch horseshoes or, since my croquet game has gotten terribly rusty over the years, swing a mallet. I did, however, leave Nevada City with a considerable accomplishment.

Having seen only the oldest of Jack's kids once — and she was four months old then — I met all 11 of them within the first 15 minutes I was there and had them all sorted out, faces and names, within the first hour.

So, Maury Pat, Katy, Colleen, MaryAnn, Shannon, Sharon, Sally, Peggy, Tim, Mickey and Dennis, if you don't believe me, there's your proof.

I once thought of family reunions the way I thought of class reunions as necessary but somewhat tedious rituals which must be gone through every generation or so for the sake of those who plan them.

Mark me down today as an advocate — and put me down for the next.

They make you proud of the past, happy in the present — and confident of the future.

Life along
the great river

AS FAR AS MY DAD was concerned, there was only one river. He was born beside it. He grew up beside it.

For all too short a time, he used to say later, he realized an ambition deep in the heart of every boy who lived in St. Louis in the 1880s and learned to love the river.

He became a cub pilot on the graceful, white packets that were as common a sight on the Mississippi between St. Louis and New Orleans as are buses on the highways of today.

In two years a boy doesn't learn too much of the torturous, changing channel of the Mississipi — but he learns a lot about boats.

And my dad remembered.

He remembered how the pilot to whom he was first "apprenticed" blew the thunderous whistle of the stern-wheeler on which he spent his first months on the river. Every pilot, he said, had his individual way of whistling for a landing, a drawbridge or a bend in the river and the people who knew and watched these once proud river queens could tell who was at the wheel by the way the whistle sounded.

Dad never met Mark Twain whose steamboat years ended long, long before his began — but he told of how the intials "H.B.," scratched on the plate glass window of the pilot house he once worked in were supposed have been those of Horace Bisby, the man who taught young Sam Clemens of Hannibal what he knew about steamboating.

It was a long time ago that I first walked down on the levee at St. Louis with my dad and we stood by the Old Rock House, a riverman's tavern of ante-bellum St. Louis, not far from the ponderous brick abutments of Eads Bridge.

130

River traffic, what there was of it, was mostly barges, towed by dingy, unromantic tugs — but my dad wasn't watching.

He looked down the sloping cobblestones to weathered, rotting piers where five or six faded beauties of the river were dying as easily as a changing world would let them.

Their white paint cracked and flaked, their railings sagged and the intricate filigree of woodlace that characterized nothing so much as it did a Mississippi steamer showed great, gaping holes where wind — and souvenir hunters, perhaps — had already begun to work.

We walked closer and were permitted to step aboard the least dilapidated — a side-wheeler named, I seem to recall, "The Stephen Decatur," whose tall-twin stacks reared empty and silent at the bright morning sky above.

I remember my dad and the way he walked up the gangplank and along the hurricane deck, past cabins and salons, empty and dark but for dust and memory, touching handrails and smiling with the feel of a deck beneath his feet.

The Texas deck and the pilot house, perched high above the river, he saved for last — then stopped once more at the dark door which led to the engine room where a satisfactory sniff of oil and smoke and burned black paint could still be had.

My dad later became an actor, a bank clerk, a railroad man and a hotel man — but I remember him first for the way he talked about the river and the boats which once were on it.

As far as my dad was concerned, there was only one river. He was born beside it. He grew up beside it.

Today, his grave in Bellfountain Cemetery in St. Louis is not far from the river he loved — where on a quiet afternoon, an errant wind can bring to anyone who listens the faint echo of a steamboat whistle.

A man's riches aren't measured in money

I REMEMBER HIM AS THOUGH it were only yesterday we stood in a dimly lit hotel lobby and said goodbye and knew, each one, that it was for the last time.

And now it's his birthday again and the memories come rushing back and the day is brighter because of them.

He knew about boats — and I remember how, on the Saturday nights when I saw him, he'd push the lamp to the center of the table and would sit for hours drawing them — paddle-wheelers, yachts, clippers, galleons, battleships and anything else that sailed or steamed.

There were other nights, when the heat had gone from the streets and the chorus of katydids droned its monotonous refrain, he'd walk to the closet and take down his hat and say, "Let's bum around."

And we'd walk and the talk would be of the town where he grew up and the river that ran by it. And sometimes, if the subject were approached right, he'd talk about show business and Al Jolson and W.C. Fields and Lou Calhern and the Barrymores and how, if a man had to sing for a living there was nothing in the world like traveling with a light opera company. It was on one of those walks I first heard about a man named Fred Stone and a show called "The Red Mill."

There hasn't been a Fourth of July since that I haven't remembered the long, hot day he spent cutting strange shapes of tissue paper and glueing them together and then sticking a stump of candle in a wire frame at the bottom.

Then after dark, he took it carefully out to the side yard and lit the candle and we all watched as the fire-balloon lifted up in the still night air and disappeared.

He made home-brew during Prohibition and persisted in claiming relationship to Aaron Burr, an attitude that more than once distressed some members of his family.

He was a man who knew how to do things, things unusual and unexpected. He stopped by a school one morning and watched as a janitor tried to raise a flag in the wind that whipped its folds about him.

He took the flag, refolded it, and fastened it to the halyard. The compact package moved to the top of the pole before he tugged at the rope and the flag spilled out and flew free.

"That's how we did it on the boat," he said. And to this day, janitors at that school raise the flag the way he showed them whenever the day's too windy.

I never asked him how it was done. It didn't seem important at the time.

This man who was at once unbelieveably stern and indescribably gentle had two words which he used more often, I think, than any others.

One was "dignity."

The other was "respect."

The worst thing he could say of any man was the quiet but, as I came to learn, deadly comment: "He is not a gentleman."

Will Rogers — another of whom he recalled from earlier years — is the one who said he never met a man he didn't like. But I heard it first on one of those long-ago walks.

We never knew, of course, how many men he did like until the morning we came to the little church and saw the crowd that spilled out the door, filling the lawn and overflowed past the brick sidewalk into the street.

His estate, when he died, amounted to the $1.89 found in his pocket.

Yet my father was the richest man I've ever known.

She had a way
of handling things

EVERYONE HAS — or must have had — an Aunt Lou somewhere in the family.

I hope so, anyway.

The one I knew would have been 109 years old today, if she had lived — and, chances are, she'd have been as young in heart as she was the way I remember her.

Aunt Lou — who was really Great-aunt Lou — was a year old when the Civil War ended. Born Mary Louisa Reed, she was the oldest of nine children and yet, to the day she died, the youngest.

She never married

There was always a brother or sister that needed caring for. Later, there were nieces and nephews.

There wasn't a wedding in the little Ohio town where she lived that was considered complete without her.

There wasn't a baby born that, sooner or later, didn't find itself cradled in her competent arms.

Having her in the house, somehow, did much even when the presence of death brought with it the familiar hush, and the strange quiet.

Aunt Lou always called it "handling things."

When a mother was sick, "handling things" meant taking her place until she was up and around again.

"Handling things" was an extra pie for the family with unexpected visitors and an extra ruffle sewn on a little girl's dress. "To perk it up," she would say.

"Handling things" included flowers on Memorial Day for those who had no one left to remember them.

Aunt Lou — had she been able — would have voted for William Jennings Bryan. But, lacking that, she did what she could to get the vote for women, even though it would add barely 100 tallies more to the small town's election books.

From the cause of suffrage, she moved her allegiance to Frances Willard, leader of the Women's Christian Temperance Union.

But, here again, Aunt Lou went her typical way. She called herself a "white ribboner" — but blackberry cordial and elderberry wine didn't count.

"Medicine," she'd say, "isn't the same as liquor." And nobody, according to Aunt Lou, could deny the medicinal effects of cordials or wine.

She took her first automobile ride in 1922, remarking as she climbed in the back seat of the Maxwell touring car, "If I'm going to be killed it might as well be in one of these as in a buggy."

Aunt Lou, who never missed a high school graduation, a Fourth of

July parade — or her Wednesday night prayer meeting — didn't get killed in either a car or a buggy.

She died very quietly in her sleep one night and people walked around town all the next day and wondered why it seemed so empty.

And no one thought it strange when, three days later, she was carried to the plot she picked out years before by six young men who came home from college when they were asked.

They remembered, every one, how Aunt Lou once had carried them.

Life has
its ups and downs

THERE ARE LIMITS, I contend, to avuncular responsibilities and I reached mine a couple of week ago while vacationing in Butte with my womenfolks.

I have recounted elsewhere in these tales of my Silver Bow county in-laws and the resultant collection of nieces and nephews which, over the years, has helped me make Uncle Wiggly look like a real loner.

But, up to this summer, I was lucky.

A rattle here, a rubber duck there — and a few pats on the head and cheery smiles of greeting were more than enough to get me through a visit when they were little.

This year, however, was different.

We were headed, I was informed on my arrival, for an afternoon at the Gardens, the Gardens being, of course, Columbia Gardens, an ingenious device of early day Copper Kings designed to keep Butte grownups so stiff and sore they couldn't cause the company trouble if they had to.

Not only, I learned, were we going to the Gardens but we (and "we" in this case meaning me) were going to ride the roller coaster.

Now there are few Montanans who have reached either the age of consent, the age of reason or the age of enlightenment who don't know about the Columbia Gardens roller coaster.

They've heard of it in folk tales handed down through generations. They've had grandparents who have told of having ridden (or watched others ride it) — and there are some who have even gone so far as to ride it themselves and have lived to tell of it.

Little did I ever dream I would become a member of that hardy band — but, I'm getting ahead of my story.

The Columbia Gardens roller coaster — for those of you who don't know — was brought over to this country on a ship which landed a century or two ahead of the "Mayflower" — but there is little else known of its early history here.

During the Revolution, soldiers reportedly used portions of it as fuel at Valley Forge but zealous custodians of the national tradition salvaged the charred timbers and after adroit use of glue, picture wire and white-wash, reassembled it so that not even a practiced eye can detect the repair job.

There was a rumor shortly after the Civil War that John Wilkes Booth's original plan was to send Lincoln a pass on the roller coaster but thought better of it when Ford's Theater was brought to his attention.

There was recently a move to send it to the Smithsonian Institute as a major example of historical America — but it fizzled out when technicians agreed it would never make the trip back East.

I was, of course, aware of all this when I boarded the roller coaster, accompanied by jubilant nieces and nephews all of whom wanted to hear "Uncle Bragg yell his head off" during the ride.

They could have saved their money.

If they'd been at their grandmother's house the day before when the announcement was made that I was going on the roller coaster, they could have heard Uncle Bragg yell his head off and it wouldn't have cost them a dime.

I lived, as you can see, to tell of the ride — but I'm keeping my fingers crossed.

The next time we go to the Gardens, I was told as I staggered to the car and home, we're going on the airplane swings.

The airplane swings at Columbia Gardens, I have it on reliable authority, were da Vinci's original working models.

Just a jingle
can give you a tingle

THE THOUGHT OCCURRED to me recently what a loss to Montana's economy it is that my sister, Judith, lives in Kansas instead of here.

Well, not the entire economy, perhaps.

Just that part of it involving Mountain Bell.

I have little doubt that with Judith on their books the phone company would have no need to go to the public service people, hat in hand, to ask for a rate increase.

Her long-distance tab alone would put them permanently in the black.

Like, as I said, the morning last week.

135

My phone rang.

"Hi," came the familiar voice.

I think if my sister were to call the White House she'd start the conversation with "hi."

"Hello — that you, Judith?" I mumbled. (I always mumble when I'm waked at 6 a.m.) "What's up?"

"Nothing," she said. "I just wanted to wish you a happy doomsday. Now you can go back to sleep."

The phone went click. I went back to sleep.

That, of course, was the most recent word from the sister who at times behaves as though she, not Alexander Graham Bell, invented the telephone.

Family birthdays, legal holidays, income-tax deadlines — even the launching of a new nuclear submarine — are all grist for Judith's long-distance mill.

Or she'll call at any hour of the day or night merely because a name bothers her.

"Who," she called once to ask, "is your friend from Cody we met last summer in the Northern?"

Wore a cowboy hat, she'll add. Judith's a stickler for detail.

I tried recalling. "Tall or short?" I asked.

"Dunno," said my sister. "He was sitting down all the time."

I was sorry I couldn't help. We talked for a while and she hung up.

An hour later the phone rang.

My sister had remembered the name and called me to tell me who it was.

She puts more post scripts to phone calls than most people do to letters.

Judith, who is women's physical education director at Allen County Community Junior College in Iola, likes keeping me posted on what's happening in the old home town.

She'd save money by sending me the paper — even if it were personally delivered.

I hear about births, marriages and deaths. I even hear about who went to jail, whose dog died and whose house burned down.

Most of the time Judith, who sounds on the phone like she's either about to catch a plane or has the rest of the evening to talk, gets the who, what, where, when and why down pretty well.

There are those calls, however, when she obviously hasn't done her homework.

"Hello," she said the day she found me at the Northern. (Judith knows most of my watering holes.) "Been trying all over town to get you."

"What's up?" I ask.

She gave a name and told me he'd just died.

"Thought you'd want to know," she said.

136

"Who?" She repeated the name.

"Gee, Judith," I told her. "I'm sorry but I don't think I knew him."

She asked if we weren't high school classmates. I told her no.

Grade school then?

Sorry, Judith.

"Oh," she said, relief in her voice. "I thought you did."

End of conversation.

Or again, Judith will call to tell me she had something important to tell me but that it slipped her mind. "Keep talking," she'll say, "I'll think of it in a minute." We keep talking, she never thinks of it and we hang up.

Moments later my phone rings.

"I just thought of what it was I had to tell you," says Judith.

I ask what.

"Never mind," comes the cherry response, "it wasn't all that important."

Talking to Judith on the phone is, as you may suspect by now, sometimes like stepping on a step that isn't there.

Occasionally my sister, in trying to locate me, will reach a bar or restaurant here we've visited together. My not being there doesn't faze her in the least.

"Judith called earlier tonight," I've had a bartender or waitress tell me often. "You weren't here so she talked to us."

There was no need, I'd be told, to call back.

Judith calls Sam and Kay Decker in Cody to ask how their dogs are.

She calls me to find out how Zellah Yegen and Gretchen Egan are. The three of them met on an elevator in the Hart-Albin Building one afternoon ten or more years ago and Judith never forgot them.

"Tell 'em hello for me," she'll say.

Sure thing, Judith. What else is up?

"Nothing," she chirps. "Just got to thinking about 'em, thought I'd call to tell 'em hello."

Of course, next time I see 'em I always tell 'em.

Does this give you an idea, telephone people, what you're missing?

With my sister on your accounts receivable list you could well spend winters in Arizona.

Not to mention you U.S. Postal Service employees were my sister to stop using a telephone and start buying stamps.

Her letters alone could cut the department's red ink bill by half.

On the other hand, I prefer my sister to stick with the telephone.

St. Patrick's Day would be a complete bust without a call from her.

Not to mention March 14.

That's a cat's birthday at my place.

And she hasn't missed one yet.

Mother was
a great witch

FOR SOME REASON or other, whenever Halloween comes around I always think of my mother.

Wait a minute. What am I talking about — for some reason or other?

There are plenty of reasons for my associating my mother with Halloween — and vice versa.

She was one of the best witches in town.

She also was a pretty convincing gypsy fortune teller. So convincing, in fact, that kids who didn't know her as well as we did were scared she might steal them.

Add to these top-drawer qualifications the fact that my mother knew more ghost stories than even Edgar Allen Poe and you had yourself a whole Halloween party wrapped up in one person.

And if there was anything my mother loved it was a good Halloween party, complete with bats, goblins, skeletons, ghosts, witches on broomsticks silhouetted against the moon — and, certainly, a lighted pumpkin or two.

Her gypsy fortune teller act was pretty good. She managed a great accent, dug assorted veils, scarves, bracelets, earrings, baggy sleeved blouses and archaic skirts out of an upstairs wardrobe trunk and dyed (with what I don't know) her face and hands coffee-brown.

As I said, my sister and I thought she was great. She scared some of the kids half to death.

And there were more than a few grown-ups in the little town we lived in who thought she was the real thing when she made her party rounds. (Back then a Halloween party without a gypsy was like normalcy without Harding.)

She enjoyed witching as much as gypsying and — to my mother's credit, let it be said — she thought of witches with green hands and faces long before Margaret Hamilton showed up in "Wizard of Oz".

As a gypsy she told fortunes.

As a witch she told ghost stories — including the classic one about the man with the golden arm.

She did them for schools, churches, clubs and house parties and enjoyed it so much she actually felt let down when Halloween came and went and the gypsy's crystal ball and the witch's broom went back into the attic for another year.

What people didn't know about my mother was that she brought considerable authenticity to both characterizations.

Where, back in those days, people shunned the occasional caravans of gypsies that came through town, my mother sought them out, talked

138

to them and wrote stories about them.

And where, again back in those days, people only spoke about but stayed clear of houses supposedly haunted, my mother sought them out, dug up their history — and wrote more stories.

In at least two cases it was my mother who laid ghosts that kept houses they supposedly haunted off the market for generations.

The man who sold one of them paid her a commission.

The people who bought the other practically made her a member of the family once they moved in.

Yes, my mother would agree, it was very nice. The money came in handy.

And the old place on the hill was so lovely to visit.

On the other hand, she'd sigh, haunted houses don't grow on trees.

"It seems such a shame," she said once, "that people don't realize that and keep a few around — especially when it gets to be Halloween."

Life is counted
in precious minutes

THIS MIGHT HAVE been a different story — had it not been a particularly fortunate combination of circumstances.

My wife's heart attack could have happened 24 hours later than it did when she was home alone.

Or, on that Sunday morning early last November, she could have been helped upstairs by someone who didn't recognize it for anything more than a fainting spell.

The way things turned out, emergency treatment for what later proved to be an acute myocardial infarction, was instituted at St. Vincent Hospital within — at most — 20 minutes from the time she walked up to a friend at church bazaar booth and said "Catch me, I think I'm going to fall."

It started, really, hours before when she was the first one up that morning and looked out to see a couple of inches of snow on the front walk.

When she'd finished the shoveling job, she noticed the pain in her left arm — but didn't let it bother her.

Who's to fuss, she thought, over what was probably a pulled arm muscle?

After dropping her off at the parish school about 10:45, I went on to town, checked the mail and dropped by the office and then the store where I picked up the pack of cigarettes she'd asked me to bring back.

Piecing things together — as best I could do — the sequence of events went like this:

Within minutes after complaining of pain, she was carried upstairs, laid on a couch and covered with coats by two friends, one of whom was a registered nurse.

A veteran fireman went outside and drove his station wagon up to the door.

All three had marked the pallor of her complexion, the blue lips and the cold, drenching sweat.

And all three recognized it immediately for what it was.

"If Dolores is sick," someone suggested, "and you're looking for Addison, he's gone uptown. He should be back before long."

The fireman — or the nurse — or the other friend — didn't waste time discussing the matter.

"When Addison gets back," one said, "tell him we've taken her to the hospital."

As close as could be determined — in the hours that followed in that long, long day — the artery which fed the heart muscle was clogged or pinched off at about 11:25 a.m.

Her chart showed her first medication administered at 11:40 a.m.

It was a few minutes before noon when I stepped off the elevator on the third floor and met her doctor coming out of the intensive care unit.

"It's definitely a coronary," he said. "We've got her stabilized and at this moment she's doing good."

Then he added:

"But it would be foolish for me to tell you right now she's going to be all right. We see too many of these cases where they're doing good — and then go all to pot within a matter of hours."

So the waiting began.

Every hour you put behind is a point in your favor. Then every six hours. Then 12. Then 24.

Then you start thinking — after 72 hours — in terms of days.

And while you're thinking — and waiting — you learn things about coronary heart disease.

One of the first things, you learn, believe me, is that it can happen to you — or to your family.

And one of the next — and most important — things you learn is that the sooner the victim gets to a hospital, the better the chances are.

More than 65 percent of all coronary deaths occur before the patient reaches the emergency room.

Once there, the mortality rate used to drop to about 25 percent.

Today the coronary intensive care unit has given the coronary patient an even better edge. The mortality rate now hovers in the 12 to 15 percent range.

The ICU may be a frightening place, with its tubes, its wires, its tiny oscilloscopes where the beat of a heart marches across in little peaks and valleys of light.

But it spells life to those who go there more often than not.

My wife came out in four days.

She came home Thanksgiving week.

It makes you think, now that those first few tenuous hours are months in the past.

It makes you think even more about that moment in time when it happened.

I thought to myself then — and have thought many times since:

If it had to be, thank God it happened when it did — and where it did.

There were people around who knew what to do.

What's more important, they wasted no time doing it.

Those 15 or 20 minutes that Sunday weren't much in terms of time.

But had it not been for the way they were used — as I said at the beginning — this might have been a different story.

If, indeed, it would have been written at all.

Mothers just don't appreciate creativity

NOSTALGIA, SOME SAGE once observed, ain't what it used to be.

And you're never more convinced of the fact than when you see some of the electronic games for kids you can find on today's market.

In a way, though, I suppose it was inevitable.

With some of the stuff that passes for entertainment on television today they had to find something to make development of the cathode ray tube worth while.

Which is how it happened that the younger set — along, more often than not, with their parents — can now play tennis, hockey, space invaders and war games rather than watch faded reprints of "Our Gang" comedies, Nat Levine serials and B-grade westerns.

It leads one, though, to wonder what kids did to pass time in that dim era before TV games — or even television, for that matter.

And — luckily for you — I just happen to be an authority on the subject.

We made spool tractors.

We polished pennies.

And if we were lucky enough to get away with it we took our mother's scissors and cut buzz saws out of tin can lids, ran a string though two holes in the center and went around sawing notches in kitchen chair legs.

It wasn't, admittedly, a giant step forward in technology — but it kept us busy and out of the way.

Take penny polishing, for example.

Back in a time when a penny was worth — as they say now of the dollar — a whole penny, they weren't the easiest things to come by.

And they were invariably dingy.

Even the dullest, however, could be restored to an impressive brilliance simply by rubbing it back and forth on the carpet.

And the penny-polisher always had something to look forward to.

The day could come when he could start shining nickels — or dimes.

It's been a year or more since I heard anyone mention spool tractors — and that was to ask me what in the world they were.

Spool tractors, I think, were invented just before — or along with — the wheel. They didn't break, wear out — or clutter up the floor.

And the really great thing about them was their simplicity.

You waited for an empty spool from a sewing basket, you found a rubber band, two kitchen matches, cut a corner off a piece of soap, notched the ends of the spool, put the thing together and you were in business.

Mothers, as I recalled, liked spool tractors.

They didn't damage kitchen chair legs.

They didn't raise carpet dust that penny-shining often did.

And they were quiet.

My grandfather taught me how to shine pennies.

A neighbor kid showed me how to build a spool tractor.

But the tin can lid buzz saw was my dad's contribution.

It worked the same way a button does when you thread it on a loop of string, wind it up and then pull out on the ends causing the button (or saw) to spin first in one direction, then the other.

Buttons, my father told me, were all right — but they didn't do anything.

It was a matter of less than 15 minutes for my father to come up with something that DID something.

It took less than one minute for my mother to finish it.

In the meantime, however, I'd sawed through the cover picture on the latest Saturday Evening Post, scratched the edge of the piano bench, snagged a kitchen curtain, caused a sawdust hemorrhage in one of my sister's dolls — and scared the wits out of my mother by ratcheting it across a china platter.

"I don't care if your father did show you how to make it," she said, "we've had all the buzz-sawing around here we're going to have."

Can lid and string disappeared forthwith.

My mother was that way about some things and were she around today, I think she'd be that way about television whether people were watching it or playing games on it.

And I'm not too sure she wouldn't be right.

Characters

& V.I.P.s

CHAPTER 6

Kentucky colonel
wears the green

THE NEXT TIME YOU run into Colonel Charles J. Heringer Jr., it won't be necessary to salute.

One of the newest members of the Honorable Order of Kentucky Colonels — who's also our town's most perennial Irishman — agrees a simple "Erin Go Bragh" will be sufficient.

There are, he said, already many Irish Kentucky colonels.

"We can always use more," he added.

The Billings oilman's new commission hung on his office wall Friday, empowering him to exercise the "rights, privileges and responsibilities" as a Kentucky colonel on the staff of Governor Bert Combs.

Col. Heringer confessed he wasn't too sure of just what they were.

"I guess," he began, "one of my rights is to get to hang that on the wall."

He shuffled through letters on his desk.

Maybe one of his privileges, he guessed a second time, is to be called "Colonel."

This, he pointed out helpfully, amounts to picking in tall cotton for a former Army man who got as far as first lieutenant before he ran out of war.

He scratched a crew-cut head.

"Lesee," he said, "we're down to responsibilities, right?"

Right.

A gleam came into Col. Heringer's eye.

"My main responsibility," he said, "is to find out for sure just what my rights and privileges are."

Maybe, said Col Heringer — who incidentally, wears neither a broad-brimmed hat or a white goatee — his old friend, John J. O'Hara, commonwealth attorney who, after a visit with the Heringers in Billings last week, recommended his appointment, could supply the information.

"Ah'd be proud, suh," said Heringer, warming to his new role, "to aisk him."

A wallet-size card, attesting his appointment, especially pleased the colonel.

It was green.

He'll be able to carry it, he said, on St. Patrick's Day.

Being a Kentucky colonel, according to official literature of the organization, doesn't cost a cent. No fees, no charges and no dues.

"Nor do we," an explanatory letter added — somewhat primly — "sponsor or publish any newspaper."

And there's only one social event of the year.

The morning of each Derby Day in Louisville, said Heringer, Kentucky colonels from all over the country meet at Churchill Downs to drink breakfast as guest of Calumet Farms.

"I just might get back there one of these days," Col. Heringer mused.

The time, he explained, is about right.

They don't run the Derby until the second Saturday in May.

That's almost sixty days after St. Pat's Day.

Col. Heringer — native Kentuckian, adopted Montanan and confirmed Irishman — figures he'll have recovered by then.

Say good-bye
to 'Good Old Days'

"I NEVER WANT TO SEE those days come again."

The speaker was Percy Banner, Billings musician. His subject, Chicago in the "roaring twenties."

At a break Friday during his organ-piano stint in the Golden Belle, Banner took a cigarette, crumpled the empty pack in an ashtray and flashed teeth in a quick smile.

"They wrote good music then," he said, "but that's about all that can be said for it."

The cigarette smouldered and its ash grew long as memory rolled back the years.

The young piano player who left a theater job in Kokomo, Ind., to work in Chicago in 1921 found himself with a ringside seat to a way of life that is now almost legend.

It was the jazz age, the time of the speakeasy, bootleg gin, hip flasks and those who fought for control of the illegal traffic in alcohol.

It was the day of the bullet-proof limousine and a swarthy little man in a pearl grey hat who needed its protection.

"I saw Al Capone a lot," Percy recalled, "and his brother, Ralph — I worked in a couple of clubs he ran. He didn't know who I was, of course — but I've gotten tips from him."

Banner's home in Chicago was on Prairie Avenue, right across the street from where the famous underworld leader's mother lived.

"And she was a nice woman," he said, reflecting. "As nice a woman as I've ever met."

Always ready for a raid, club owners in that era often used the piano to conceal the trapdoor to their emergency booze cache. "There were plenty of times," Percy recalled, "they'd move my piano, stow the whisky below, slam the trapdoor, move me back — and there I'd be, playing away like mad when the cops came in."

Speakeasy patrons, Percy admitted, drank rotten alcohol, worse beer and questionable gin. "The only safe drink," he grinned, "was home brew — if you knew the person who made it."

Gang members, he said, were easily recognized wherever they went — even though their faces might not be familiar.

"Good dressers, all of 'em," he said, "Pick 'em out a mile away — and they almost always were chewing cigars."

Percy remembers one of those who would come to him periodically, hand him a diamond stickpin and ring — "big as hen's eggs" — and ask him to hold them "until I get back."

"I got scared every time it happened," he said, "for fear I'd lose them or have them stolen — he'd be gone for days."

Banner once worked for a club owner who was a gangland-killing victim. Another acquaintance was one of the seven men who stood against a wall on a remembered St. Valentine's Day and fell under a hail of machine gun bullets.

"They were interesting times," he agreed, "but they were rough times. I was just a piano player — I didn't know what was going on and I didn't want to know. You stayed alive longer that way."

A fresh pack of cigarettes came out as Percy looked across at the clock.

"Gotta get to work," he said, moving toward the piano. He sat down started a chorus of "Hindustan."

The familiar Banner grin came up and over a hunched shoulder as his left hand thumped out two-four accompaniment.

"They wrote good music," he said, "and people still want to hear it — but the days were bad. I'm glad they're gone."

Purt' near ever'body knows 'Peanuts'

CLAUDE OWENS SHIFTED his seat on a bicycle rack near the Gazette building, and squinted thoughtfully at a parking meter.

"Yes sir," he began, "I'm 73 now, been here since I was 9 years old and know purt' near ever'body in the country.

The man with the baseball cap, the western shirt and the charm-heavy watch chain could, of course, be wrong.

But one thing's certain — purt' near ever'body in the country knows him. Not by his real name, perhaps, but as "Peanuts." The city's number one sports fan and the closest thing, probably, we've ever had to a town crier.

The opening of baseball, football or basketball season — as well as any other important athletic event — is sure to find him plodding in and out of downtown restaurants and bars, familiar megaphone over his shoulder, to announce a game, keep a crowd posted on the latest score or list a last-minute change in a starting lineup.

Between seasons Claude Owens keeps busy — marching or riding in parades.

"You had a story about me in the Shrine parade," he said in his characteristic clipped speech. "Had on my fez cap. I cut it out, had it framed. When'll this be in the paper?"

He admitted with a grin he kept a scrap book. "Stories with me in 'em, though, I frame."

He peered over his glasses. "You know where Custer Hotel is? You know that place right back of it where they survey land? I take it there and they put it in bigger letters. Then I frame it up, put 'er on the wall."

Crafty Claude Owens won't commit himself on favorite sports. "I take 'em all in." He's just as cagey about being pinned down to favorite teams, even leagues.

"Fella doesn't let on who he likes," he confided, "gets lots more bets that way." This, he added, even includes the controversial New York Yankees.

"I won't say anything about 'em," he said, "either for or against. Might wants make little bet."

Who'd he pick in the world championship fight? The smile broadened beneath the broken nose.

"I lost twelve dollars on the Swede," he admitted. Then stoutly: "A lotta people besides me lost money on him."

He passed up the chance to comment on lagging interest in Pioneer League baseball. "Well, sir," he hedged, "I may have some idea but I'll just keep quiet. I don't wants say anything make Enright mad."

Claude Owens stood up.

"Guess that's about all I oughta say. You just make a little writeup, there. Got enough? Plenty for a big story looks like to me. That do it? There you go. Yep. Now you got 'er. Atta boy."

His windup of the interview brought to mind another Claude Owens hobby — and one without which downtown Billings would seem more quiet.

He works at it while not otherwise busy in plugging sports events and marching in parades.

You remember — it's directing pedestrian traffic at busy intersections.

Everyone knows
when Murray's in town

WALKING TWO BLOCKS along North Broadway with Murray McBride is like trying to carry on a conversation with a highball freight.

A man less than 6 feet tall with a voice problem doesn't stand a chance.

Murray, who blew into town Tuesday on one of his biennial whirlwind visits, had a word or 50 for practically everyone he met — and if they didn't hear him they're worse off than they think.

Maury Enright, for example — who's had an off-season to begin with — barely got out the words "Well, when did you ...?" and the McBride torrent was turned on.

"Here," he said, one hand pumping Enright's, the other on the shoulder of a companion, "is baseball's greatest manager. I mean it. Stengel, believe me, has nothing on him, nothing. Except a bank."

He paused, looked over Enright's shoulder and spoke to a friend who happened to be passing a block away.

Teeth flashed in the familiar McBride grin above the familiar bow tie as the ever-present cigar was flourished in greeting.

It was like that most of the morning.

There was no question Murray felt good about being back in the city — Portlander though he has become — he still calls Billings "my town."

There was no question that people were glad to have him here.

Bewildered, of course. But glad.

One old friend who — by long experience — had learned how to get a word in edgewise noted that Mac had lost some weight.

"That's right, buddy," he said, "that's absolutely right. I'm down to 205 now and I wear one size smaller shoe. Used to wear 14's and now I'm down to 13's and it's a great thing. I've just been in Wayne Lucy's barber shop and made arrangements to get shoe shines at the regular price. Save a lot of money that way now."

At the Midland National Bank he looked across the lobby to a desk where a friend sat talking to a bank customer.

"Like to shake hands with Glenn Rye," he said, "but I see he's busy giving away dollars."

At the First National Bank where startled cashiers and customers alike eyed the well-dressed hurricane, he roared a farewell to another banker, also talking to a customer.

"Give that man all the money he wants," he called from the door, "he's a friend of mine."

The two-block walk — which turned into four — would have taken the average person ten minutes at the most.

It took McBride almost an hour.

It included an inspection of the Fox Theater marquee. "I used to change that marquee," he said, "and I want to check and see if they're still spelling all the words right."

Con Kelleher — who sings tenor to McBride's bass — stepped into a sheltering doorway to escape the wake. He wanted to know if Murray had a lunch date.

"I'll declare an intermission," came the window-rattling reply, "as soon as we finish this job of rearranging this part of town. I see some signs that have been around here a long time — they'll have to come down and then there's a few store fronts I want to switch. Cornelius," he concluded, "I'll call you."

So it went.

This was one McBride.

The other is the McBride who, since he left here in 1955 — he now lives in Portland, Ore. — still calls Billings "my town."

"This," he said, "is the greatest town, really the greatest. It's clean, it's refreshing, it's up-to-date and there's not another city in the country can beat it."

It's a town, he went on, that's "changing all the time."

"You may not realize it here," he said, "because you're so close to it — but that's what's wonderful about it."

Problems that Billings has now, he said — streets, traffic, highways, schools — don't mean that there's anything wrong with the town.

"You've got 'em," he said, "because you're growing and this I love to see, believe me."

This is the other McBride.

You can take your pick.

They're both great guys.

Never a lack of interesting people

AN OLD CHICAGO-TYPE new spaperman once wrote a book called "Such Interesting People," the title of which, incidentally , I borrowed for a weekly feature I did for The Gazette for 15 or 20 years. In the book the author explained how he decided on the title.

A woman once remarked to him that, being in the newspaper business, "you must meet such interesting people."

Yes, the writer told her, adding:

"And most of them are in the newspaper business."

Well, the Gazette — in case you hadn't suspected — has had its share.

I'm thinking, for example, of the well-read, well-traveled veteran reporter and copy editor who unfortunately had his problems with the bottle but who, nonetheless, was deemed competent enough that the Gazette risked putting him on the payroll.

He showed up for his first shift at 8 a.m.

He went to coffee at 10 a.m., was drunk by the time he got back at noon.

Since the editor had already left for lunch the man wasn't fired nor did he formally quit.

He walked out and never came back.

But despite the fact he put only two hours in on the job, the Gazette paid him for a 40-hour week.

The last I heard his check was still waiting for him 20 years later when he died, having never left Billings.

In the MacArthur-Hecht play "The Front Page" there was a reporter named Benzinger who, fearful of catching someone else's cold, carried his own plastic telephone mouthpiece with him.

Back in the early 1960s a sports writer from the West Coast reported for work at the Gazette carrying his electric typewriter under his arm.

He brought it to the office daily and took it home with him at night for all the few months he was here.

Bob Lane, a wire editor, came to work with a trombone under his arm.

He never played it and we never found out what happened to it.

Bob became memorable, however, for making the Gazette city room the equivalent of a town house.

His desk drawers contained canned soups (which he ate cold for breakfast on those mornings after a bad night), plastic spoons, a clean shirt and a razor.

We could always tell when Bob had a bad night.

He shaved dry at his desk while reading copy and would invariably nick himself up a bit.

The Gazette's all-time hold check champion had to be Sam Blythe, the political writer and city-county reporter.

We'd get paid Monday noon and Sam would spend part of the day picking up the hold checks he'd written the previous two weeks. By the time he got off at 6 p.m. he'd be writing another two weeks worth of hold checks.

It wasn't all that much trouble for Sam to pick up those checks.

He had only to visit the Heidelberg and the Empire Bar — and in the five years he was here he never missed a one.

We had another Benzinger on the Gazette, only his war was against smoke, not germs. Daily when he came on duty, out came his can of room deodorizer.

He replenished his protective cloud from time to time as the Typhoid Marys of the city room's tobacco lobby inadvertently polluted his corner of the office.

I've been wanting to write this next bit about Hal Seipp, retired Gazette editor, for a long time and he's always managed to talk me out of it.

But here goes:

For as long as I've known him — and even before — Hal has collected misspellings of his last name.

And in the mail a newspaper editor named Seipp gets, they can mount up — Sipes, Siepp, Sepps, Sippy and Speiss, to list only a few.

But look who's talking.

Continental Air Lines for years sent me mail addressed to "Addison Bugg".

They stopped — but not because of any of the protesting I did to their public relations department.

Taking my case to Continental's highest court, I wrote the president himself — and I think my misspelling of Robert Six's last name was what turned the direct mail tide.

In my time I've worked for an editor who insisted — on pain of death — that one animal story appear on the front page at least once a week.

And I worked with a reporter who would make the Washington Post's Pulitzer prize winner look like a piker with the features he turned in regularly for nearly three months.

They were brillantly written and fascinating in their subject matter.

And they were about people who never existed.

Finally, I worked for a Gazette editor who never mastered even the hunt-and-peck system of typing.

Bill Roesgen wrote fast and furiously, using only one finger.

But don't get the idea I'm knocking him.

Bill's now publisher of the Bismarck Tribune.

But just think.

If he had no fingers at all he might have owned his own newspaper by now.

The sky seems empty without him

YOU TAKE THE 30,000 hours and you break them down into the seconds and minutes that make up a pilot's life.

You parcel them out carefully, into the time he watches the brown and green of the earth drop away and return again, into the blue of a sun-washed sky or the blackness of a star-drenched night.

You put aside the seconds lighted by the tiny reds and greens of an instrument panel at midnight and the minutes given life by an engine's roar.

And you take the sounds of flight and the feeling of the sky around you and you fold them into the pages of memory — and if your name is Earl Hale, you've had more than your reward.

The man who took Northwest Orient Airlines Flight No. 7 from Tokyo to Seoul, Korea, eight days ago — then rode back to Tokyo as a "deadhead" because he'd reached retirement age during his Seoul layover — stubbed a cigarette out in an ashtray.

"Whatever you write about me," Hale grinned, "just don't put in any baloney."

Here, then, is Hale, third ranking pilot for the airline at the time of his retirement Sept. 5 — the day he turned 60 — without baloney.

He came up here from his native Harrold, Tex., in the early 1920s because he wanted to play baseball — and he'd heard that Billings was a good baseball town.

He took the money he made catching in a game at Ryegate and gave half to his wife, the former Blythe Williams. Buy a dress with it, he told her.

The other half he took up to Logan Field — and paid for his first airplane ride.

From this to flying lessons and from a pilot's license to a job with a Wyoming air service, flying passengers on its Billings-Denver route, was Hale's no-baloney road to a career as a commercial airline pilot.

He joined Northwest May 1, 1933, and left the Billings airport two days later with a trip to Bismarck, N.D. After a year on the run, the Hales moved to Seattle where he's been since.

The planes flown by Hale sound almost like an aviation "Hall of Fame."

The Hamilton, Lockheed's "Orion" and "Zephyr," Ford tri-motor, the DC3 and DC4, Boeing's Stratocruiser, the DC6, the Constellation, and the DC7.

He remembers them, as does any pilot, with affection.

The "Orion", for example: "One of the best airplanes I ever flew. You pumped up the hydraulic gear on this one after takeoff. It took exactly 165 strokes."

The DC3: "That's the airplane that made aviation what it is today."

The Stratocruiser: "A pilot's parlor, we called it. All the room in the world in the cockpit — and I remember when I first started flying passengers the pilot could look down and see their feet sticking out of the cabin under his seat."

Hale's voice still retains a touch of Texas. He speaks easily of flying, a profession in which he grew up and one which, in a way, grew up with him.

153

He's a four-stripe captain who never flew co-pilot. He remembers when flight engineers wore coveralls and were called mechanics. He was the line's chief pilot for a while and the line's check pilot for many years — in addition to his other duties.

He doesn't drink.

He's taken more than 70 physical examinations during his 29 years with the airline. The last was in August — and the only restriction appearing on his airman's certificate reads:

"Must possess corrective lenses for near vision while exercising airman's privileges under this certificate."

It doesn't say, Hale grinned, he has to wear glasses, only "possess" them.

The 30,000 hours of flying time Hale is credited with isn't exactly baloney — but, he admitted, it might be a bit on the generous side.

"My log book showed 29,643 in August," he said. "And I've done some flying since then — I guess, maybe, 30,000 is close enough."

Hale has been responsible for several company "firsts."

He flew the first run from Seattle to Anchorage, Alaska.

He flew the first flight from Seattle to Billings.

He landed the first Constellation to touch down at the Billings airport, bringing it here from Seattle for the first Jaycee Air Fair.

He's one of the few airline pilots in the country who also holds a government rating as a mechanic.

Hale would probably be the last to admit it — but he's a sentimental man.

That's why he made a special request of the company when he retired.

"I put on this uniform in Billings," he said, fingering the sleeve stripes, the diamond-set 25-year pin and the gold wings, "and I wanted to take it off here."

That was the reason for the luncheon at the airport Thursday and the old friends who came.

It was the reason for the nice things that were said — and the nicer things left unsaid.

And it's the reason the sky, for a lot of pilots who knew him, seems a little empty now — now that Earl Hale isn't up there.

Bess Truman was
a mom to servicemen

WELL, THEY BURIED Bess Truman last week in Independence, Mo., and hearing and reading about it and watching it on televsion brought back a lot of memories.

They were of Washington, D.C., and the war — and of a great place called the 18th and H Street U.S.O.

The war ended and not too long after, they tore down the abandoned church which the U.S.O. had taken over; and now Bess Truman's dead.

The book is closed now — but the story, I think, is still worth telling.

The time was 1944, when the sight of a civilian in downtown Washington was as rare as the sight of a uniform there today. And where the military went, the U.S.O. followed.

There was the Stage Door Canteen in the old Belasco Theater just off Lafayette Park across from the White House.

There was the second floor of an old building at about Eighth and Pennsylvania Avenue they called "Mother Steed's."

There was the Pepsi-Cola Canteen about four blocks north.

And there was the 18th and H Street U.S.O., almost in the shadow of the sprawling State Department building which now houses the Executive Office of the president.

The first three drew, for the most part, on transient or temporary military.

"Customers" at 18th and H Street were mostly servicemen and women stationed in the Washington area. It was, in fact, about as close to having a family in Washington as many of us ever got.

And Bess Truman was one of our mothers.

There weren't many people in the country — or even in the service, for that matter — who could have breakfast cooked for them three times a week by the wife of the Vice President of the United States.

And the first two or three times I went there I didn't even know who she was — other than that she seemed to be a friendly sort who talked a little like she came from my part of the country and who handled a skillet as though she knew what she was doing.

Later, after I got to know her, we talked about mutual friends — mostly those involved in politics — and towns we'd been in or where we had friends in either Kansas or Missouri.

She was that way with all of us.

She also fussed over us a little and when, in her opinion, occasion demanded, put in her two cents worth about how we were or were not getting all the sleep we needed or whether we did or did not eat what was good for us.

To the best of my recollection, Bess Truman was the only person I ran across in my four years in the Army who fretted about my not eating bread crusts or drinking enough fruit juice.

I guess I got a scolding from her every week or two for that alone.

She was also interested in our families (especially our mothers) and how things were with them back home.

Bess Truman — and I don't think there was a single 18th and H Streeter who didn't feel this way — was like having an understanding, but stern, aunt around to keep you in line.

And she was the kind of a person who, by the time you found out or realized her husband was who he was, you felt so comfortable with that you didn't let it scare or impress you a bit.

During the year or more I was a member of the 18th and H Street family I never even got to see Harry Truman, let alone meet him, despite the fact that he'd pick Bess up a couple of times each week when she'd finished in the kitchen.

One Sunday night, I recall, I came in from a weekend in Pennsylvania and got to the 18th and H to learn that the Vice President had just finished an impromptu concert for two dozen or so regulars there.

Bess, it seems, was delayed in the kitchen. So her husband played the piano until she was ready to leave.

The time finally came when I had to eat my last breakfast, drink my last cup of coffee and say my last goodbyes to 18th and H Street.

Bess Truman stayed in character.

"Goodbye," she said, "now take care of yourself."

Months later, overseas, I had a letter from my mother who bubbled over (in pen and ink) with the news that she'd had "just the nicest note ever" from Bess Truman in Washington, D.C., who said how we'd got to know each other and that she hoped things were good in Kansas and hoped that I was taking care of myself.

"Wasn't that thoughtful?" my mother asked.

I knew the woman in Washington better than she did.

"Taking care" meant only one thing:

Bess Truman was still fretting about my not eating bread crusts or drinking enough fruit juice.

He can paint, but can he cut hair?

SOMEHOW AMID MY frequent flights of imagination, I've never pictured myself an artist — or, more specifically, a Western artist.

Which, come to think of it, is strange.

At one time or another I've gone into Walter Mitty-like trances where I've been a cowboy, a horse cavalryman, a scout and a cattle baron. Once I was even a rustler — but the price of beef at the time was so low the profession didn't pay.

I was thinking of heading for New Orleans and becoming a riverboat gambler when my high-school history teacher slammed a ruler on my desk, told me to stop daydreaming in class and gave me an extra chapter on the industrial revolution to read and outline for the next day.

But paint and canvas — let alone fame and fortune — stayed pretty much out of my wool-gathering.

In fact, the only time I came close to palette and easel in my dreams was back when I collected stamps and was introduced to Goya's famed Duchess of Alba, a lady of considerable station (as well as proportion) who posed for Goya in the buff.

Her subsequent appearance on a Spanish stamp found me one afternoon wondering if I should leave philately for art, where, it seemed, the action really was.

It was years later before I got interested in Western art, and I guess the reason I never dreamed of becoming another Russell, Remington, Rains or Ralston was because from what I read of some and knew of the others, they didn't look or act arty in the least.

As a matter of fact, I'll put Western artists in a class of their own simply because they're about as honest about what they do for a living as a truck driver — or even some newspaper people.

I've never seen a piece of work by a Western artist that had to be explained or interpreted.

After all, a horse is obviously a horse, an Indian's an Indian — and a cowboy shooting up a town on Saturday night doesn't need a critic to point out the dramatic nuances, the emotional undercurrents or the vivid, unconventional use of color and line which led to the evanescent, primitive force behind the emerging of a truly new talent in the field.

The first time I met Harry Jackson — 25 years or more ago — he'd just been kicked in the eye by a horse. He was much more interested in talking about that horse than he was in talking about art.

And, looking at how far Harry's gone in the art world since, I can't see that having been kicked by a horse has done him all that much harm.

Ken Ralston's another no-nonsense guy where Western art is concerned.

Ken looks like an old cowboy — which he is. He talks like an old cowboy.

And you can spend hours with him and come away having learned more about Montana history, cattle spreads and life in the West the way it was — and the way he lived it — than about perspective, purpose or message.

And Ken's a pretty fair country artist into the bargain.

Jay Contway — who draws terrible but whose bronzes can sit alongside Russell's with Russell coming out second best — is another in the crowd who you'd never mistake for an artist even at an auction or a gallery.

He dresses Western because those are the only kind of clothes he's ever worn.

He knows the animals and the people that go into his work and respects them. And what's more important, they know and respect him.

I guess about the only Western artist I've known from the beginning is Bill Rains — and I knew his dad, Whitey Rains, long before I met Bill.

The Forsyth kid who's made his way quickly — and successfully — in the world of Western art was a barber when I met him.

But there were three pen-and-ink sketches hanging on the wall of his shop.

"One of these days," Bill told me when he'd finished with a customer and had time to talk, "I'd like to do art for a living. Really, I guess my one ambition is to make a career as a successful artist."

And it happened for Bill. His paintings are all over. His prints sell at top prices. His work in bronze has achieved the sort of recognition that has put him in the Country Music Hall of Fame in Nashville.

Bill Rains, in short, is a successful artist. And I think that's great — especially for Bill.

You know — he never could cut hair worth a damn.

Only a chicken could love an egg

Aside from frying them for breakfast and boiling them to dye at Easter (or to drink with beer) my affair with the Incredible Edible Egg has never been what could be described as heavy.

I have, for example, never been invited to an Egg Roll on the White House lawn. For that matter, I've never ordered egg roll in a Chinese restaurant.

You might say, I suppose, that as far as eggs are concerned, we, the egg and I, have existed on a live-and-let-live basis — until recently when I was invited to an omelette breakfast.

Now the art of omelette making is indeed that — an art. Custom must be followed, tradition observed in its preparation, cooking and serving.

An omelette must be beaten (with a fork) not too much, not too little.

It must be properly browned (over the proper flame), properly stirred (with a spatula) and properly folded and buttered.

I have, of course, tried omelettes on my own. They end up looking like scrambled eggs, lumpy eggnog or, as happened once when I let it brown too much, home plate.

As the critic once observed: "I cannot lay an egg — but I can tell when one is bad."

So with me. I cannot cook an omelette but I can tell — along with everyone else who's looked at the color photographs in Gourmet Magazine and in various books by Julia Childs — when the bounds of common decency in French cuisine have been overstepped.

My friend — and despite her omelette she is still my friend — obviously attended the scoop shovel school of French cooking.

I found things in that omelette that I wouldn't even expect to see in chili.

And the omelette itself was a thing of both beauty and utility. However, you could say the same of a Frisbee.

In all honesty I must say I survived the breakfast.

In Christian charity as well I must admit that my friend's omelette was no better or worse than others I've experienced.

I guess it all comes down to the fact that no omelette ever turns out the way the cook book pictures look.

So I suppose, if invited again, I'll go again — even if she tells me of plans to perpetrate another omelette.

But of one thing I'm sure:

If those chickens are still picketing her front door I'll turn around and go home. Oatmeal and milk may not be French or fancy — but every time I fix it it turns out looking exactly like it does in a color photograph.

Potpourri

CHAPTER 7

Some things
never change

O OG CALLED THE MEETING to order by banging on a hollow log with a dinosaur bone.

"The question," he told the Cave Elders, "we must decide tonight is whether we take over the Mud Flats across the river and develop them as a people attraction.

A rumble of dissent came from a group of fur-clad Elders, huddled in a corner of the cavern which even the leaping flames of the council fire failed to light.

Their spokesman, Wah, growled his disapproval.

"Before we start wasting time and energy on the Mud Flats," he said, "there are some things about these caves that could stand some fixing up."

Besides, he pointed out, there was little chance people would come to the Mud Flats once they were developed.

"The Oldest Among Us," he said, "remembers how 23 snows, 2 winds and a dust ago, a Cave Council tried to develop the Flats and the only one to visit them was a member of Ug's tribe who sought the job of caretaker — and he was eaten by a sabre-tooth tiger."

Wah's companions clamored agreement and were gaveled (or boned) into order by Oog.

"The Mud Flats," Oog insisted, "have a great future."

Gnurr, a junior member of the council, scrambled to his feet. "The Mud Flats are too far away," he said. "What happens to them is none of our business and moreover ..."

Oog interrupted.

"I said when I took office I would not be cave-limited," he told Gnurr, "and I think we have a responsibility to these Mud Flats."

They would, he added, be part of the Cave Dwellers future.

Wah, Gnurr and a third Elder shook their heads.

"You dream too much, Oog," they said. "First, you proposed that idiotic business of throwing meat in the fire before eating — and then you tried to foist that ridiculous thing you called a Wheel off on us — and now you expect us to go along with your silly Mud Flats scheme."

If these weren't bad enough, Wah added, there was Oog's attitude in letting anyone who wanted to come in and draw pictures on the sides and roof of the Council Cave.

"Just suppose," he said, "someone comes along after we're all gone

and finds our cave all scrawled up by a bunch of paleolithic Picassos —
what'll they think?"

Oog considered the question.

Maybe, he said, it would be a good thing.

"I can even," he said, "see the Mud Flats people coming out here to
look at us."

Hoots of derision drowned out Oog's futile pounding.

"Question," yelled Wah.

"Question," echoed Gnurr and the rest.

The development of the Mud Flats was voted down by a substantial
margin, to Oog's dismay.

So the Mud Flats weren't developed for a long, long time.

Oog, who eventually accepted his defeat with good nature, spent his
remaining years as the sole occupant of the Cave.

The Elders, legend has it, moved across the river to live on the Mud
Flats — and some say they live there still.

But the buns
are just great

W HEN, IN SESSIONS OF sweet silent thought, I summon up
remembrances of things past, I always wonder:
What ever happened to the hamburger?
I hasten to add, in the event hate mail starts arriving
from the McDonald, Wendy or Burger King people, I'm not talking about
the hamburger the way it is today.

I refer to the product as it was back in the days when a ten-cent
hamburger was the norm, a "double" went for the going price of 25 cents
— and a "deluxe" included french fries as well.

There are, surely, decent and good hamburgers made today.

They come in plastic bags, in cardboard boxes and an assortment of
other containers.

But somewhere, to quote an old city editor of mine, we've lost something.

Sometimes I have the feeling that the hamburger of the computer
age — the "fast food" product, if you would have it so — is put together
by a computer.

In contour and dimension it smacks of a perfectly engineered piece
of meat, geometrically round and honed (or sliced) to micro-smooth-
ness.

The bun on which it is served is — to read the glowing praises on the
menu — nothing short of magnificence in both texture and decoration.

And today's hamburger is cooked rare, medium or well, in a matter of seconds by the most recent arrival on the electronic scene.

I can almost see a computer programmer, bending his software to the utmost, to produce the new ultra plus of hamburgers.

My vision, however, is obscured by the memory of a black, greasy and smoking grill, presided over by a man in a T-shirt, rolled-up sleeves bearing tattoos of a past hitch in the Navy — and the solid "splat" of a broad knife or spatula smashing down a hunk of ground beef in the middle and rounding out (approximately) its sides.

I also remember the slices, thin and fresh, of raw onion as well as the proportions of the tomato slice which blanketed the finished product.

Back then hamburgers came rare, medium or well.

Buns came as they were — unless the waiter followed the order with a hearty order to "burn the bun."

Anyone lucky enough to have ordered a hamburger back in those days had no need of potato chips, french fries — or even a portion of cole slaw to fill out the meal.

Back then you didn't have to ask for lettuce or mayonnaise. It came with the territory.

You didn't even have to flatten the finished product with the palm of your hand so you could take that first bite without dislocating your jaw.

The cook did it — with a deft swipe of his spatula — for you.

And the hamburger arrived, hot, moist, dripping grease and bulging with the red and white of tomato and onion.

Don't get me wrong.

I take nothing away from today's hamburgers. I still eat them. I still enjoy them.

But not like I used to enjoy watching steam locomotives.

I suppose that's why I still keep looking for someplace where I can eat a hamburger after having watched it and smelled it — being cooked on a grill by a guy in a sweaty T-shirt who doesn't have to ask me what I want on it, how I like it cooked — or whether I want it on wheels.

And if you remember what that expression means, you remember the same kind of hamburgers I do.

Just for the record he's tired of records

THANK GOODNESS the World Series is over — and I'm not just saying that because I couldn't stand the suspense.

It's just that I get fed up to here with the "all-time" records and the "first time in history of a seven-game Series" that

165

sportscasters feel compelled to sprinkle their play-by-plays with.

We heard Thursday, for example, that "never before in the history of a seven-game Series" did the team that scored first fail to win.

If, by chance, Boston had gone on to win, we'd have had "the first time in history of a seven-game Series the team that scored first didn't win."

I'm just as fed up with "all-time" records, one of which St. Louis manager Red Schoendienst tied when he used eight pitchers in Wednesday's game.

Two can play at this game, you know — and I'll prove it by saying that Wednesday marked the first time in the long history of the game of baseball that any manager nicknamed "Red" used even one pitcher. In the sixth game of a seven-game Series. Played by a St. Louis team. On a Wednesday. Where the other team was from Boston. Managed by someone with the nickname "Dick."

This record-setting business gets even more ridiculous.

"This is the first time in World Series history a left-handed batter ever popped up to a right-handed centerfielder after hitting an outside curve thrown by a left-handed pitcher. In the third inning of the second game."

I forget who that last quote came from — but you can bet your bottom-dollar (and tie an all-time record of bottom-dollar betting) that some announcer said it somewhere, sometime.

If historic firsts and all-time records have to be reported, I say report them — but keep them interesting.

For example:

"For the first time in World Series history, opposing teams are made up entirely of men who wear glasses.

"The game today set an all-time record as the first World Series game that was ever called due to a total eclipse of the sun."

"Never before in history of the Series has a home plate umpire had the initials R.B.I. and the first base umpire the initials E.R.A."

I realize there's little use trying to break people of the habit of finding a world's record for doing (or not doing) something in a World's Series — no matter what happens. Or doesn't.

But I'm waiting for the day, duckies.

And it'll be here when we hear an announcer, his voice trembling with emotion, tell us:

"This fans, is the first time in World Series history that a World Series ever broke all existing records for firsts in World's Series history."

Eternal city
is dream come true

WHILE I'D BE HESITANT to stake my last dollar on it I'd still be willing — for a reasonable amount at reasonable odds — to bet that no prospective visitor to Rome spent as much time reading up on the city, past and present, as did I.

And precious little of my information came from either a guidebook — or travel articles on what to do and what to see there.

Rome, for me, was a dream that began long ago in a little Ohio town even before I started the first grade.

I learned to read from an old history text called "Goldsmith's Ancient Rome."

I pored over the engravings of the Appian Way, Hadrian's Tomb, the Colosseum, the Forum — and tried as best as a five-year old could to piece together shattered marble, tumbled arches and crumbling walls into what writers then, as now call, "the glory that was Rome."

I could tell the Arch of Septimus Severus from that of Constantine, the temple of Saturn from that of the Castors — and I knew the names of the seven hills of Rome long before I learned the names of the Seven Dwarfs.

My favorite of them all, however, was the Arch of Titus. Why, I don't know.

Maybe it was because of its simplicity, or its commanding position between the Forum and the Colosseum.

Or maybe it was because my mother once for my birthday gave me a framed picture of the arch which hung on my wall until I was almost through high school.

"Someday, maybe," she said, "you might get to see this. Rome isn't all that far away.

In a way, she was wrong. Rome was — up until last month, anyway — every bit that far away.

But I finally got there.

I walked around renaissance Rome and felt I'd really seen it when I had dinner one night in the Tratorria Polese, a restaurant just outside Vatican City which became a must on my list the moment I heard it was located in what once was a Borgia palace.

I spent three days at St. Peter's, visited all the "major" basilicas (and a couple of minor ones), toured the Catacombs, watched a soccer game in progress in the long grassy quadrangle which was once the Circus Maximus and on my last day there climbed the 357 steps to the cupola of the dome of St. Peter's — after taking an elevator halfway up — and looked out past the Bernini colonade, across the Tiber and saw

Rome, its hills and its monuments, its traffic and its winding streets, its domes, spires, trees and gardens in the afternoon sun that broke infrequently through the clouds.

It has been called the Eternal City so often one would think the term overworked.

That's before you see Rome and feel the past at your elbow.

You have to walk through grass-grown ruins where once Caesars walked and hear the night wind through the pines on the Palatine Hill over the sound of traffic in the distant Via del Fori Romani where it intersects the Via Cavour for only then can you have the sense of the eternal that is Rome.

For all its naked brick and stained granite, tan and brown in the sun — and for all its popularity as a tourist attraction — the Colossium still smells of death.

For all their marble, gold, bronze and for all their art and sculpture the basilicas of Rome still stand foremost as monuments to faith.

How long, a recent Pope was asked, does it take to know Rome?

"Two days, good" he said. "Two weeks, better. Two years — not long enough."

I'll go back one day to Rome. I know I will because that's why I threw the coin in the Trevi Fountain.

And there's much more to be seen — even in the Forum where I spent four hours one afternoon.

But looking back, I guess the high point of the whole trip was when I paused on the Via Sacra, the Forum's "main street" and looked up toward the hill and saw framed in the trees that lined that stone-paved Roman road over which centuries ago triumphal chariots rumbled, a long familiar sight.

And when I finally reached the arch itself, I waited for a moment, looking at the ruins of temples, palaces, ancient shrines, and at the long shadows they cast in the sun before I walked slowly through the Arch of Titus.

The chill that went down my back was, I think, understandable.

A long time ago Rome was only a picture, hanging on the wall of a small boy's room.

As I stood beneath Titus' arch, it became a dream come true.

The best is at
the bottom of the barrel

SOMETIMES I FEEL THE IMP of the perverse is never so strong as he is when, on occasion, I find myself required to perform even the simplest of household tasks.

The mere installation of a new towel rack in a bathroom is enough to send me back to an accredited engineering school.

Long ago, after subjecting myself to one drenching after another, I decided that the replacement of a washer in a leaky faucet was something that called for a master plumber where my well-being — as well as my peace of mind — was concerned.

Which brings me to the latest domestic fiasco in which — if you hadn't already guessed — I played a leading role.

In short, it takes a pretty dumb person to screw up emptying the garbage. But I managed to do it.

We have a new thing about dumping garbage out where I live, which involves my loading the two-day accumulation in the back of my car and making the dump stop on my way to town.

A couple of times, naturally, it slipped my mind.

I ended up with a sack full of garbage in my back seat — but with a wide choice of how and where I could get rid of it.

The Gazette won the first day. Sambo's was a possible second.

And, of course, there was always the Northern.

One morning last week, a Thursday, I noticed the sack in the back of my car.

Obviously, I had forgotten again. Well there was no problem.

But, I thought as I carried the sack to the boxlike metal contrivance a truck picks up and engorges once a week, this day's garbage was heavy.

Very heavy indeed, I decided.

Nonetheless, I walked to the dump, gave the sack the old heave-ho and heard it thud satisfactorily into the mound of garbage already deposited there.

But I kept thinking about the weight as I walked back to my car.

Had I, I wondered, thrown out any cans of outdated food?

Was there in the sack, perchance, a pound or two from the freezer that I'd figured had gone past both its time and its prime?

Had I thrown out any bottles?

Bottles.

It was only then I remembered.

Two days before I'd stopped by the liquor store and walked out with a supply of scotch, rum, wine and brandy, which I stowed in the back seat in approximately the same place I stow my dumpable garbage.

169

This was what I'd given the old heave-ho.

It was only a matter of a moment — well, two seconds, actually — for me to get back to the dump and correct my error.

And let me tell you:

It's dark in there.

And deep.

Besides, there's always the chance of someone seeing you, half in, half out of a garbage container.

In the sort of neighborhood I live in, they'd probably say nothing — but they'd wonder a lot, I'm sure.

Luckily, not a single bottle was broken.

Luckily, I managed to retrieve all four fifths.

And, luckily, no one saw me.

For which, and duly, thanks be.

Can you imagine how embarrassing a thing like that would be if anyone were to find out about it?

Take two ads and call me in the morning

ANYONE WHO CAN REMEMBER "pyttirosporum ovale" can go to the head of the class.

The rest of you dullards can sit there and scratch your heads.

Because that, after all, was what you did — or were supposed to do — once you contracted this dread affliction.

For pyttirosporum etcetera, which doubtless found its origin in the brain of a Madison Avenue idea man, was what back in the dark ages of the ad biz they called whatever it was that was supposed to cause dandruff.

And having dandruff in the era of the Oxford gray jacket or the blue serge suit was the equivalent of being caught at the beach weighing only 97 pounds.

To cure dandruff you bought that special kind of soap.

To deal with the sand-kicking bully at the seashore you mailed the coupon to Charles Atlas.

There was, come to think of it, something eminently comfortable about advertising before ethics reared its ugly head and the industry began policing itself.

When I saw a picture of some guy in a white coat with a mirror strapped to his head I didn't worry about where he went to dental school.

170

He looked like a dentist and when he voiced his warning about pink tooth brush I by heaven paid attention.

(Pink tooth brush, in case you've forgotten, was only one of the host of other ailments, conditions, symptoms and syndromes which once crowded magazine and newspaper pages — like halitosis, stomach gas or lazy bowels, to name only a few.)

Having a pink tooth brush was almost as bad as having dandruff except that it wasn't quite as public.

But one got the impression early on — even without the surgeon-general of the United States getting into the act — they were nothing to fool around with.

Pink tooth brush was frequently a factor in broken engagements, lost jobs and gradual deterioration of the smile of beauty.

Dandruff had been known to send more than one worrier to his best friend seeking a solution to his problem.

Best friends were good things to have around then.

But only if you had pink tooth brush or dandruff.

There were some things about which even best friends wouldn't tell you.

Halitosis, if I remember rightly, was one of them.

But, like I always said:

It's better to have halitosis than no breath at all.

I used to love reading those letters from Mrs. F.D., Lancaster, Pa., who admitted daily in newspapers all over the country that she had been troubled with stomach gas for years and that now, thanks to whatever it was she was taking, her bloated condition was a thing of the past.

But my favorite of the lot was that prize of the laxative ad copy writer's genius which urged a nation to "Pull the trigger on lazy bowels!"

I hate to say it but medicine and dentistry suffered a setback when truth and honesty came into advertising.

Ads don't scare us as much as they used to — but on the other hand we lost a lot of incentive for that quick trip to the corner drugstore in time to cure what might well have resulted in terminal athlete's foot.

Ask not what your keister can do

THE PRESIDENT, I think, did us all a favor a few weeks back when he expressed the way he felt about leaks from White House offices.

And in case we missed it that time, he reminded us again

when he spoke out recently about lobbyists attempting to emasculate a piece of legislation he's sent to the Congress.

I don't know how you all feel about it, of course.

But I both praise and applaud what Ronald Reagan has done for the language.

Because, quite frankly, I've had it up to my keister with time-worn quotations and famous sayings which over the years have lost much of their punch.

I'm not suggesting, mind, that we should start rewriting the history books.

But think of how they might have read had some of our more quotable leaders or men of prominence followed Reagan's example.

"I regret that I have but one keister to lose for my country." — Nathan Hale.

"Damn the keisters, full speed ahead." — Admiral Farragut.

"Ask not what your keister can do for you, ask rather what you can do for your keister." — John F. Kennedy.

"Millions for defense — but not one cent for keisters." — Charles Cotesworth Pinckney.

"The vice presidency isn't worth a bucket of lukewarm keisters." — John Nance Garner.

"There's a keister born every minute." — P.T. Barnum.

"What this country needs is a good five cent keister." — Thomas R. Marshall.

"I have said not once but many times that I have seen keisters and that I hate keisters." — Franklin D. Roosevelt.

"That's one small step for a man, one giant keister for mankind." — Astronaut Neil Armstrong.

"We are not interested in the possibilities of keisters." — Prime Minister Margaret Thatcher, quoting Queen Victoria.

"The Surgeon General has determined that keister smoking is dangerous to your health." — Warning on keister packages.

I suppose by now you've the idea, the potential of which is, of course, boundless.

Let us, then, conclude this exercise with a final expression of hope:

That this nation, under God, shall have a new birth of language and that government of the keisters, by the keisters and for the keisters shall not perish from the press.

Thirty days
hath the groundhog

SINCE CONFESSION IS supposed to be good for the soul, I've got a couple of things I want to get off my chest — such as it is.

I have never believed in Santa Claus.

And for good reason.

Any guy who'd spend Christmas Eve clattering across rooftops waking citizens whose only offense was to envision dancing sugarplums deserves to be complained about, not believed in.

Also on my list of Utterly Impossibles is the Tooth Fairy.

I stopped believing in he, she or it back when I found a dentist who not only didn't believe in the Tooth Fairy but who also was highly skeptical of the anesthetic qualities of novocaine.

It was he who convinced me when I had my first molar pulled that a shot from a bottle had pain-killing (and mind-easing) qualities far and beyond those of a shot from a needle.

When you can trade a tooth for something like that who'd settle for a shiny nickel?

And back in Kansas where I grew up they still sit around at Easter time and recall how I dealt with Peter Cottontail the first time I saw him hopping down the bunny trail.

As a longtime reader I had nothing but respect for Uncle Wiggly — not to mention Nurse Jane Fuzzy Wuzzy.

But rabbits who run about the neighborhood hiding eggs should, I contend, be in a home — or a hutch, if you want to split hairs over it.

I do, however, believe in the Groundhog.

Each year when the second day of February rolls around, you'd find me scanning the headlines for the latest word from Punxsutawney, Pa.

There, by tradition, is the world capital of Groundhogism.

As Punxsutawney goes, someone once said, so goes the nation. (This held true for decades, I'm told, until 1936 when a get-out-the groundhog-vote campaign saw Punxsutawney solid for Alf Landon.)

But though I believe in the Groundhog I have trouble remembering what happens with the shadow.

If he sees it does that mean six more weeks of winter?

Or is spring here?

If he doesn't see it, does that mean spring is here?

Or are we in for more thunderous applause from the ski buffs?

I can remember thirty days hath September and "i" before "e" except after "c."

I can even remember how to tell a stalactite from a stalagmite.

But if there's a Groundhog formula, so far I haven't run across it.

So don't start reminding me that if Candlemas dawns bright and clear there'll be two winters in the year.

How can I be sure that second line doesn't say something like "it means that spring is drawing near"?

But, foggy though I may be about groundhogs and their shadows, I'll still take them over the meteorologists every time.

They may be wrong as often as they're right — but they don't cost the taxpayers a cent.

Earth rejects
Brown Thumb's offerings

I KNOW THIS IS the wrong time of the year to be writing about gardens — but then where gardens are concerned I've always been a day late and a dollar short.

In fact, had it been me in Eden instead of Adam, the Lord wouldn't have to wait around for the funny business with the Tree and the Serpent.

He would have just taken a look at the way things were growing with me in charge and I'd have had my walking papers then.

Let's face it:

I can't grow things.

I can look at the catalogs and explore the seed packets in the store and plant according to directions.

I can weed and water assiduously.

And I can fill my head with all the wisdom found in a summer's worth of garden columns.

But I still end up with something in the backyard that looks like a cross between Death Valley and a jungle scene from "King Kong."

I have considered the possibility of enemy agents, bacteria from outer space or just plain chinch bugs — but it boils down, I'm afraid, to one thing.

By the time I reached the head of the green thumb line they ran out of food coloring.

That's why long ago I gave up trying to grow my own lettuce, cucumbers, radishes, cabbage, squash, beans and spinach — not, let me add, that I care especially about eating the aforementioned viands. They just looked good in the color pictures on the seed packets.

I'm reminded of my many horticultural deficiencies every year at this time since that's when the people who know their way around gardens start unloading their surpluses.

Overnight, boxes (or bags) appear on Gazette desks or bookcases accompanied by "Help Yourself" signs.

174

I do, of course. I help myself to cucumbers, zucchini, tomatoes, squash, bell peppers and an occasional ear of corn.

Once there was even a surplus of green onions.

And the exasperating thing about it, of course, is that all this bounty is regarded by the growers with the same unconcern they'd give the slopover from a hastily filled glass of water.

The zucchini, one will say, "got away from me this year."

Another will have run out of jars before all the tomatoes were canned.

The thing is — these people not only can grow things, they can over-grow things. And they can accept it as calmly as they'd accept the presence of a fly on a screen — outside.

I have never in my life grown a tomato.

The one cucumber that emerged from a former gardening effort of mine looked for all the world like a shriveled cork from a wine bottle.

My radishes could have, save for their color, been mistaken for peas.

And theologians, had there been any around at the time, might have disputed for days over how many angels could dance on the head of one of my cabbages.

Perhaps it's just as well.

The way it is I don't have to worry about planting a garden.

All I worry about is that my friends continue to overplant theirs.

After all, it's pretty hard to beat tomatoes at nothing a pound.

The wheels of progress are turning backward

EVERYONE KNOWS THEY didn't of course — but just suppose stagecoach lines in the old West operated the way some airlines do today.

A typical day in the Popskull, Wyo., office of Southwest Occident Stage Lines might have gone something like this:

"Good morning, sir. May we help you?"

"Gimme a one-way to Deadwood — and hurry it up."

"One-way, Deadwood. Yes, sir — and you had a reservation?"

"Tried all day yesterday but your window was crowded. Figured you'd have room anyway."

"That we do, sir. That we do. We're sorry about the window, though. We've had a request in to the main office to cut us a couple of more windows — or maybe set up a table in front — but that was a year ago. Baggage?"

"Just the shotgun. I'll carry it on. Is the stage on time?"

"We've just gotten a one-day delay — but they should make up some of that. There's some pretty bad Indian activity between here and Twin Snags and the driver thought best to bypass it. Passenger comfort, you know, comes first with us."

The Deadwood passenger remembered the last time he traveled to Twin Snags.

"We lost a horse just out of Pig Buttes," he said. "Had to spend the night there." The stageline, he recalled, bought the first round of beers.

There are, the agent agreed, worse places than Pig Buttes to be stranded overnight.

"But how," the passenger said, "they managed to lose my baggage when I didn't even change stages was beyond me." The agent clucked sympathetically.

"Our man at Pig Buttes can't read, you know. He just matches up the look of the bag with the looks of the passenger — and up until we got to be the biggest stageline in these parts it worked out pretty good."

The Pig Buttes Chamber of Commerce has been after the company to improve its baggage handling by hiring a man who can read, the agent said.

"They don't seem to want to spend the money," he added.

The passenger for Deadwood nodded.

"Seems like if they could put these spring-cushion stages on and add two horses to each run they could provide better service at their stops," he said.

The agent counted out the man's change.

"Now, if you'd like to step across the street to the saloon, we'll call your trip when it's ready."

The passenger turned toward the door just as a rattling, dust-covered coach drawn by lathered horses pulled up in front.

"There you are, sir," the agent said cherrily. "The Deadwood stage."

The traveler looked surprised.

"But you said a one-day delay — " he began.

The agent was patient.

"That," he said, "was on today's trip. This is the trip due in last week."

It was delayed, he said, by a priority wagon train, two hold-ups and severe tumbleweeds. The passenger killed by stage robbers would be marked on Popskull passenger manifest as a "no show," thus opening a seat to Deadwood, the agent explained.

The passenger climbed aboard and waited for the "Fasten Your Gun Belt" sign to go off.

He sometimes wondered if after all, his grandfather had been right.

"If the good Lord had wanted you to ride," the old man would grumble on hearing of his grandson's travels by stage, "he would have given you wheels."

176

Chili wasn't
created for sissies

GAZETTE COPY PAPER, I'll admit, is a poor substitute for a drum head — but if you'll throw another log on the campfire and hand me a quill with a decent point — I'll get on with what I was saying about these being times that try men's souls.

It's time, fellow patriots, we spoke out.

It's time we take up arms, if need be, to preserve a heritage as American as apple pie and, to my mind, twice as filling.

It's time we took chili away from the Betty Crockers and the Prudence Pennys and the Clementine Paddlefords and put it back where it belongs — in a restaurant kitchen in the hands of a man whose sole claim to immortality is making a bowl of chili with no nonsense.

Time was when you could sit down at a counter and order a bowl of chili — and see it put together right in front of you.

The beans were ladled out of one pot, the meat and grease out of another.

You had your choice. Chili or "dry" chili. (When you said "dry" this meant not so much grease.)

You spooned it up, lovingly, watching the beans and chunks of meat swim in reddish-golden grease through the tears that welled in your eyes after the first swallow.

Here, indeed, was a bowl of chili with authority — and I never miss it so much as I do when run afoul of a contemporary substitute whose only resemblance to chili is that you eat it with a spoon.

You can take a can of vegetable soup, sprinkle red pepper in it and come up with what in the minds of some is quite an acceptable chili. (And THEY, incidentally, spell it c-h-i-l-e.)

I know people who use kidney beans in making chili. I know others who put tomatoes and carrots in it. If a Senate subcommittee is prepared to listen, I can testify to having been attacked once by a bowl of chili that contained two peas and a stalk of celery.

And I shall shudder at the memory of one recipe for chili which omitted chili powder altogether. ("Many don't care for the hot seasoning used for chili in some parts of the country," it added.)

If anyone's tampering with the soul of this country, I contend, it's the crowd trying to foist off on us a watered-down, anemic, greaseless, mild and innocuous pot of vegetables that, thanks to the addition of a judicious amount of red food coloring, passes for the Real Thing — until you take the first spoonful.

It's late — but not too late.

Write your congressman. Write the White House. Demand a return to the chili we once knew and enjoyed, remembering the words of that great epicure, Jose Martinez y Roderiguez, who once said, "The only way that poor chili can triumph is for good men to do nothing."

Wake up, America!

Give a man enough rope....

WHEN A FRIEND gives you a cake of soap for a birthday present you can assume any one — or all — of three things:

- Your present soap isn't doing the job the foghorn people claim it should.
- The friend is trying to be original;

Or, there was a cake of soap left over from Christmas — and it saved a trip downtown.

- Injury, minor or otherwise, didn't enter into the picture.

So, at least, I thought before I unwrapped a brithday present a week or so back.

By way of opening argument, ladies and gentlemen of the jury, let me say that in my years in the business I have never had problems in hanging onto — or recovering in a matter of minutes — a cake of soap in either tub or shower.

I have, admittedly, ended up with wet hair when I intended no wet hair.

I have as well spent an additional minute or so scrubbing soap from under my nails from hurried grasping of a soggy, slippery cake.

But I have never felt — nor do I now — the need of any attachments to my personal bar of soap to aid me in recovering it should it pop out, so to speak, of my dripping grasp.

In short, soap on a rope, to my way of thinking, is an idea whose time has not yet come.

Not in my life, anyway.

Nonetheless, that was what I found among my anniversary goodies.

Exactly how, I wondered as I prepared to use it for the first time, does one go about dealing with a cake of soap on a color-matched cord?

I tried the obvious. I hung it around my neck.

As far as I'm concerned, St. Christopher medals work better.

A football-shaped piece of soap around one's neck not only looks silly, it feels downright uncomfortable.

I tried swinging it casually at my side, much in the way you see a woman swinging a purse — or a policeman a nightstick.

That looked worse.

But appearance isn't the only thing working against you when you're trying to deal with that sort of a problem.

Your hands get tangled in the rope — which, by the time you've decided to have a go at it anyway, has become as slippery as the soap itself.

The washcloth gets entangled in it.

And I discovered early in the game that a bar of soap falling freely in a shower is duck soup to losing grip on one on a tether.

The free-falling soap bangs on the bottom of the tub.

You bend over and pick it up.

No problem.

Letting a new bar of soap on a rope pop out of your hand can result in as nasty a bang on the sternum as you've had in months.

It's also physically restraining.

I like being able to take a bar of soap and go anywhere I want with it.

When it hangs around your neck like an albatross, you can't get to a foot or a calf without doing deep knee bends.

And try, just try, I beg you, to work up a good lather on your scalp without getting soapy rope burns on your eyelids.

Mind, I have no complaints about the product — as long as it stays outside the shower.

Soap on a rope smells good.

It cleanses satisfactorily.

And I suppose it lasts as long and is as economical as anything on the market.

But for those of us who bruise easily it's about as practical as a petrified cotton ball.

As elsewhere noted, I hit myself a couple of good ones in the chest that first time.

I got my thumb caught in the cord, causing the bar to strike me smartly on the cheekbone.

Without thinking, I turned quickly under the shower.

The soap swung out on the cord and ended up hanging down my back.

On attempting to retrieve it, I dropped it on my head.

The cord came free.

And there was my so-called "unlosable" soap on the bottom of the tub.

The entire experience was — if you'll allow me the liberty — a cleansing one.

By the time I emerged from the shower I knew what sailors felt like when a cannon broke loose on deck in a storm.

You can't even consider yourself out of danger once the soap is in the dish.

The cord dangles. You get an elbow in the loop.

And the bar crashes down on your foot.

179

The Ancient Mariner, in my book, didn't know when he was well off.

After all, he had only to worry about blood and feathers.

But for every problem, I always say, there's a solution — and it took me about five minutes to reach mine.

I now have as fine an example of cordless soap as you'll find in these parts.

And once I heal up, I'm going to try to find a market for the soapless cord.

If all else fails, I can always use it to strangle the people who put it on bars of soap to begin with.

She boils
an evil brew

U P TO NOW, me and the New York Times have gotten along just peachy.

Having been for years an avid National Review fan, I've been able to take the editorial fulminations (and vacillations) of the Good Gray Lady cum grano salis, as it were.

And not being able to number myself among those elect who count the day lost when it doesn't begin with reading the funny papers, I've never missed — in fact, I've cheered — the Times for its long-standing no-comics policy.

In short, the Times, in my book, has been a nice, heavy Sunday newspaper.

Up, as I noted earlier, until now.

But — and I mince no words — the line has to be drawn when the Times, in the person of one Jane Brody, takes out after coffee.

In fact, I found myself sufficiently incensed at Missus Brody's diatribe against the heavenly brew which appeared in The Gazette a week ago that I had to stop reading in the middle to get up and make another pot in order to finish it with an acceptable degree of aplomb.

I can understand Missus Brody not caring for coffee on the grounds (oops, sorry) that she doesn't like the taste, that it keeps her awake — or that possibly she's a Mormon. All these are reasons both cogent and valid.

But I resent bitterly (sorry again) her carrying on as though one of the greatest pick-me-ups in the history of civilization were only slightly less lethal than opium, heroin or even hemlock.

She writes, for example, of coffee as a mood-altering drug, an artificial mental and physical stimulant and calls upon her lexicon of scare-words to gain the attention of those "plagued by a host of withdrawal symptoms that are quickly relieved by a dose of caffeine."

Heavens to Elizabeth, if you listened to her long enough you'd think coffee was something you smoked in a pipe while lolling on a bunk in a Limehouse opium den or injected in your arm with a needle.

Missus Brody should be ashamed — especially considering the way she earns her living.

Ask anyone who works — or who has worked — on a newspaper.

Many a copy boy has risen to publisher on intelligence, initiative, energy AND coffee.

And what of the armies of this world who travel on their stomachs?

You can bet any mess hall would shut down in a matter of hours were the anti-coffee lobbyists to have their way with the Quartermaster Corps.

Not to mention what would happen on a ship of the line were the captain to discover that he has sailed without sufficient coffee to get him through an engagement.

Madame Brody, obviously reveling in recounting the litany of the physical and mental discomforts which she believes stem entirely from a morning cup of the healing, lists such symptoms as sleep disturbances, headache, irritability and stomach pains. Among others.

All I can say in reply is that reading Brody on Coffee is enough to keep me awake, make me irritable, give me a headache and a pain as well — but not in the stomach.

It also, in case you're wondering, makes me want to pour myself another cup.

But I think the climax was capped when, after her recital of a long list of "withdrawal symptoms," Missus Brody told of how she went about weaning her moody, irritable, anxiety-ridden and depressed husband from The Awful Coffee Habit.

She tampered with the family coffee pot, mixing in more and more decaffeinated coffee until she cut his daily dose to one-third.

"After a few weeks," she wrote, "his episodes of irritability, anxiety and depression had all but disappeared."

All I can say is that had I been married to the New York Time's Jane E. Brody, so, at about that stage of the game, would I.

It's bad enough we have people in the world who don't like coffee, period.

We don't need a bunch of Lucretia Borgias running around dropping decaffeinated coffee in our morning cup and expecting to get off scot-free with it.

So for the time being at least, the Times and I part company.

As far, that is, as Brody is concerned.

And one final liberty — for which I apologize in advance:

Jane, baby — You don't know beans about coffee.

Tom Swift
changes with time

ANY BOY OF a generation ago who unwrapped a Christmas present and found himself with a book could give odds that it would have a tan cover.

Right smack in the center would be a sketch of a grim youth dressed in a pinstripe suit and wearing a snapbrim hat, pulled rakishly down over one eye.

Surrounding the portrait were sketches of a variety of machines and contraptions that flew, crawled, exploded, sailed or performed other useful — and exciting — tasks.

The reader who could identify them all as electric runabouts, motorcyles, flying machines, giant telescopes, racing cars or airships could establish his bona fides in any crowd of his contemporaries.

He was a Tom Swift fan.

Tom Swift books — written by a man with the unlikely name of Victor Appleton — were practically staples with what today has become the Cub Scout and Little League set.

Young Swift, according to the libretto, was the son of an inventor who, besides providing his off-spring with complete laboratory and plant facilities in a place — appropriately enough — Shopton, had the foresight to bring him up in a community that provided all the necessary characters for an adventure series.

There was, of course, a close friend and companion named Ned Newton who managed to accompany Tom where ever his inventions took him.

And there was, most certainly, a villain — a red-headed bully named Andy Foger who, when not busy cleaning his zip gun or putting a high shine on his leather jacket, occupied himself by harassing the boy inventor.

And who can forget pretty Mary Nestor, Tom's girl friend whose father owned the bank?

For comic relief you could always depend on a bustling eccentric named Mr. Damon who was constantly blessing things. "Bless my ailerons," he says in a book about a "flying machine." "Bless my diving plans," would be his reaction to a submarine cruise. Or, in a suspenseful story of a balloon trip, dependable Damon could always be counted on to exclaim at least once, "Bless my gas bag."

I don't suppose for a moment I'd have thought of Tom and his friends — as Appleton used to put it — if I hadn't been passing a downtown bookstore and noticed two Tom Swift books in the window.

But, alas, this is not our Tom Swift — not the one we knew. He's Tom, Junior, son of the son of Shopton's aged inventor. (Whose mother, we hope, is the Mary Nestor we used to know.)

But try as I might, I couldn't find any mention of Ned Newton, Andy Foger or Mr. Damon — no matter how hard I looked. (Bless my eyeglasses!)

Even the titles are strange.

"Tom Swift and His Atomic Blaster," "Tom Swift and His Outpost in Space," "Tom Swift and the Caves of Nuclear Fire" — (Remember "Tom Swift and the Caves of Ice"?) — and "Tom Swift and the Cosmic Astronauts."

Don't get me wrong — I'm still as much of a Tom Swift fan as I ever was but I can't help feeling that if they're going to modernize Tom, who else is safe?

Every dog
has his day

DEAR AL:

Well I suppose youre wondering how the old gang is so I thot Id drop a line & at least tell about how things are going here which as you may guess are not too good. I could of told you when this bisness started what would happen but you know how it is Al no one ever asks a dog his opinion & about the best any dum beast can expect is a pat or 2 on the head and if hes lucky maybe peace of lunch meat that was gonna be tost out anyways.

As I was saying you could see the handwriting on the fents a coupla weeks ago when the councel put this quarentine across & I think I could take it maybe if it wernt for the jokes you hafta put up with. Like what happened the 1st day I mean Al.

I am minding my bisness and not hurting a fly let alone tearing up any ladies rose bush & here comes the Man out the door with a strap. You cant blame me Al I thot acourse something was spilled & here I was stuck with the blame for it & then he showed a lotta teeth in what they call a smile & said thisll give you a new leesh on life. Instead of letting me have it across the hunches Al he snaped it on my coler & hookt the other end to the clothsline & here I am yet but as I said its not so much the boredom as some of the ½-baked jokes you listen to.

Theres this fella lives acrost the alley Al who thinks hes a rel comick & ever oncet in awhile hell stick his hed over the fents & say every dog has his day but it looks like you got 30 ha ha ha. Its enuff to make a fella sick. At his stummick if you know what I mean.

I don't say anything Al because dogs arent sposed to talk let alone write but no ordnanse was past to keep us from thinken which is exackly what Im doing along the lines of giving him the old 1-2 to the ankel with maybe a lightening slash in the trowsers. Just to show him an old dog may not lern new tricks but he dont forget the old ones as you will no dout agree.

When you come right down to it Al I guess even the joking is bare-able but Im fed up up to here with the attetude of this holier & thou cat who for the last 3 or 4 days has been walking around like she is the Dog Worden his self looking down her nose at me & smurking you know the type Al. It uset to be practicly like pulling teeth to get her outa the house but now shes gone ½ the day & comes back sneering & licking her pause & it would not surprise me 1 bit to lern after this is over in 2 weeks that she is pretty adepped at tearing up a rosebush or 2 herself if you dont mind me descending to the level of making a catty remark.

Well I guess Ill close now but remember Al when we get through this we should get our heds together & do something about the counsel either lobbing for more rits for dogs or else fixing it sos these cats are in the doghouse with us for 30 days in other words whats soss for goose is soss for the gander.

Hoping you are the same,
Ed.

When a machine answers, hang on

I SHOULD, I SUPPOSE, have known better.

I was warned.

But I went ahead anyway.

I bought a machine to answer my telephone.

From there, as the saying goes, things all went downhill.

I've gotten a few calls, admittedly, that I would have hated to miss.

None, of course, came from the White House, the Joint Chiefs of Staff or David Rockefeller.

But I can tell you there were four lunches, one dinner, two cocktail hours and an opportunity to buy a box of Girl Scout cookies which would have gone down the tube had it not been for this miracle of the telecommunications age.

Let us, however, look at the other side of the coin.

"You get one of those things," a travel agent of my acquaintance told me, glowering, "and I'll sure as hell leave you a message."

She did. Though the people who sold me the machine were painstaking in pointing out all the things I could do with it, they never mentioned putting it to the use my friend suggested.

I have another friend. He's from Texas and he's in the oil business.

For the many years I've known him I have never known him to growl at anyone.

He growled at me when I told him, "If I'm not home, leave a message."

Cleaning the Texas out of his language, it boiled down to something like this:

"I hate them damn things."

Since then I've come to know what to do if I come back, play the tape and find a series of barks and growls on it.

Telephone answering tapes have their amusing aspects, however.

One came the other day when, after hearing the tone signal, I waited for the message.

There was a moment of silence, then slowly, wonderingly:

"You ... mean ... this ... is ... being ... recorded?"

There was a click as the caller hung up.

One of my favorites is the woman who talks to the machine, not me.

After listening to my cheery, apologetic and polite (I hope) message about not being able to get to the phone and the invitation to tape a message, she obliged as follows:

"Listen. Tell him when he gets home to call me. And I don't have to leave my number. He knows it. OK?"

Maybe the quality of the tape had something to do with it — or possibly it was the way I sounded.

Whatever the reason, not long ago I was treated to a full 30 seconds of giggles.

I'm still wondering what I missed out on there.

My sister, Judith, didn't know about my electronic secretary — but she was equal to the occasion.

Knowing her, she probably figured as long as we were being impersonal she'd go along with the idea:

From her taping I got Iola's time, temperature, her weight, blood pressure — and the latest report on her blood sugar.

"Why," a colleague in the news business asked me just yesterday, "can't you stay home and answer your phone like other people?"

He didn't add "God knows, we see enough of you around here" — but I knew what he was thinking.

And all I thought I was doing when I bought the thing was making things less complicated. I have since found, however, that answering machines can sometimes turn on you.

My son pointed this out early on when he called from Oregon and said he'd tried to reach me without success since my line was busy.

I told him I just bought an answering machine and, new at the business as I was, I had possibly gotten it hooked up wrong and that caused the busy signal.

He was silent for a moment, then:

"Or maybe," he said, "your answering machine was talking to another answering machine."

I think he had a point there.

When in doubt
just ask the editor

ONE OF THE FIRST things you learn when you go to work on a newspaper — besides "i" before "e" except after "c" — is that you follow the newspaper's style.

It isn't, however, all that easy.

Newspaper style, like love, is a many splendored thing.

And it's also, like love, as difficult to find as it is to define.

The first source you go to, of course, is the newspaper's style book.

This tells you, in effect, to forget everything you learned in journalism school or at your mother's knee (if an editor hasn't gotten around to telling you that already) about spelling, capitalization and punctuation.

After pages of examples involving names, titles, numbers, scientific and technical terms, slang and that sort of thing, the style book comes up with the Catch 22 of practically every city room in the country.

"When in doubt," the newly-arrived reporter is told, "consult the city desk."

It figures.

No matter how much time, research, thought and effort went into the making up of the style book, the newspaper's style still is nothing more or less than what an editor says it is.

During my years on the Gazette I went through three or four style books.

The first — and as far as I'm concerned, the most sensible — was a shirt-pocket size pamphlet of 30 or so pages which, citing Webster as the ultimate authority, advised midwestern transplants accustomed to writing stories about cars leaving highways and ending up in ditches that a ditch in this country was something that carried irrigation water.

A car leaving the road in Montana had no place to end up in but a borrow pit, not — the style book meticulously pointed out — a barrow pit.

People who died were buried, not interred, regardless of what the funeral home called it. Too often it happened that a printing error made it "interned" which, of course, carried the implication that there was a possibility of getting out.

The Gazette also aligned itself opposite the greatest legal minds in the county who kept insisting that, while not guilty pleas were common in courtrooms, there was no legal precedent for anyone pleading "innocent."

Drop one word from a "not guilty" plea, Gazette stylists pointed out, and you not only had an inaccurate story but a good chance of winding up in a libel suit.

The Gazette began as a "down style" paper, an expression meaning that a capital letter was never used when a lower case letter served the purpose just as well.

Accordingly, we wrote, "God" and "Cornelius F. Kelley" (when he was chairman of the board of the Anaconda Company) — and saved our few remaining capitals for such things as the name of the publisher, United States senators — and the cola beverage with which things go better.

As years went by the Gazette pamphlet was replaced with first the Associated Press style book and — not too long ago — a second Gazette style book which, in addition to weighing a pound or more, was put together in loose leaf format which facilitated corrections, revisions or additions on almost a daily basis.

The worst thing about it was that it was more difficult to misplace (or lose) that the first one I worked with, and the best thing about it was that the One Inviolate Rule of all newspaper style books still prevailed:

Newspaper style — including here at the Gazette — is still what an editor says it is.

And if you don't like it, do what we reporters have been doing in this business for as long as I can remember:

Hand your copy to an editor who agrees with you that the proper way to abbreviate "Monsignor" is "Mnsgr." — not "Msgr.".

Eloquence abounds in a floral corsage

THE PEOPLE IN the floral business who suggest from time to time that I say it with flowers are wasting their time if they think for one minute they'll get any argument from me.

I've been saying it — whatever in the world "it" means — with flowers for years.

But more often than not my symbolic voice is either muffled, incoherent — or I come off with a bad case of floral laryngitis.

That's why I leave it up to the people who know.

Ever the traditionalist, however, I bow to custom and go as much whole hog as mood and money dictate, particularly when it comes to corsages.

I never think of sending flowers for funerals, illnesses, birthdays or grand openings — but give me an evening for two on the town that includes dinner, dancing and something a bit more formal than faded Levi's and a sweatshirt, and you'll see me scurrying off to the nearest flower shop looking for all the world like the White Rabbit trying to make points with the Duchess.

Having learned very early in life that a corsage wasn't something like a corset — even though the two words sounded dangerously similar in grade school — I heeded the advice of my elders when, through some streak of luck, the very first girl I asked agreed to go to the Junior Prom with me.

"You must buy her a corsage," my mother said, proceeding to tell me one didn't simply order flowers for such an occasion the way one ordered a ton of coal or a cord of wood. "Find out what flowers she likes, what color her gown will be, and would she prefer a hair, wrist or shoulder corsage."

My mind boggled. After all, if a girl sent a guy flowers it would, to begin with, be only one and there'd be only one place it could be worn — unless, of of course, he wanted to spend the evening looking like some sort of weirdo.

But I listened dutifully and followed instructions. I don't remember much about the evening, but my corsage — or hers, rather — was a whale of a success.

It was the only orchid at the prom.

Since then I've bought gardenias (which turn brown), sweet peas (which are about as easy to come by as ambergris), roses, carnations and goodness knows what else.

The people who got them wore them on their shoulders, their wrists, their heads and other places where skin didn't show. I remember one girl who pinned hers to her purse, which seemed kind of dumb to me until I realized I was one of the few guys at the party who didn't have to keep an eye on his date's purse while she danced.

As I say, I've had no trouble with my corsages — as long as I leave it up to the flower people. I give them a dress color, a flower preference, the place where she's going to pin it — and believe me, SHE pins it. I've had this nightmare for years that I'll either draw blood or else drop a pin where it'll take a trip to another room to retrieve.

I also give my florist an ideal of proportion, corsage to wearer. You don't want a corsage that shows up on the girl who's wearing it like a saddle on a Pekingese. On the other hand, when you've drawn a battleship in the social whirl you do your best to see there's enough greenery to make the launching as esthetic a success as possible.

In short, when I say it with flowers only my lips are moving.

The voice belongs to people who know a lot more about the business than I do.

Everything you need to know about editors

I SEE WHERE MY old friend Larry Siegel has ascended to the hierarchy of this business by becoming publisher of a newspaper in Ottumway, Iowa — or is it Ottumwa, Ioway? — and is looking for an editor.

I can hardly wait for him to get my letter of application.

In fact, since I am by nature — and have been for a long time by inclination — a lousy correspondent I'm not even writing Larry a letter.

I'll just clip this once it's printed, stick it in the mail and see what happens.

I may not get the job — but that's okay.

It won't be the first time that experience, competence, originality, talent and sheer personality have gone begging.

To begin — are you listening, Larry? — I know all about being an editor since I've been a reporter long enough to have seen editors come and go. For that matter, I've seen reporters come and go, too, but then again that's their job.

Reporters come and go. Editors sit at their desks and wonder where reporters went and when they'll be back. This is called supervision.

As an editor I'd be a good supervisor because as a reporter I learned all the places where reporters went — and knew how they acted on coming back to make an editor think they hadn't been there at all.

We had a reporter once on The Gazette who never let a Friday night go by without celebrating the admittance of Alaska to the union or the tricentennial of the execution of Charles I. This, of course, resulted at times in a rather foggy Saturday morning. But he was equal to the occasion.

He'd arrive on time, uncover his typewriter, drink coffee and leave the city room, headed for Smith's Funeral Home where there was once located (in the back office) a large, comfortable leather couch.

After about two hours sleep he came back. The reporter — who later became a radio newsman — called this "checking sources." The editor believed him, of course, since the idea had never occurred to the editor that sources could be checked by catching 40 winks in a funeral home.

Editors not only have to deal with reporters, they deal with the public (or reader) as well. And I know something about readers.

Editors must bear in mind always that most people don't read stories in the paper. They read headlines. And if the headline doesn't say what they think it should say, they're convinced the story never appeared in the paper. (Taking this entirely understandable vagary one step further, if the story doesn't appear on the front page — where they think it should have appeared — they're equally certain that it wasn't printed at all.)

In such situations editors must be patient, understanding and, above all, diplomatic.

I've watched this happen so often I'm able to exercise the patience of Job, the understanding surpassed only by a certain peace — and the diplomacy of an undertaker looking sad at a $5,000 funeral.

Finally — are you still there, Larry? — I can act like an editor.

I can yell loud enough to be heard across a busy city room — and now that we have computer terminals instead of typewriters this is easier than it used to be. I can swear at reporters for not putting quotation marks OUTSIDE punctuation marks (or is it the other way around?) and long ago I learned that when you're dying for a decent picture to fill out a page all you have to do is to find someone who grew a squash that looks like a turtle — or heard of a turtle that looks like a squash. Which, come to think of it, can happen if a luckless turtle tries to cross a busy highway.

But I guess the main reason I'm writing, Larry, is to say that I'd enjoy working for you (I think) since you got to be a publisher without ever being an editor and are therefore not experienced in finding an editor who comes and goes and you're sitting there wondering where he's gone and when he's coming back.

After all, old buddy, us editors have our tricks of the trade, too.

And if you think I'm going to let you in on any of them, guess again.

We learned them a long time ago — back in those days when we were reporters.

Isn't it about time for another centennial?

HERE AT THE GAZETTE — in case word hasn't leaked out yet — we've been working on a centennial editon.

Files have been gone through, scrapbooks borrowed, senior citizens interviewed, libraries prowled and reference works consulted.

And it's all occasioned by the fact that exactly one century ago —
give or take a few months — Billings became a town.

This isn't the first newspaper centennial edition I've been involved
in.

Twenty or so years back we did a bunch of special sections and
called it our "Parade of Progress" edition.

We also published some special thing (but I forget what) in 1964
when Montana had its centennial celebration.

Also, when I was working on the Wichita (Kan.) Eagle, we did something similar designed to convince readers that, second only to Rome,
Wichita was the center of trade, culture, industry, science, sports — and
had the best wheat in the world.

People love centennial editions. They buy extra copies to send to
friends and relatives. They stow them away like stamps and coins, certain that in years to come they'll increase in value.

And any centennial edition, whether published in Billings or Wichita,
is good to have around in settling bets.

However — if you hadn't noticed — I've spoken only of those who
buy and read the edition in question.

Reporters and editors look at it from another angle.

Bear in mind, for example, that centennial stories are written by reporters in addition to their daily stint of covering the news — and sometimes it isn't all that convenient. One deadline a day sometimes is
enough. With a centennial edition in the offing a city hall or courthouse
reporter can end up with two or three deadlines.

The cross borne by the centennial edition editor can be even more
heavy.

What, specifically, should be chronicled for those past 100 years?
What should be left out?

No matter how objective the editor, things are going to be left out.

Other things are going to get in.

And people, organizations, activities — and history buffs — are
going to be unhappy.

On the other hand, there'll be happy people, organizations, activities
and history buffs which — as long as a newspaper is in the centennial
business — makes all the time and work worth while.

Herewith, then, is my all-encompassing thumbnail Centennial
Edition for Billings which has (I think) three things going for it:

It's easy to read and remember;

It costs only a fraction to print and mail;

And it's comprehensive enough that no critic, however biased, can
complain of sins of either omission or commission.

HISTORY — Billings was founded in 1882. A lot of people have come
to live here. Most of them are still around. Its chance of becoming a
ghost town (however attractive the tourist potential) are nil.

TRANSPORTATION — Trains replaced stage coaches. Diesel

trucks replaced freighters. Buses, airplanes and automobiles replaced buggies. Joggers proliferated.

CULTURE — The city's first painting to be viewed by hundreds, even thousands, came unfortunately before art preservation became popular. That's why only those who know where to look today can make out the paint on the east Rims which spells out "Yegen Bros."

INDUSTRY — Billings has a water plant and a steam plant. Now that we're celebrating our 100th birthday there's some talk about greenhouses here running specials on century plants.

INDIANS — Things are looking better for the Indians in the area. Thanks to Earl Rosell — and the railroads — there are more buffalo around here now than there are passenger trains.

AGRICULTURE — Progress has made things less difficult for the Billings-area farmer. It is, for example, much easier to go broke on a farm today than it was a century ago.

EDUCATION — There was a time when at least one teacher in Billings lived on a diet of chalk. She turned out a lot of good kids who grew up to be bankers, editors, lawyers, doctors, insurance salesmen and preachers who still remember her and who wonder if maybe some school district budgets shouldn't have included more money for chalk.

RECREATION — In the beginning there was the Lucky Diamond. We now have baseball, football, rodeo, golf, hockey, basketball, soccer, horseshoe pitching, skeet shooting, square dancing and dining out in a place called the Lucky Diamond. To get into the true spirit of the centennial, look down from the new Diamond across the tracks where the Montana Power substation is and you'll be looking at where the old Diamond used to be. (Nostalgic sighs are permitted.)

I think you get the idea.

There are, admittedly, omissions — but consider.

We've another special edition due out in another 100 years.

Why put everything in this one?

'Aircraft carrier' desk grounds old pilots

WE HAVE A NEW desk in the Gazette newsroom.

They've already started calling it "the aircraft carrier" and once you see it it's easy to understand why.

It's a gem of design, a proud example of the cabinet maker's trade and, I'm sure, is without peer in functionalism.

It's also a monster.

Unlike, however, other city room monsters that I've dealt with in my years in the business, it'll take some time getting used to — even for the guys who work at it, let alone having to wander in, out and around it in getting from one place in the room to another.

I prefer (in case you hadn't guessed) the monsters of yesterday.

They were recognizable as desks by their general shape, the fact that they included three drawers and a typewriter well and that, during working hours, there was at least one pair of feet up on top.

Newsroom desks, whether they belonged to reporters or editors, were well scarred. They were burned by cigarettes and cigars. Still - distinguishable rings and smears on working surfaces marked where coffee cups sat or drinks were spilled.

They could also be lethal. I remember one city editor's desk with a spring-operated typewriter table that popped out and up, invariably getting a reporter on the knee when he opened it. (And what OSHA would have said about that!)

We not only sat on desks at the Eagle in Wichita where there was a constant shortage of chairs, we walked on them. A reporter leap-frog-ging typewriters and broad-jumping aisles between desks scarcely lifted editorial eyebrows at the Eagle — as long as the phones were answered by the second ring. It may have seemed unconventional — but it was quick. Besides, aisles were more often than not crowded with reporters sitting on wastebaskets while the city room visitors occupied the only available chairs.

I don't know what happened to those dingy old desks, including the one I shared with two other reporters. (We were assigned one drawer each.) But I miss them — even the ones from the old Gazette.

Newsroom desks, as I say, have changed.

But, on the other hand, so have newspapers.

And his make-up
wasn't too hot either

AFTER HEARING THE State of the Union address night before last, I was treated — as were all of us who watched and listened after the President had finished — to the sight and sound of White House newsmen telling us what the President meant by what he said or did not say.

As one who has seldom had to ask for consecutive translation where the English language is concerned, I don't mind saying that I can do without the rehash which inevitably accompanies such presidential appearances.

And I think a lot of us could.

After all, we do understand the language; so why, then, is it necessary, once we've heard from the man himself, to be told what he said, what he meant by saying it — and how much more significant (or insignificant) the speech was by reason of what he did not say?

I can't help but imagine what might have happened to Lincoln' Gettysburg Address had there been back then a trio of Washington experts who accompanied the president to the ceremony who, when it was over, delivered themselves — to a breathless audience — of their version of the famous speech.

It might have gone like this:

"Well, Sam, let's start with you. You've been traveling with this man since Springfield. How do you think the President came over in this latest speech?"

"Hard to tell, Harry, as short as it was. He was obviously unprepared — or stalling for time — as you could tell by his saying 'four-score and seven years ago' when it would have been much simpler to say '87 years.' There were reports on the train coming up here that he wrote it on the way on the back of an envelope and there's actually a lot about his talk that leads me to believe it. It's just another case, I'd say, of this man's procrastination. In other words, he put off writing this speech until the last minute the same way he put off issuing the Emancipation Proclamation until the war being fought to free the slaves was two years old."

"You mean he had no other choice?"

"Exactly."

"Excuse me, Harry and Tom — but while you were talking a thought occurred to me and that is — did the President really address himself to the issue at hand which was the dedication of a cemetery? Remember, that's what he came up here — at government expense — to do. It seemed to me that he sidestepped the issue by saying that was what he was here for, then later saying 'in a larger sense, we cannot dedicate ...'"

"You're quite right, George — and thanks for calling that to our attention. The key phrase, of course, was buried in presidential rhetoric. First he said 'we have come to dedicate' then a few words later said 'we cannot dedicate.' This is a good example of White House equivocation as I've seen. The point is well taken, George, and thank you."

"Could I say something here, Tom? After all, Edward Everett, who, you must remember, is a former president of Howard University, a secretary of state and senator from Massachusetts, spent two hours giving the audience a complete history of the battle here, a battle which the President seemed to mention only in passing. It makes one wonder — at least I wonder — whether the President thought by ignoring it, he could take the country's mind off the fact that we are, indeed, still at war."

"Yes, Sam I think you've hit on an important aspect of what this

194

President meant by, in this case, what he did not say. In other words, he skirted — or completely avoided — any reference to the war, how it's going or whether we are winning or losing it, a fact which the people have a right to know. Of course, with an election coming up in two years, it's understandable, I suppose, why he chose not to say anything about it."

"If I, George and Sam, could interject at this moment, do you recall the remark he made along toward the end of what, I think we all agree, is one of this President's less inspiring speeches, particularly where the Congress was concerned. He mentioned 'people' three times — but not once did he refer to the legislative branch of government. Are we to infer from this that he is moving toward a position from which he will ignore the Congress altogether in taking such issues as he may be able to dredge up directly to the voters? No president that I can recall has ever made such an appeal, not once, but three times in a single speech. We may be seeing a dangerous precedent set here, gentlemen, and one that I don't think will set well with either the House or the Senate."

"An excellent point, Harry. Now, returning once more to the brevity of this speech. I think everyone noticed that the single photographer didn't even have time while the President was on the platform to set up his camera. Was this an intentional slight to the press? Or was it, some of his friends would have us believe, entirely accidental? In other words, did the President really want news coverage — or did he deliberately cut his remarks short so that the people of this country wouldn't see him speaking at a solemn occasion like this without removing his stovepipe hat?"

"Thank you, Gentlemen. I think, in summing things up, that the essence — if one can be distilled from this speech — is that we have a President who obviously came here unprepared; who chose to speak only briefly despite the many people who came here to see and hear him; who contradicted himself at least once; who played politics by first ignoring the war and then by going over the heads of the Congress to the people and who finally was either less than cooperative with the press or downright secretive with the American people.

"On one point, however, I think we are all in agreement with the President. The world will little note, nor long remember, what he said. It was, unfortunately, that kind of a speech.

"Thank you, gentlemen, and good afternoon."

Forgive him Damon,
he's only kidding

I T IS EIGHT BELLS of a Thursday morning when The Driver, stick man for the guys and dolls who write stories and one thing and another for the paper, calls my name and says to me like this:

"It is a year and maybe more since you go to the Midland Empire affair and report on the citizens who come from around and about to drop a few potatoes on the horses."

Besides, he says, he gets a headache from watching me sit around with my nose in a Damon Runyon paperback. "It is a pleasant thought," he says, "to imagine you in the cattle barns and sitting out a few seidels of root beer with the 4-Hs and the FFAs who are making their first scratch in the cow business."

I do not throw my hat in the air, mainly because it is like killing time at a movie you've seen eight or ten times before for me to go to this Midland Empire affair. I write about it two or maybe three times and then it comes very easy indeed.

Also I do not like to go because I meet this same horse each year and though he changes his name each time I always recognize him because he does not make it to the post without developing a severe case of sore feet. However, I do not remember this from year to year and it is more or less common knowledge among one and all that I drop more sugar on this one hide than a kid does in a bowl of breakfast food.

As I know from past performance, Halleluja Harry, who stages this Midland Empire affair for many years, waits for me in his office and gives me a large hello before saying as follows:

"I do not see you here before," he says, "and I wonder if you are mad or perhaps you go to some other affair than the one I run which is the best in the state as you will no doubt agree."

I tell him I am busy writing and trying to make a score now and then and what with one thing and another I do not get to his affair before this because I do not have the scratch to make a trip to a two-dollar window worthwhile.

"I see a schoolteacher and a banker and stenographer I know at these windows," I say, "but I feel a guy is loved more by these parties when he puts on few potatoes on a hayburner he likes in the fourth than if he merely walks up and says hello and then walks away." It is also more discomfiting than somewhat to the citizens who stand in line behind him and hear this conversation, I add.

I wait for Halleluja Harry to offer me a note to see me through the afternoon but he does not hear me because he is busy getting mail for an elderly carnival doll who comes in and she is the only one who walks out with a note.

I walk through the cattle barns as The Driver tells me, watching my step as I do not like to trip over ropes or hay or whatever else lies around and about on the floor, and then I head for the action.

I am no sooner through the gate when I see One-shot Leo, a party who I know off and on for maybe eight or ten Midland Empire affairs, who tells me he had a a walkaway quinella in the fifth and do I want in. I thank him for the tip but I do not take a piece of Leo's action as I am already in on a sure thing which a high shot gives me in return for a cigar which I get from a friend whose ever loving wife has a baby at post time for the third Monday.

I do not see my horse finish because I am not anxious to hang around the track that long but this is not the worst. On the way out I see One-shot Leo who waves his quinella ticket at me and yells and though I do not hear what he yells I do not recall seeing a loser carry on in such a manner at the Midland Empire or any other affair.,

When I am back in the office The Driver looks at me and says like this:

"I do not see you this sad when you leave the office. Can it be that you drop a few bobs on the ponies while you are there?" I do not see the percentage in arguing the point and I tell the whole story except to say that I do not drop anything but shoeshine money.

The Driver does not agree, saying that a couple of bucks is considered a sizeable amount of scratch to pay for a shoeshine even by large operators.

The reason he thinks this way is because The Driver never buys a shoeshine after spending an afternoon at the Midland Empire affair. You do not win them all and I know by experience you do not miss them all.

The hound
of the Baskervilles

THERE IS, I SUBMIT, nothing quite so unnerving on a stormy Sunday night when you're trying to get in a little TV time than to look away from the tube and see a towering black Doberman regarding you silently from a dark corner of the room.

It is doubly unnerving when you don't own a Doberman.

There was, of course, no mystery about how he got there.

I'm in the habit of leaving one or both doors of the apartment open on occasion and as has often been the case, a friendly Dachshund named

Gretchen, a white poodle named Brandy and a yellow cat (who thus far has stubbornly refused to present any identification whatever) have wandered in, sniffed about and padded on their way.

I have no objections, understand, to having my digs serve as a wayside chapel for assorted dumb chums who feel the need of meditation and companionship. I've even offered them a seat on the couch, a sip or two of water or a nibble of cat food. (Wandering cats, as you may know, are notorious gnoshers.)

I have, in short, never drawn a line at Dobermans — but only because, never in my more nightmarish moments, did I dream that one would appear.

"Materialize," I think, is more the word I want.

Anyway, there I was, watching a documentary on how one of these days if we're not on our toes, the bugs are going to take over, lock, stock and barrel — when my attention was distracted by a shadowy movement in the corner.

At least when the poet's raven dropped in he had the decency to tap on the chamber door before parking himself atop the pallid bust of Pallas and going into his Nevermore act.

This Doberman didn't knock. He was just all of a sudden there. And I found myself wishing he weren't.

He was, I'll admit, quiet, mildly curious and a complete gentleman. He inspected a bookcase, sniffed at a chair, strolled over to the kitchen door and eyed my refrigerator, came back and regarded me silently from across the coffee table.

How, I remember thinking, does one tell a Doberman to leave?

Diplomacy, I felt, was called for here as never before.

"Please leave," I said in what I hoped was my best non-belligerent, conciliatory voice. The Doberman just looked at me.

"Go away," I said, my voice a bit louder. I had the presence of mind to add: "Nice doggie."

Still the Doberman looked at me.

"Scat," I said. I'll admit I thought of trying "Raus" — but there's no point in stirring up a Doberman, especially if at the time he's doing nothing but acting the soul of propriety.

He looked at me once more, then turned and walked out as quietly and mysterious as he had entered.

It was but the work of a moment for me to shut (and lock) both doors, mix myself another drink and return to the couch where I sat — rather breathlessly, I recall — and realized for the first time how Sir Hugo Baskerville must have felt.

There's not, I'm sure, a moor within miles of my apartment but at that particular moment, with lightning flashing and thunder rumbling outside, nothing could have convinced me that a moor wasn't exactly what my uninvited guest was headed back to, leaving I daresay, gigantic footprints in the grass on the way.

The ending of all this was prosaic to the point of being downright beautiful.

The Doberman, I found later, wasn't a he but a she named Shadow — who was visiting a neighbor downstairs.

Shadow was, I was assured, a gentle soul who loved people.

Apparently the only thing that keeps her from being a Rotarian or a Lion is that neither club has instituted a Doberman category yet.

So I'll be ready for Shadow the next time she shows up — but I'd prefer it in the daytime — and in good weather.

Thunder is bad enough. Lightning is worse. Rain and wind only add to my terror.

And when they come at night all I need to turn into a terminal case of the heebie-jeebies is for a big black dog to appear without warning.

So the next time, Shadow, please knock.

Okay?

There's a good girl.

Every kid deserves a kite

ANYONE WHO'S BEEN flying kites off and on for 75 years deserves to be heard on the subject. And Harry W. Hill of 322 No. 30th St. — over a cup of breakfast coffee Thursday — was glad to oblige.

"Kites?" Hill asked. "Sure — I made 'em for myself, then for my kids, my grandchildren and now I'm making 'em for my great grandchildren."

Kite-flying, said Hill — who was busy at it as recently as a week ago — is fun. And it's even more fun when you build them yourself.

He unfolded a paper napkin, clamped an ever-present cigar in his mouth and started sketching.

"I build a six-point kite," he began. "You need a tail to balance, of course, but they fly a lot steadier and go a lot higher than a four-pointer."

He stopped for a moment and looked at a finger on his right hand.

"See that?" A thin white scar showed on the tip. "I cut myself there with a jack-knife back in the 1880s — building a kite when I was a kid in Iowa."

Hill's recipe for kite-construction is simple — a jack-knife, sticks for the frame, newspaper, string and flour-and-water paste. "Last one I made," he said, "I had to get some wrapping paper — wind was a little strong for newspaper."

Anyone who runs with a kite to get it up, Hill said, isn't playing the game.

"I never ran to get a kite in the air in my life," he declared, eyes snapping.

The Hill-approved launching method consists of letting out about 200 feet of string, securing it to a post or tree and then simply boosting the kite into the air.

"If there's not enough wind to take it up that way," he said, "you might's well forget it."

Hill's latest kite was made for Richard and Steve, sons of Mr. and Mrs. Jack McBride, who live at 5 Adams St.

There was no special reason for making it, Hill said. He just heard the boys wanted a kite.

"And when a kid wants a kite," Hill said, "I make it for him. What's important to a kid is important to me."

While spring — by tradition — is the approved season for kites, Hill feels the true kite-builder is not one to be shackled to a calendar.

"The best time to fly a kite," he declared, chewing on the cigar holder, "is when you feel like it."

An epitaph
for a grand old lady

SHE DIED WITHOUT fuss or show the way all grand old ladies die.

"Brakes," said Capt. Vern Carlson, the man who landed the last DC-3 to fly a commercial airline route in Montana as he parked on the airport ramp for the last time.

"Set," First Officer Roger Thompson replied.

The two flyers went through what was a requiem for the airplane men have called the "gallant lady of the skies."

"Set," First Officer Roger Thompson replied.

"Ignition," said Carlson.

"Off," Thompson replied.

"Gyros."

"Caged."

"Master batteries."

"Off."

"Gear and flap handles."

Thompson — who was barely learning to walk when the airplane he was flying first left the ground — answered quietly:

"Spread."

This was how it was Sunday night at 7:10 when Frontier Airlines ended DC-3 service in Montana with a final trip from Williston, N.D., to Billings.

There were few to mourn its passing.

Among the two dozen or so passengers the plane carried during its round trip which left Billings Sunday morning, was John Herr Jr., 14, of Denver who was headed for Miles City and a summer on his godfather's ranch.

Sunday was the first time he'd ever flown, said John. And he wasn't hesitant about comparing his flight in the "antiquated" DC-3 with his Denver-Billings ride in a near-supersonic jet.

"This is really neat," said John. "You can see things down below."

Mr. and Mrs. Neil Stadmiller of Billings boarded the aircraft No. N4998E for the trip to Williston and the trip back to Billings for strictly sentimental reasons.

Mrs. Stadtmiller, as Frontier's first chief stewardess, brought the airline's first DC-3 trip into Billings nearly 18 years ago — and she wanted to be on the last.

"I flew on Threes for five years," Irene Stadmiller said, "just not an airplane like 'em."

Her 1968 counterpart, Fran Knobbe, agreed — emphatically.

"I love the airplane," said the stewardess who started 15 months ago on three-engine jets, changed to twin-engine turbo-props and finally settled on what the industry calls aviation's Model T. "Everyone thinks it's a funny airplane," she said, "yet everyone who's flown over a period of time has a lot of affection for it."

The DC-3, said Fran Knobbe, is the one passenger plane left in which "you really get a feeling you're flying."

The confirmed Three fan doesn't mind the steep slant of the cabin floor as he first gets on board. He settles good naturedly for the heating system which necessitates blankets as standard equipment for each passenger. And the high pitched whistle of the hydraulic brakes on taxiing, along with the absence of roaring from reversed props on landing, are part of the song of the DC-3.

The airplane, they admit, isn't perfect — except when it's flying.

The story is still told about the DC-3's leaky windshield — and how pilots calling in weather would often report "light rain outside, heavy rain inside."

Captain Carlson had heard the story, of course — and could well appreciate it.

"Things haven't changed a bit," grinned Carlson, turning in his cockpit seat and pointing to the lower part of his windshield.

There, wedged between the glass and the rubber frame, was a length of white surgical gauze and cotton, already damp from the rain that accompanied Sunday's flight for most of the way.

As it has done since it was built at Santa Monica, Calif., in 1942 as a military transport, Aircraft 996 droned its placid way through overcast skies, its two 1,200-horsepower Pratt & Whitney engines never missing a beat in maintaining 180 miles an hour one mile more or less above ground.

It was in 1947 that a Canadian airline bought the plane and converted it for passenger use. Frontier acquired it some years later.

Irene Stadmiller wasn't in the least doubtful that some of her time had been put in aboard the aircraft she found herself on Sunday.

"I can't say I recognize it," she said, "but if it's a DC3, I know I've flown on it many times."

And No. 996, she added, was most assuredly a DC-3.

A few photographers took pictures at stops along the way.

Two or three station agents remembered to comment about Sunday being the "last time for this old gal" — and a passenger who said he hadn't realized he was making the last flight of a venerable airplane agreed that Montana was "looking at the passing of an era."

And then, much too soon for some people who find it possible to fall in love with an inanimate object of steel, aluminum and rivets, No. 996 had braked to her last stop.

The rays of a late afternoon sun broke through clouds and brightened the green-padded cockpit where two pilots went through the final motions of shutting the airplane down.

Their voices could have been an epitaph — had not a much better one been spoken two decades ago by an American general in wartime England of a plane which could have well been the one in which Carlson and Thompson were seated:

"All the rest are just damn machines," the general said. "This, by God, is an airplane."

It takes two
to have a conversation

I T MAY COME AS a surprise to those of you who know me as the brilliant conversationalist I am to learn that there is one thing in whose presence I am struck inexplicably dumb.

It's a simple thing. It is relatively common — and is found in abundance on streets, in stores, at church and most often, of course, in the home.

I refer, in these general terms, to babies — around whom I invariably find myself at a loss for words despite the urging of my womenfolks to "say something" or "go ahead and talk" every time a baby and I come within spitting distance of each other.

This, let me assure you, is not a crochet of advancing age.

I experienced the same sort of non-verbalization (as the sociologists would put it) around my own children when they were small.

In short after I've nodded and smiled pleasantly and said something like, "Hello, there, baby how are you?" my conversational bolt has been shot.

Any further communication I leave to people like my wife who not only can talk at length with babies but who can actually understand what they're saying in reply.

"Anyone," she told me once, "with any sense at all knows how to talk to a baby."

Which should give anyone with any sense at all a rough idea of where that puts ME on her list.

But let's face it.

Babies and I, after all, have little in common — and when I say "babies" I'm talking about any kid who hasn't yet reached the age where he understands such gems of the art of small talk as phrases like "Why don't you go out and play?" or "Can't you see I'm busy making this beer can ready for recycling?" or "Be quiet and watch the nice television."

I suppose, too, that my tongue-tiedness around very small children (or "babies," as they call them) results from the basic fact that they have the drop on me, psychologically speaking.

Unequipped as they come with any suitable sort of handle, I've never been able to hold a baby without being afraid every minute that they're going to squirm out of — or drop through — my arms right onto the floor.

And while this, come to think of it, would allow me to improve my baby-talking vocabulary by adding to it the phrase "Oops-a-daisy" or "Now there's what I call a real bouncing baby boy" — I doubt whether it would be worth the trouble.

I suppose, when you get right down to it, my relations with the younger set can be described in about the same sort of terms the State Department uses when it talks about international diplomacy.

And a communique, were I ever to issue one, would describe our meetings as "beneficial and rewarding" and express the hope that "an easing of tensions leading to a rapprochement" would not be "entirely beyond future probability."

But let me make one thing clear.

It would not include the phrase: "We engaged in mutually rewarding conversations."

Maybe he should have
gone out for track

NOW THAT BASKETBALL is over and done with for the season — and since I find myself in a mood both introspective and retrospective — I have the feeling the wide world of sports just might be ready to hear the story of my meteoric career as a star of the great game of thump-thump.

You wouldn't realize it to look at me, I'm sure.

But there was a time — I still think of it as my one brief moment in the sun — when my name was on the lips of every high-school student (and not too few of their parents) in Iola.

And it all happened because of my playing in a game of which I knew nothing, about which I cared not a whit — and in place of which I'd have settled for two hours in study hall any day.

Let me take a moment to tell you how they ran basketball back in my high school

Everyone had to play it, the same way everyone had to go out for track.

The kids who were good at it got on the first team.

The kids who weren't, managed to make what was called the "scrub" team.

After one look at the way I played my first time out, Coach Harlan George organized what — for lack of a better term — I must describe as remedial basketball.

I couldn't dribble. I couldn't run. I couldn't shoot.

And my concept of guarding was to keep both arms in front of my face to prevent being hit by the ball.

Besides all this, my uniform didn't fit.

Put all these athletic shortcomings of mine together and you can understand why I needed those A's in history and English and all those B's in geography and language.

With the D's and F's I made in physical education, I'd have never graduated without them.

But to the point of this exercise:

Despite my many shortcomings on what has been referred to as the "friendly fields of strife" I found myself one afternoon in the starting line-up of an intramural game, a game in which, I was told in no uncertain terms, I had to play.

I suited up — if "suited" is the word I want — fastening my too-large trunks with the safety pin I kept in my locker.

All went well for the first ten minutes. I didn't fall down. I managed to stay clear of anyplace where the ball could be passed to me, and not once did I bump into anyone — our side or theirs.

Then suddenly, as I was running down the court on a turnover of the ball, I felt something give.

It was a safety pin which proved to be no safety net. Now, Coach George was a thorough man. He'd told us how to handle any number of emergencies which can come up in a game, how to deal with unexpected setbacks and how to act in times of stress or crisis.

But he never mentioned a word — not to me, at least — about what to do if, while running the length of a basketball court before hundreds of watching students and parents, you feel your shorts dropping down around your knees.

Not surprisingly, it slowed me for a moment — but only a moment.

I stopped, my trunks dropped to my ankles, I stepped adroitly out of them and continued running — straight toward the hallway door, out into the hall and into the nearest restroom.

The sign on the door said "Girls" — but I was not in a nitpicking mood.

I was, of course, rescued eventually by a classmate who scooped up my discarded item of uniform, brought it out to me and showed me how to get to the locker room without going back through the gym.

The names of the other players on that team — let alone who won or lost — have long since been forgotten, but for good or ill, mine lives on.

The subject was last brought up at my 40th high school class reunion by a friend who from that distance in time could, along with me, manage to look on the bright side.

"Sure, Bragg," he said, "it was embarrassing — but consider the fact that you not only made Iola High School basketball history, you also got the biggest hand of any player in the game that afternoon."

He had a point.

Packing chills
the thrill of travel

I LOVE TO travel.

Years ago I cut my teeth on travel by reading such legendary junketeers as Richard Halliburton, Carveth Wells and Talbot Mundy.

And I started traveling (at the age of five) by rail.

However, and to be completely honest, a 50-mile trip on the Erie Railroad can hardly be considered traveling — in the strictest sense of the word.

It was years later — nearly 20, in fact — that, thanks to World War

II and the U.S. Army, I managed a cruise to the Far East.

It was, beleieve me, no Love Boat experience — even if you took the Red Cross girls into consideration.

But I enjoyed every minute of it.

There were, in the years which followed — both military and civilian — various tours and junkets — but, try as I might, I couldn't place myself in the same league as Messrs. Halliburton, Wells or Mundy.

A year ago, thanks to my children who thought it would be a great retirement present — I spent a week in (or on) the Caribbean aboard the S.S. Norway.

I'm grateful — after reading the latest dispatches — I made the trip before things went downhill in the food and fire departments.

But don't get me wrong.

I debarked from the Norway with no more ill effects than a sunburn — and a malfunctioning flash on my camera.

In other words, traveling — in war or peace — doesn't bother me.

It's the packing for the trip that drives me up a wall.

All I needed for that first 50-mile rail journey was a paper bag with a sandwich in it — and a baggage tag around my neck telling those in charge whom I was to be delivered to in case I got lost.

The Army was equally solicitous when it came to baggage.

We had a list of what went in "hold" baggage and what went in the duffel bag we carried with us.

If anything was missing it was, after all, the Army's fault.

Long ago I stopped worrying about what to pack — and when to pack — for a trip.

There was a time, I admit, when I made out lists and began stowing neatly folded essentials and accessories into a suitcase weeks ahead of time.

I always had reason to both regret — and swear.

The razor was among them, along with the shaving cream.

And the comb.

And the pajamas. (Let's not kid each other, guys. There was a time when I only owned one pair myself.)

The day finally came when I realized that every time I was to leave on a trip I spent a week or so before living out of a suitcase.

And that wasn't all.

No matter how complete my list or how meticulous my packing I always ended up — once I was on my way — with something left behind.

The last time this happened was on a vacation on the Flathead.

I packed carefully, consulting my list frequently.

I included everything — even down to an extra ink cartridge for my fountain pen and enough vitamin pills to get me through the week.

It wasn't until I got there and unpacked that I realized that I'd left home with socks, shorts, tee shirts and hankerchiefs neatly stacked on the bed back home.

Another time I went to Washington for a tour of active duty at the Pentagon and discovered the day I reported to duty that I'd left my orders, my ID card — AND my address book — at the Gazette.

If I hadn't known a WAC major at my reporting office I could have been in big trouble.

So now I don't worry about packing ahead of time.

You can forget just as much in a week, I've learned, as you can in three hours.

And whether you're headed for a weekend in Miles City or 10 days in Rome, you're as bad off without a razor in one place as you are in another.

When you've called the cab for the airport, I always say, start shoveling the stuff in the bag.

The odds are even that you won't end up any worse off than if you'd reserved it for a week.

Waiting
for a Chinook

"THE NORTH WIND doth blow and we shall have snow,
"And what will the robin do then, poor thing?"
"She'll sit in the barn to keep herself warm
"And tuck her head under her wing, poor thing."

I don't know exactly from how far back in my literary past I dredged that particular bit of doggerel but it somehow seems to fit our weather.

Besides, when I think of all the people in the Gazette city room who have started off pieces by quoting poetry — most of which has been considerably more high-faluting than the above — I figure I've put in enough time here to do a little quoting myself.

On reflection, however, a bit of Keats on St. Agnes Eve might be more fitting when you consider the thermometer. The way it's been around here for the last couple of days reminds me much more of feathered owls all acold and trembling hares limping through frozen grass than it does of robins in barns with their heads under their wings.

I've found in the years since I've been able to say — and with considerable pride — that I'm from Montana, that people, particularly, easterners, think we're the next worst thing to Siberia — without the language problem.

"Montana, huh?" is the usual reaction. "Gets pretty cold out there, right?"

207

In the past I've tried to explain such things as a reading of 40 below in West Yellowstone when at the same time in Billings we can have temperatures in the 20s but it does little good.

My eastern friends try to be understanding.

"On the other hand," they say, patronizingly, "it's a dry cold you've got out there."

Dry or wet, I tell them, cold is cold.

"The important thing," I told a New Yorker when I was there last week, "is knowing how to handle winter. We get enough practice at that to make below-zero seem like kid stuff."

"Maybe," he said, "but if it's this cold in New York I don't see how you guys live out there."

I tactfully refrained from telling him that Montanans live through cold by adapting to, not fighting, it — and by maintaining the attitude that this, too, shall pass. He swore again, stamped his feet, blew on his hands and shivered.

"I don't know how you guys live through it," he said again.

The temperature at the time was five degrees above zero. There was little wind.

I remember a time I went to Washington, D.C., just after John F. Kennedy's inauguration when, you may recall, a snow storm hit the city and almost wiped out the social events planned for the night.

My cab driver nodded when I told him I was from Montana.

"Yeah," he said, "we could sure tell who you Montana and Wyoming people were that night."

I asked how.

"You were the only people who had cars on the road," he said. "Everybody else had stalled out or spun off in the ditch. Yessir, you people know how to drive in snow."

Then there's the story — a classic among Butte newspaper men — of the call made to Butte by a newspaper man in London.

He'd read of Butte's 35 below temperature and wondered how anyone lived through it.

"But I mean to say," he asked a Mining City reporter, "in all that, how do you get about?"

How do we get about what? came the typical Butte reply.

The Londoner explained.

Do people freeze? Did cars start? Were schools open?

And what about business places? Did they function?

The only thing different in Butte at 35 below from a Butte basking in 35 above temperatures, the Montana Standard reporter told him, was the time it took to get a drink.

"Takes longer to boil water for a hot whiskey," he said.

The London newspaper got a firsthand report on mile-high Butte in winter.

And the Montana Standard got a front page story on its phone call from London.

Personally, I don't let the cold bother me.

I manage to get about — and never mind what.

And as long as there are bartenders around who can still boil water I'll be thanking my lucky stars I'm not a robin, an owl — or a rabbit.

You can hear that
lonesome whistle blowing

IT'S COMFORTING, in a way, to hear some of the talk about saving Montana Avenue's most prominent landmark, Union Depot.

But, in another way, it's sad to think that any railroad station — with the possible exception of the tiny red frame buildings which once marked whistle stops all over the country — needs a committee and a movement to ensure its continued existence.

On the other hand, I suppose, the threatened and disappearing stations are another offering we place, for good or ill, on the altar of progress.

The great stations left are, at best, empty shells when you think of what they once were — and the worst part about it was watching them die slowly.

The trains left and took the people with them.

And the preservers — with, I'm sure, every good intention in the world — turned them into office buildings, shopping centers and museums.

Whatever purpose they now serve, you can never forget how they were once the nerve center, the heart and, in a way, the life blood of the cities they helped build.

Let's start with Grand Central, if not the most magnificent in the country, at least the best known. After all, it did have a long-running radio program named after it.

Grand Central had grandeur, it had status and it had people, millions of them, leaving, coming home, meeting (at its famous clock over the information desk in the cavernous lobby) or simply stopping by (if they were tourists) so that they'd be able to say in years to come: "Grand Central Station? I've been there."

Kansas City's Union Station wasn't all that metropolitan, but it had — in addition to the distinction of being among the last few "great" stations to be built in the country — a touch of the sensational others lacked.

It was there that, during the gang wars of the early 1930s, the famous "massacre" took place when federal agents shot it out with gangsters trying to rescue a gang member headed for prison. Men died on both sides, including the man to be rescued, and the building became as famous as the Chicago garage where the St. Valentine's Day massacre took place.

It was a dingy place the last time I saw it. The waiting room was as empty as the track yard behind the building, and there was no difficulty finding a parking place in the entrance plaza.

I think of Penn Station in New York, Union in Chicago — along with Dearborn, 14th Street and LaSalle — and I think of those familiar Milwaukee Road tiled towers from Portland to Butte.

And I remember well — and miss more than a little — the white marble magnificence of Union Station in Washington, D.C. They turned it into a visitors center a few years back, and the last I read someone was worrying whether it was worth the money to patch its leaking roof and repair the damage already done to its elegant lobby and waiting room.

Mausoleum of the passenger train era — that's what they called Cincinnati's Union Station when it was completed just before World War II. I was there in 1964 to watch part of its dying.

I'll never forget the first time I saw Union Station in St. Louis, said to be the second largest in the world. Not an hour passed without announcement of an arrival or a departure, day or night.

It was confusion, noise, thrills and adventure all rolled up in one package — and for a youngster barely out of the fourth grade, it was like being set down suddenly beside one of the Eight Wonders of the World.

The last time I was in St. Louis I made a special trip just to see the place — but I wonder now if I should have been content with my memories.

I stood at the head of the long, wide stairs at the main entrance.

I looked down — and thought of a tomb.

In the auditorium-size waiting room, hundreds of empty benches stretched away into the darkness at the far end.

And the only sound was the clank of the handle on a mop bucket as a stooped figure, alone in all that emptiness, worked to restore some of the brightness to a marble floor.

Sainthood is
just a puff away

WHEN, IN THE course of human events, it becomes necessary for a man to dissolve the ties that bind him to a motley collection of pipes, lighters, cigarette packages and ashtrays, there's one way of making certain he sticks to his non-smoking resolution.

He tells his friends about it. Condescendingly, of course, trying with difficulty to conceal his pity for those still chained to the habit.

That's what I've been doing the past two weeks — but it's gotten to the place where I can't find anyone who'll listen anymore.

Actually, they don't know what they're missing. Like Mark Twain, I've come to the point where I can speak as an authority on Getting Rid of the Nasty Habit — I've done it so often.

The first time I quit I stayed off for two and a half years. The second time I stayed on the tobacco equivalent of the wagon for three months — the last time, about a year ago, I was nicotine-pure for all of six weeks.

How long this'll last, is a good question — I may not make it through Tuesday night.

So far, though, I've done pretty well. I've gained five pounds — and on me that's considered breaking even. I have not screamed at my wife, beaten my children or kicked the cat.

I've taken up none of the "compensatory" vices of the non-smoker such as chewing gum, rattling mints around in my mouth — nor have I tried to convince others they should follow my example.

As a matter of fact, I've become so all-fired saintly since I stopped smoking that I might run for president myself ...

Seriously, it's a great experience — everyone should try it.

Your sense of hearing is sharper. Everywhere you can hear people tearing cellophane off cigarette packages and crunching tobacco into pipes.

You can smell things better — you can tell the difference between cigarette and pipe smoke, you can even smell the micronite in a package of filter tips.

Your vision is more acute. You can tell at a glance the approximate number of puffs left in a cigarette as it smoulders on a tray. You can also tell whether anyone's watching to see if you'll pick it up.

But mostly, once you've quit smoking, you become more tolerant. Your morphine bill goes up, of course, but you become more tolerant — even to the point of supplying friends who left their cigarettes back in the office.

That's why — in case you were wondering — I'm carrying the pack-

age around in my pocket. Of course it's not for me, silly, it's in case anyone needs a cigarette in an emergency ...

And to show you how tolerant I've become, if no emergency comes
up, I'll smoke 'em myself.

March ushers in
a bright new season

IN LIKE A LION, out like a lamb.

That's what they used to say about March.

There are other things, just as graphic — and as applicable —
to be said about the time of year when nature begins to take that
first tentative, halting breath and stir itself for the unfolding soon to
come.

There's a sense of waiting and anticipation — whether you look at
the month just beginning with the eyes of a child whose memory holds
less than a dozen Marches, or from the plateau of years where single
years have long since blended into decades, even generations.

March is the year beginning to gain momentum.

It's the world around, holding its breath.

Soon to vanish in the new fresh smell that comes one morning to tell
you, in the words of the poet, that the hounds of spring are indeed on winter's traces, are the snows which ushered in the new year and the raw,
chill winds that followed.

March, on whatever calendar, is a time of beginning again.

It's cold rain and warm wind, clear skies and gray clouds — and the
first, almost imperceptible hint of green in brown grass on rolling hills.

It's that time of the year when skeletal tree branches begin to lose
the harsh outline which has been theirs since the last leaf fell, as new life
rises and buds.

March, for children at school, means three months until summer vacation.

For grownups, it means lawn caring, garage cleaning, putting
houses in order — and filing income-tax returns.

But for those around who still live occasionally in that mystic mid-
region of yesterday, the treasures of March are only slightly mildewed
with age.

I doubt little but that there are still those who walk to a creek on
that first warm day of the month to watch the ice break up — and collect
a handful of pussywillows on the way home.

And in some half-remembered closet or drawer, I'm equally certain, there's a wooden top — and someone who still knows how to spin it.

March as well is — or used to be — a time for flying kites or playing marbles.

There's no law that says when either starts.

Except that it's sometime in March.

A kid simply wakes up one day and decides to fly a kite — or play marbles.

And the thing both interesting and wonderful about it is that every other kid in town gets the same idea — the same day.

March has always been the month of beginning.

In like a lion, they still say of it, out like a lamb.

But it's also good to remember that March is also that time when, of all times:

"The year's at the spring, the day's at the morn;

"Morning's at seven, the hillside's dew-pearled;

"The lark's on the wing, the snail on the thorn,

"God's in his heaven, all's right with the world."

Intentions were made to be broken

WHEN IT COMES to making New Year resolutions I'm as dependable as the next guy.

The first day of the year always finds me with a list

I've come, over the years, to call it my Decalogue of Good Intentions.

But by the time Groundhog Day gets here the native hue of resolution has been sicklied o'er by the pale cast of, among other things, realism.

My GI decalogue has, in short, gone down the tube.

Like the guy who can resist anything but temptation, I can keep any New Year resolution so long as it isn't binding on me.

Like writing letters, for example.

That's always number one on my list.

I think a lot about writing them. I save addresses. I have paper, envelopes and a new ribbon on my typewriter.

But if I'd have been St. Paul you can jolly well bet the Romans, the Corinthians, the Ephesians and the Galatians would have still been sitting around waiting for the latest word from the missionary circuit.

Remembering birthdays and anniversaries is another place where I'm very big in the mea culpa department.

I remember them, of course — but I never get around to sending cards.

"Send birthday, anniversary, thank you, get well, etc. cards," reads another of my resolutions, year after year.

This, I suppose, would be either forgiveable or acceptable.

But tell me, then, why I keep buying cards — and letting them yellow with age in a dresser drawer before I ever get around to signing, addressing, stamping and dropping even one in the mail?

Dresser drawers, come to think of it, are subjects of another perennial resolve.

I try to start off each year by cleaning out the junk of the previous 12 months.

The project never gets farther than the first odd sock, the cigarette lighter I thought I'd lost early in the summer — or the missing key to the trunk of my car.

I started, for example, to clean out a drawer the afternoon of New Year's Day.

And there, tangled up in some kite string which had eluded me since April, was a piece of paper I was certain had long since been consigned to the trash.

It was like seeing an old friend — only too late to truly relish the experience.

It was a copy of the resolutions I'd made last year.

This year, however, I'm determined.

I will be methodical about it. I will be — is "resolute" the word I want?

Yes, resolute.

And above all, I won't fall into the usual trap that in the past has spelled doom for more resolutions of mine than I care to think about.

I will not procrastinate.

I won't, of course, start right away.

I've still got that other sock to find, a couple of birthday cards to pick up and — if the weather stays like it is — try out the kite I got for my birthday last fall.

It's around someplace, I'm sure.

Cleaning out closets is something I never put on my list of resolutions.

After all, a guy can only do so much.

Friends Departed

CHAPTER 8

Spike Van Cleve
lives on in his words

W hen I heard last week about Spike Van Cleve my first thought was to get out his book and read it again, especially those parts where Spike, the man, came through best.

It was pretty hard to skip even a single page.

But the time always comes, though, when people, those we love, those we respect and those who just give us a good feeling when we're around them, have to take off and leave us. We don't like it a bit but that's the way it is and there isn't a lot we can do about it.

But we're lucky — when something of a man's life can stay around after he's gone. It gives us encouragement, it gives us hope and it brings a lot of light into hours and days that would, without it, be pretty quiet and lonely.

And it makes us feel like he's not all that far away.

Of course, I knew Spike long before he wrote "40 Years' Gatherin's."

But it was only in recent years that I got to know him and his family well enough to call him friend.

Make that good friend.

And that's why that night a week or so back I mixed myself a drink and stayed up late. And I felt I was doing more than reading just another western book by just another western writer.

It was like sitting across a table with Spike with drinks in front of us — as I did once a couple of summers back at his ranch — and hearing him again.

And, in Spike's own words, it was a damn good feeling.

As far as I'm concerned, Spike Van Cleve was the West as it was — and is — but at the same time he could hold his own in any company, anywhere — under any circumstances.

I guess that's because he was about as honest and open a guy as I've ever known. I got that feeling talking to him.

You can get it from reading what he wrote.

So that's why, remembering Spike, it was good to have him there again in a way and to feel once more the sensitivity and the truth that was in him.

Spike wrote about a lot of things.

Of his marriage: "Barbara and I quit college — we were too far apart and I was afraid somebody'd undercut me — and got married in the fall of 1934. It cost me a Harvard degree, but hell, lots of men have those and I'm the only one who has Barbara."

About horses: "In my considered opinion, one of the greatest pleasures God gave man is running horses — filly-chasing. Unlike sex it is of necessity an outdoor proposition, and although it, too, is an all season deal, it can get pretty wild when the ground is iron hard and slick with snow, particularly in the rough country, but Lord, it's fun."

On ranch hands: "I remember those ... who worked for us, in one instance from before I was born until well after I was married, with a good deal of affection. Good men. Men who took pride in their work; men who put the welfare of the livestock in their care well ahead of their own. They helped raise me, and many's the time it must have been a pretty thankless proposition."

On stringing along dudes: "I'm almost ashamed of myself once in a while about the things I sometimes get away with telling people at the ranch. The outfit is run pretty much ahorseback. We ride every day, as a rule all day, but on Sunday the horses get a well-earned rest, always. Well, I was chatting with a pair of new guests one Saturday evening and mentioned we wouldn't be riding until Monday. When they asked why not I told them that Sunday was the day we washed the horses. They jumped on the idea like a duck on a June bug. I forgot about it after they went to their cabin, but it sure was brought to my attention the next morning when I went down to tend the wrangle stock. Here these two were, loaded with cameras and waiting for the washing to begin! Nothing I could do but admit my perfidy, and it was some little time until they fully trusted me again. If ever."

If you knew him, it's easy to see and hear Spike on every page.

He was that kind of a man. He was, as well, that kind of a writer.

There was one paragraph that I read more than once.

And I thought about it as I sat that Monday afternoon in St. Joseph's Church in Big Timber and I thought about it later at the ranch where a lot of Spike's friends went to be with his family.

It was pure Spike.

"Somehow the hereafter is the least of my worries. It's a cinch I'll foregather with more than a few of my friends in hell, if I end up there, and some of them will be old filly chasers with a hitch in their getalong. If not, what could be finer than a bright, spring day in the lovely country under the Crazies, at a long lope on a good horse, with the wind in my face, the smell of lupine and sage in the air, and a string of slick, spooky colts to be gathered. Hell, I've already had heaven!"

I've been thinking about it and I think the best way to wind up these few memories of a real man and a good friend is to recall what the poet said:

> **"The riders are home from the milling herd,**
> **Which fades in the darkening day;**
> **The ponies drink at the cool, clear creek,**
> **And slowly graze away;**

While far from the sage blue circling hills,
Comes a coyote's evening lay;
All is rest and peace, at last,
For a son is home, to stay."

You know who the poet was?
Spike Van Cleve.

A newsman who
was something special

D on Anderson once gave a speech at the University of Wisconsin which he titled "Newspapering — Something Special".
He sent me a copy of it years ago and I ran across it the other night, read it again for the umpteenth time and thought I should be writing Don a letter.

The letter, unfinished, was still in my typewriter when I heard Wednesday afternoon of his death.

So, as Don Anderson talked of newspapering as something special, I'd like to talk a minute about Don Anderson as someone special.

I think the greatest thing about him was how he never let his almost boyish curiosity and enthusiasm about things and people — anything and anyone — grow stale or flat.

Don could get just as enthused about a crack in the sidewalk as he could about a session of Congress — if he thought a story could be gotten out of either.

And he was one of the greatest editors I've ever known in the years I've spent in this business about encouraging people. It didn't matter to Don whether it was a veteran reporter or the greenest kid in the newsroom.

If the talent was there, he brought it out.

And he wasn't satisfied with just bringing it out. He kept it alive and growing by his almost constant encouragement and approval.

I think of Don Anderson and I think of a guy with a great reservoir of energy and a grand sense of humor. I think of him as a publisher who could never forget he was an editor — and an editor who could never forget he was a reporter.

I don't know how Don felt when he was called once "the Abraham Lincoln of Montana journalism.

All I can say is that once he came out here from Madison, Wis., to take over as head of Lee Newspapers of Montana, a whole lot of fresh air started blowing through newsrooms in Helena, Livingston, Butte, Missoula and Billings.

And Don Anderson was never one to let a fair wind go to waste.

We grew in it, we moved with it — and we alld professionally profited by it.

There's little I can say about Don that hasn't already been said — and I'm grateful that a lot of it was said when he was still around to hear it.

He was an inspiration, he was a gentleman, he was a friend — and he was one hell of a newspaperman.

It was not only my privilege to know him — but I consider it a sort of badge of honor in this business to have worked for him, however short a time.

They tell the story — and it's true, of course — that when Don Anderson got ready to retire he got wind as well of plans for a barnburner of a retirement banquet his paper was going to throw for him.

Stuff and nonsense, said Don Anderson — though not exactly in those words.

If there was to be a party, said the Wisconsin State Journal's publisher, he was going to throw it — and throw it he did at his home in Madison for the entire Journal staff, husbands and wives.

And he was almost too busy waiting on his guests to listen to the chorus of "Good lucks" and "God blesses" that sounded throughout the evening.

And I think that's the way Don would have wanted this sort of thing to go — so I'm not going to get sentimental about it.

I just want to join the crowd talking about him right now and, with a drink in my hand, add my voice to the chorus.

Here's to you, Don.

Good luck.

And God bless.

A sunburst
will never fade

ONE DAY LAST WEEK I watched a sunset over Flathead Lake and sat for a long time thinking about Rhoda Hanson. I got the call that afternoon from Paul Husted in Miles City, telling me of her death.

Later I talked to her family, then I fixed a drink and went down to the dock to look for awhile at where the red-gold of the sky met the dark blue of the water and to remember an old and dear friend.

Up until then I had never thought of Rhoda in connection with the sunset.

For that matter, she wasn't the sunrise type either.

Sunburst, I think, would describe her more accurately, for I don't know of anyone who could explode on a scene the way Rhoda could — and did — for as long as I knew her.

Undoubtedly her first explosion in this part of the country came when she arrived in Miles City with her new husband, Roy.

There, with her Boston accent, her eastern mannerisms and her ready opinions, Rhoda took some getting used to.

We talked about that once.

"I had the feeling sometimes that people didn't like me," she told me. "I didn't seem to get across to them."

I told her it was understandable.

I felt the same way when I first met you," I said. "It lasted about five minutes."

Rhoda was quick, abrupt, outspoken, crisp — and acted like she was running 10 minutes behind schedule every hour of the day.

An invitation to lunch or for a drink with Rhoda was never so much an invitation as it was a command.

A suggestion that I do a story or a column — and over the years, Rhoda made a lot of them — on something or someone never began with "What do you think ..." but rather, I think you should ..."

She was never sparing with her compliments. She was never shy about voicing her criticisms. But once you got to know her, she was as generous, thoughtful, caring and honest a woman as I've ever known.

I guess this was what made Rhoda good at whatever she did, whether it was writing, selling insurance or the travel business.

I guess, too, it was part of what made her the good wife and mother she was.

I always felt Rhoda was lucky to have the energy to live the mile-a-minute life she led, for this was a woman never without a goal, never without a cause — and never without the time to help others equally driven even though not, perhaps, in the same direction.

And never once — and I knew her pretty well for a long time — did I ever hear an expression of worry, discouragement or doubt from her.

Even when it came to teaching me how to speak better French.

If there was a love in Rhoda's life outside her family and her friends, it was for France and its people.

She knew the country like the palm of her hand and little wonder, since she had made more than 40 trips there. I couldn't help feeling she behaved sometimes as though she were an unofficial ambassador for the republics on both sides of the Atlantic.

She brought France to Miles City — including its now famous Bastille Day celebration — as it has never been brought before. French diplomats, as well as many visitors from the country, were guests in her home.

There are people from France in this country today who wouldn't be here but for Rhoda Hanson. And there are people in Montana who never would have studied or worked in France had it not been for her.

And all this didn't happen, I must add, because Rhoda was all sweetness and light in selling France, or for that matter, selling anything else. She laid out a proposition, challenged someone to find something wrong with it, then pushed it to a conclusion. People were always glad in the end that she did.

I told her once that when she set out to storm a barricade, be it social, political or personal, something always happened — and usually, to the barricade.

Rhoda was a "liberated" woman, long, long before the term became fashionable, because essentially she was a free soul whose main interest in life was encouraging and helping others to be just as free.

This included especially her husband, Roy, her daughters, Erika and Torha, and her sons, Andy and Kurt. She was most proud of them, and I know they were, and are, most proud of her.

I last saw her about three weeks ago after the usual Rhoda-type phone call.

"I'm at the Northern on my way back to Miles City. We have about two hours for a drink and lunch. When would be a good time to meet you?"

Since I learned a long time ago that turning down lunch with Rhoda was like passing up a weekend in the country, within an hour we were chattering away over two beers and two reuben sandwiches. The conversation ranged (as usual) from Paris to pack trips, writing, politics, Red China, family, food, history, travel and friends.

The time was up before we knew it.

"We never know when we say goodbye for the last time — and with Rhoda, it was always "Au revoir" or "A bientot," never "Adieu." — and perhaps it's just as well.

I remember her flashing smile, the hint of challenge in her voice, and the touch of impatience as she'd look at her watch, gather up her bulging purse and announce her departure as though she'd lost another 10 minutes in an hour.

I remember the way she wore her hair, up and coiled tightly in braids around her head, and down. (I liked it down better.)

I remember her hats; they were both pert and dramatic. I even remember the black, wide-brimmed floppy one (my favorite) about which she once told me her friends would be "horrified, absolutely horrified" if they knew where she got it, how long she had it — or how little she paid for it.

But most of all, I remember a woman who gave much of herself to her family, her friends and her community. We are all of us better for having had her around as long as we did.

Mickey Cochrane;
last out for an era

H E WAS A KID who loved baseball.
It was hard, his father said once, to find the boy when there was any work to be done around the Cochrane home in Bridgeport, Mass.

He was always somewhere — playing ball.

The family called him "Mike" — but to nearly two generations of sports fans he was "Mickey."

Mickey Cochrane, a star with the Philadelphia Athletics under Connie Mack after joining the club in 1925.

Mickey Cochrane, a star with the Detroit Tigers when he moved to that club nine years later, first as a catcher, then as manager.

Mickey Cochrane, who found his way from a corner lot in a little New England town to baseball's Hall of Fame in the course of a life that lasted 59 years.

And everywhere Thursday they talked about Mickey — as a great ballplayer, as a great guy.

Grover Resinger, manager of the Billings Mustangs, didn't find it too easy to talk when he heard the news. Resinger, whose career in professional ball began about the time Mickey's playing days ended, called him a hero.

"There was just nobody like him," Resinger said. "This was a guy who, when you saw him play ball, your mouth flew open — and there wasn't a kid or a grownup who didn't feel that way."

A Chicagoan who guessed he'd watched Mickey in a hundred or more games called him "a real pepperpot."

"Boy, I'll tell you," said Frank Harmon, "that guy was the one that kept a club together — every minute of a game. Nobody laid down when they played baseball with him."

It was pretty much like that through the day.

People remembered Mickey Cochrane — as a gentle, quiet man. As a great ballplayer.

They told him he had about two years when leukemia was first diagnosed.

That was almost five years ago.

And Mickey outfoxed the doctors — just as he outfoxed the pitchers, coming out of 13 major league seasons with a .320 batting average.

And he stayed in baseball until the end. His contract as a scout with the Tigers, the club he sparked to two pennants, had still a year to run.

His last visit to Billings was a year ago this month. He'd planned on coming out again in July.

Montana was his second home. He discovered it nearly 25 years ago

223

after a fast, inside pitch on a three-two count in Yankee Stadium ended his playing days.

Two innings before — through Mickey didn't know it then — he got his last hit in a major league game.

Typically, it was a home run.

Then Bump Hadley's pitch struck him in the head and an era in baseball ended.

Recuperating on the 4-K Ranch near Absarokee, Cochrane discovered Montana — the way his two brothers, Archie and Burt, and his father, John, discovered it earlier.

And for 20 summers after, he didn't miss a trip out here.

The stock market was up 12 points Thursday morning — but no one talked about it. Not after the New York Exchange ticker flashed the word.

There were many around town who'd lost a friend. There were others who lost a boyhood idol.

And there was a new generation around to whom Mickey Cochrane was just a name.

A name like Babe Ruth. Ty Cobb. Walter Johnson. Grover Cleveland Alexander. Lou Gehrig.

A great name in stories of the game — and a name that, to them, properly belongs in baseball history.

They didn't lose Mickey Cochrane.

In a way, no one did.

He'll always be around somewhere.

Playing ball.

Don Nutter's final return to Sidney

I T ENDED WITH the muted echo of "taps" as the setting sun streaked clouds with crimson in the western sky.

It began two hours earlier when a black-robed minister stood before a copper casket in the Sidney High School gymnasium and bowed his head in prayer.

This is how a town said good-bye.

This is how a man's soul was commended to his God.

The people of Sidney and of Montana started filling the school where services were held long before the scheduled hour. They sat in bleacher seats and stood behind railings along narrow catwalks. They kept coming and those too late for even standing room watched and listened from the corridor.

They sat and heard the sorrowing majesty of the "March to Calvary" from Stainer's "Crucifixion" as a muted organ played prelude music.

They listened while the clock hands crept to three to "Traumerei" and bowed heads silently in prayer when the service began.

There was muffled coughing as the Rev. Leo H. Buechler, pastor of the People's Congregational Church, spoke the timeless truth of an English poet.

"No man is an island ... the death of any man diminishes me."

"Therefore, send not to know for whom the bell tolls ..."

The American flag that draped all that was mortal of Montana's late governor gleamed brilliantly red and white beneath the warmth of the lights that flooded the gymnasium-chapel — and a young boy high on a stairway ledge to the left of the flower-decked rostum leaned his head against the wall and looked down at it.

Just 34 minutes later the intermittent coughing stopped and silence like granite held the place as the final benediction was pronounced.

Quietly, the flag-shrouded casket moved out the main aisle toward the entrance and, as the music swelled into a recessional, the strains of "Montana" lifed up and over the slowly moving crowd.

The four soldiers in the color guard shivered at "parade rest," as the casket, gleaming copper under the flag, moved past its honor guard of Knights Templar.

Montana Highway Patrolmen came to attention and saluted. A young father lifted up his tow-headed daughter to watch as cars crept slowly on toward town and through it.

They said goodbye in little knots of grownups and children who gathered on each neighborhood corner to watch.

They said good-bye in the winking yellow of traffic lights, beckoning the procession on its way.

They said good-bye in the families that came to curtain-free windows and looked and shook their heads.

And they said good-bye, those who stood in scattered groups along Sidney's flag lined Central Avenue, heads bared in the chillness of the afternoon.

The cars moved on.

On, past the Co-op Cafe. On past the closed stores with the little white cards in the windows telling why they closed.

On, past the street where a half-block down, Don Nutter had his law office.

On through town and out, tires crunching now on the drab gravel of Cemetery Road.

On past snow-filled ditches, raw fields and grass grown rank and sere.

On, slowly on, toward a knoll in the distance where earth waited.

Above the brown wintered hill a rift appeared in the clouds and blue sky showed through as cars parked where they could in the already crowded place.

People, shivering in the biting wind that blew across the hill, looked back toward the town a mile or more away to see the unbroken stream of headlights of cars still coming.

The casket moved again — for the last time now — and stopped.

The tie-strings of his white Masonic apron were looped around the copper Grecian handles and you heard them creak in the stillness as they were moved.

Elmer Sorensen, acting Worshipful Master, spoke the opening words of the rite and his voice was strong in the wind and in the cold ... "Ashes to ashes ..." came the words.

A man stopped over the open grave then stood up.

"Dust to dust ... " they came once more.

The man stooped again.

The sky was clearing now and from somewhere overhead the muffled roar of a jet aircraft spilled down and over the silent crowd.

From the top of the hill came Lt. Louis Baxter's crisp command to an eight-man firing squad.

The volleys cracked three times and were lost in the wind swept darkening hills.

Nothing was heard but the flapping of the half-masted cemetery flag in the breeze.

Then a bugle close and clear, sounded the final call for a soldier.

The last note died away.

The echo, softly now, seemed to come from everywhere — the earth, the sky, the hills that rimmed this now-honored ground spoke softly now of sleep.

And those who loved a man looked up at the splendor of a sunset and went home.

And they really cared

C ALL IT A LOVE story if you want.

Or a story of love.

It all began six months or more ago when a teen-age girl found an old man in the county nursing home who had no one to visit him.

He had no family — unless you count a daughter somewhere back East.

He had no friends except those who took care of him at the nursing home.

And everyone should have someone, the girl felt. No one with his life behind him should be alone.

And so the girl became the old man's family and his friend.

Until, one day last March, Sam Ash died.

"We were preparing for the ususal, routine graveside service like always," said the funeral director, "until the girl walked in the office.

Would it be possible, she asked, for her to "sort of take charge" and see that Sam Ash had something more than the routine?

Things like that don't happen very often, the funeral director said. "We did all we could to help her."

This is how it happened that on a cloudy Wednesday morning not long ago Sam Ash went to the county cemetery — and he was not alone.

Six senior boys, who the girl knew would help if they were asked, carried Sam Ash's $400 coffin to the grave.

Another senior — a friend of the girl's brought his guitar and played and sang.

He sang first a song he'd written himself about what friends can mean.

Next he sang "Lovin's Really Livin'."

Then the young Catholic priest — who also came out because the girl wanted him to — spoke the words over the grave asking that Sam Ash be granted eternal rest and that perpetual light would shine upon him.

And they stood there on the rocky, bare plot of ground that is the cemetery — the girl, the priest, the guitar player, the pallbearers.

They stood there and, as the guitar, loud and clear in the silence of the morning struck the opening chords, the 35 to 40 high school seniors, who came along so that Sam Ash wouldn't be alone, sang "Battle Hymn of the Republic."

The funeral director said he hadn't seen anything quite like it.

Don't ask for names.

The only reason Sam Ash is identified is so you'll know it all really happened. If you want, you can visit his grave and see for yourself.

The kids didn't do it to get their names in the paper.

They did it because they believe that loving your neighbor is more than an empty phrase.

And Sam Ash was their neighbor.

And they also remembered another man who, after he'd died, would have merited the "usual, routine" treatment — had it not been for one who saw to his decent burial.

Joseph of Arimathea was a man who also recognized his neighbor.

Write a -30-
behind Dave O'Connor

DAVE O'CONNOR WAS one hell of a newspaper man and those of us who knew him are going to miss him very much.

(I can feel him looking over my shoulder right now, the way he did sometimes when he knew I might be fighting for an idea — or a word — and hear him saying "Just write it, Addison. You can do it. Just write it.")

Dave, whom I first knew as a reporter then came to love — and fear more than a little — as an editor, had a rare talent.

("Careful now, Addison. You're writing about me, remember, and a reporter's first responsibility is accuracy. I have many rare talents.")

He could grin at himself as easily as he ever grinned at the rest of us — and he never once let you forget that once the job was out of the way, no matter how tough it was, or boring or distasteful or whatever, the person who couldn't smile what was bothering him away with a shrug was, in the long run, the worse off for it.

("You're making me sound like a Nutsy Fagan, Addison — but go ahead and let's see what comes of it.")

Dave and I had our difference. He was an outrageous punster. He hated snow. And I used to infuriate him by asking about people I know in Butte, assuming (often just because I knew it graveled him when I did) that he'd know them, too.

("You might also mention, Addison, that in the 15 and more years I edited your copy, I was unable to teach you the proper place for a comma in relation to the punctuation mark which followed it — and I'll bet no one has yet.")

But the things we saw eye to eye on were many — like shooting rubber bands at each other or at the newsroom ceiling in the old Gazette building. Like eating milk toast as a cure for everything from a hangover to just plain stomach ache. And like playing The Game.

("I was afraid you weren't going to mention The Game, Addison.")

Dave and I played The Game over bean soup lunches (we agreed on bean soup, too) years before anyone thought of playing Trivia. Only we did it with news events (Who was the executioner at Sing Sing? How was the pingpong ball related to aviation history? What was the farmer's name who identified Bruno Richard Hauptmann as the driver of a car near the Lindberg kidnap scene?) and we both agreed there was no one who could touch us — even after we'd taught them to play it.

But when I think of Dave O'Connor now, I think of him as a guy with much understanding and sensitivity — especially when it came to dealing with us newspaper types who, whether we admit it or not, are as big a bunch of prima donnas as you'll find anywhere.

There were some, of course, who tossed off the lengthy talks Dave would have with a reporter who was having problems, professional or personal, as examples of "the Dave O'Connor School of Journalism" — but he still taught people how to write.

And he taught newspapermen to be better newspapermen — me among them.

Every reporter was different to Dave — and his was no assembly-line way of treating them. Some had to be yelled at. Or sympathized with. Some had to be kidded. Others had to be lectured to. A cup of coffee with a reporter or deskman in the Turf solved lots of problems, once the afternoon paper was gone — and Dave used it a lot.

I guess the thing I feel about Dave — and that all of us who knew him felt — is that he cared about people who wanted to work on newspapers and did everything he knew how to make them care about working on newspapers, too.

("Don't let it run too long, now, Addison — there's still such a thing as a deadline and you're pushing it.")

Dave used to say that if there was a lost art in the world today it was the art of writing a simple declarative sentence.

So here are three — just for him.

Dave O'Connor was one hell of a newspaper man.

Those of us who knew him are going to miss him very much.

And we'll remember him every time we sit down at a typewriter to write a news story.